SYSTEMS AND PSYCHOANALYSIS

Other titles in the
Systemic Thinking and Practice Series
edited by David Campbell & Ros Draper
published and distributed by Karnac

Credit card orders, Tel: +44(0) 20-8969-4454; Fax: +44(0) 20-8969-5585
Email: shop@karnacbooks.com

SYSTEMS AND PSYCHOANALYSIS

Contemporary Integrations in Family Therapy

edited by

Carmel Flaskas and David Pocock

Systemic Thinking and Practice Series

Series Editors
David Campbell & Ros Draper

KARNAC

First published in 2009 by
Karnac Books Ltd
118 Finchley Road, London NW3 5HT

British Library Cataloguing in Publication Data

A C.I.P. for this book is available from the British Library

ISBN: 978 1 85575 559 8

Edited, designed and produced by The Studio Publishing Services Ltd,
www.publishingservicesuk.co.uk
e-mail: studio@publishingservicesuk.co.uk

Printed in Great Britain

www.karnacbooks.com

CONTENTS

CHAPTER TWELVE

ACKNOWLEDGEMENT

Early versions of Chapters One, Three, Six, and Ten had an outing at an unexpectedly packed conference at the Tavistock Clinic, London in December 2006: "Extending systemic thinking: the contribution of psychoanalytic ideas". Our thanks to Ellie Kavner and Vicky Harrison for organization, to co-presenters Sebastian Kraemer and Inga-Britt Krause, to panel members Julia Bland, Mary Donovan, Rabia Malik, Jeannie Milligan, Margaret Rustin, and Bernadette Wren, and to everyone who participated so enthusiastically, thereby encouraging us in the idea that a book might well be timely.

SERIES EDITORS' FOREWORD

We are delighted to include this book in our series, and believe the book will be of interest and useful to the field of psychotherapy in general, and not just to those psychotherapists committed to systemic thinking and practice.

Both editors and contributors are recognized for the depth and sophistication of their thinking and the significant contributions each has already made to their professional discipline, as well as to the field of psychotherapy.

An aspect of this book's sophistication, in our view, is that it is an important punctuation in the ongoing explorations and conversations about the interface between systemic and psychoanalytic concepts and practices. The editors and other contributors have, over time, all held a "both . . . and . . . and more" position in any debate regarding similarities and differences between these two approaches to psychotherapy, and this book, we hope, will be seen as making a major contribution to the ". . . and more" part of any debate.

We congratulate the editors on rising to the challenge offered at the 2006 Tavistock Conference: "Extending Systemic Thinking: The Contribution of Psychoanalytic Ideas", convening such a talented group of international contributors representing a diversity of mental health contexts, and we believe this book is indeed timely.

The range and diversity of contributors' experience and expertise will go a long way to dispel any remaining need to argue a case for holding a "both . . . and . . . and more" position in relation to comparisons between all approaches to psychotherapy. The various chapters in the book demonstrate how, when positioning themselves to hold different ideas over time, accomplished clinicians can promote the emergence of a richness and creativity that appeals to practitioners, not least because of the immediate relevance and usefulness of the ideas.

Sharing with the reader their own process in collecting and ordering the chapters in the book, the editors also offer readers a view through another lens of how much a commitment to curiosity and the ideas of co-construction and emergence can yield.

As Series Editors, we hope readers of this book will find inspiration and stimulation for their own thinking and practice.

David Campbell
Ros Draper
London 2009

ABOUT THE EDITORS AND CONTRIBUTORS

The Editors

Carmel Flaskas is a social worker and family therapist, and Senior Lecturer in the School of Social Sciences and International Studies, University of New South Wales, Sydney, where she convenes the Master of Couple and Family Therapy programme. She has published a number of books and articles on the therapeutic relationship, on psychoanalytic ideas in the systemic context, and on knowledge in family therapy. In 2006, she was awarded an Honorary Doctorate by the Tavistock Clinic in conjunction with the University of East London for her contributions to systemic psychotherapy, and in 2005 she received the ANZJFT award for Distinguished Contributions to Australian Family Therapy.

David Pocock is Head of Family Therapy at the Child and Family Consultation Service in Swindon, and a visiting lecturer to the Bristol University Diploma/MSc. Family Therapy training. He is a current assessor for the *Journal of Family Therapy* and past member of the Editorial Board and previous moderator for the AFT/JFT internet discussion forum. He is a psychoanalytic psychotherapist in independent practice and a member of the Severnside Institute for Psychotherapy, where he currently chairs the Study Day Group. His published work ranges across systems theory, psychoanalysis, and the philosophical underpinnings of psychotherapy.

The Contributors

Teresa Arcelloni, psychiatrist and psychotherapist, was trained in systemic family therapy by Luigi Boscolo and Gianfranco Cecchin, works as a psychiatrist for the Italian National Health Service in Piacenza, and is part of the teaching staff of the Episteme Centre in Turin, Italy. Her present interests concern the nature of therapeutic interaction and the use of systemic theory and practice in couple therapy.

Paolo Bertrando, psychiatrist and psychotherapist, was trained in systemic family therapy by Luigi Boscolo and Gianfranco Cecchin, is the Director of the Episteme Centre in Turin, and teaches at the Università Vita-Salute San Raffaele in Milan, Italy. The author of many articles and books, his present interests concern the dynamics of systemic individual and family therapy, and the broader implications of systemic theory.

Julia Bland is a consultant psychiatrist in psychotherapy at the Maudsley Hospital in London. She has trained in both family therapy and in psychoanalytic psychotherapy. Her current position includes responsibility for training and family therapy clinics, and she leads the service development of family therapy within adult services across the largest mental health trust in the UK.

Mary Donovan is a systemic psychotherapist working with Barnet, Enfield, and Haringey Mental Health NHS Trust in London. She previously worked as a senior social worker at the Anna Freud Centre, London. Prior to her systemic training, she undertook a psychodynamic training and has a long-standing interest in themes of integration between the two orientations. She has published articles on the subject in both systemic and psychoanalytic journals.

Stephen Frosh is Professor of Psychology and Pro-Vice-Master at Birkbeck College, University of London. He was previously a Consultant Clinical Psychologist and Vice Dean at the Tavistock Clinic, London. He has written extensively on psychoanalysis and social relations and on systemic family therapy. His recent books include *Hate and the "Jewish Science": Anti-Semitism, Nazism and Psychoanalysis* (Palgrave, 2005), and a second edition of *For and Against Psychoanalysis* (Routledge, 2006).

Sebastian Kraemer has been a consultant child and adolescent psychiatrist at the Whittington Hospital, London since 1980, and was also a consultant at the Tavistock Clinic from 1980 until 2003. He writes, teaches, and lectures on family therapy, on liaison psychiatry, the training of child and adolescent psychiatrists, fatherhood, the fragility of the developing male, parenthood, and the politics of attachment.

Inga-Britt Krause is a social anthropologist and a consultant systemic psychotherapist. She has carried out fieldwork in Nepal and in Britain and has worked in the National Health Service (NHS) since 1990, where she has helped to develop specialist Asian psychotherapy services. She has published on the cultural construction of concepts of illness and emotions and on cross-cultural psychotherapy, and is currently Training and Development Consultant in the Tavistock and Portman NHS Foundation Trust.

Glenn Larner is a senior clinical psychologist with 30 years experience in CAMHS. He lectures in family therapy for the New South Wales Institute of Psychiatry, Sydney and is a past associate editor for the *Australian and New Zealand Journal of Family Therapy*. He has published in the UK, North America and Australia, and his research interests are in the intersection between deconstructive philosophy, psychoanalysis and family therapy.

Deborah A. Luepnitz is on the Clinical Faculty of the Department of Psychiatry at the University of Pennsylvania School of Medicine. She is the author of the influential book, *The Family Interpreted: Psychoanalysis, Feminism, and Family Therapy* and, most recently, *Schopenhauer's Porcupines*. She maintains a private practice in

Philadelphia and directs a *pro bono* project connecting formerly homeless adults with psychoanalysts in the community.

Rolf Sundet is a specialist in clinical psychology. He is currently working as a research fellow at the University College of Buskerud and as a family therapist at the Family Unit, Hospital of Buskerud, Norway. He has published several articles within the field of family therapy, focusing on clinical and theoretical issues.

Vigdis Wie Torsteinsson is a specialist in clinical psychology and a philosopher. She is working at the Regional Department for Eating Disorders, Ullevål University Hospital, and is a senior adviser at the Regional Centre of Child and Adolescent Mental Health in Oslo. She has made contributions to several anthologies on therapy and has written articles about family therapy, developmental psychology, and the philosophy of science.

Jeremy Woodcock is a family and couple psychotherapist who worked for many years with survivors of political violence at the Medical Foundation for the Care of Victims of Torture, London. During that work he appreciated the value of ideas that bridged systems and psychoanalysis. Recently a Director of Family Therapy Training at the University of Bristol, he is now in private/independent practice as a psychotherapist and organizational consultant.

Introduction

Quite a lot has been written, over the years, about the apparent gap between systems and psychoanalysis: whether this might be bridged by various integrative models, or carefully guarded in order not to deny important differences, or lightly stepped across just long enough to borrow some useful ideas. This focus on "the gap" can, however, draw attention away from convergent developments within systems and psychoanalysis occurring within the past two decades. Writing in 2009, it is possible to make a reasonable case that the differences within these two distinct cultures are larger than that which currently divides them at their closest point. Most systemic family therapists have long made the shift from mechanical systems to those of meaning and understanding, in which the self of the therapist is fully present within the area of enquiry. Within psychoanalysis, one major line of development can be read as having a systemic direction of travel: from the rather isolated psyche of Sigmund Freud's classical theory, via Wilfred Bion's notion of the interactive presence of a containing mind and Donald Winnicott's early intersubjectivity, through to the currently highly influential grouping of ideas—drawn from self-psychology, intersubjectivity theory, and attachment and parent–infant research—that has become known as relational psychoanalysis.

For those familiar with either systems or psychoanalysis it is easy to assume that the other is settled and easily definable, but each is, and always has been, a mixed, factionalized, shifting culture in which new and established ideas are continuously contested. So much the better, since theory needs to be fallible, and subject to critical debate, if it is to serve the subtle therapeutic task of helping to understand, rather than the colonizing task of knowing. This is why "integrations" rather than "integration" appears in our title. The project of a single grand integration implies too high a commitment to theory; all those writing here would be likely to want to hold their ideas with a reasonably loose grip.

While contributors are varied in their interest in, or commitment to, psychoanalytic thinking, they are, on the whole, approaching psychoanalysis from a position of being steeped in systemic family therapy. For example, we doubt that any would subscribe to the view—itself much less commonly held within psychoanalysis than is generally recognized—that change occurs only through a full-transference interpretation. In fact, the term "interpretation" is barely mentioned in the book other than in Deborah Luepnitz's chapter on dream interpretation with couples, where it appears within a fully collaborative context. So, although many chapters, and even the book as a whole, could be read as part of an ongoing critique of the limitations of the turn to language that so powerfully influenced family systems therapy from the early 1990s onwards, it is likely that none of the authors would be without the advantages that have followed in its wake: sensitivity to cultural difference, an understanding of dialogical process, and a critical, reflexive position on knowledge.

Systemic family therapy is a theoretically rich, progressive modality. So, the sceptical reader may ask, why bother to look to psychoanalysis at all? After all, the interest can hardly be said to be reciprocal: family systems therapy has yet to appear significantly on any psychoanalytic horizon as far as we can tell. We cannot speak for all contributors, but a common reason is the wish to draw on, presumably helpful, experiences of personal psychoanalytic psychotherapy (sometimes, supplemented by informal or formal training). It would be inconceivable to put such experiences to one side for any length of time when practising as a systems therapist, although some have experienced the discomfort of holding on to the value of analytic ideas when training to be "proper" family systems therapists.

But beyond the important urge to draw on the whole of one's accumulated store of ideas and experiences when faced with the infinite complexity of a family system, there is a further motive which runs through this book. The important gap, far greater in significance than the gap between systems and psychoanalysis, is the one between any system of thought and the never fully knowable reality of the lives of those who seek our help. A significant part of that territory is non-conscious and, while this domain has not escaped the attentions of systemic theorists, psychoanalysis has some pretty experienced map-makers.

The shape of the book

In compiling the book, we approached therapists with a known interest in systems and psychoanalysis, but made no attempt as editors to steer the content, asking only that contributors should write about what was currently of interest to them. We also decided to resist any temptation to "iron out" differences between contributors in terms of their relationship to psychoanalysis. Readers should have no difficulty picking up the varying levels of enthusiasm for psychoanalytic ideas in different chapters. As one small example, most contributors use the word "client" rather than "patient", the latter being more commonly used in psychoanalytic discourse, but some switch between the two languages, depending on the context of the discussion, and a few more comfortably use "patient" as the language of their work contexts.

Within the group of contributors, no one knew what the others would produce, beyond the circulation of the initial proposals. The result is a considerable—and, to our minds, pleasing—diversity of ideas, but also a mini-survey of some emerging developments. The influences of the relational analyst and feminist, Jessica Benjamin, the contemporary Kleinian, Ronald Britton, and the philosopher, Emmanuel Levinas, are each felt more than once. The notion of emotional systems seems to be gaining a little ground. The foundational ideas of Wilfred Bion on containment and the capacity to think are directly referenced in half the chapters. However, most significant is the profound impact of the work of Peter Fonagy, Mary Target, and colleagues on mentalizing, which is used, to a greater or lesser degree and in differing contexts, in no less than eight of the twelve chapters.

As editors, we deliberately left the question of the grouping of the chapters until we had them all in hand. We were quite ready to let them just sit alongside each other if the diversity of offerings negated an overarching frame of section headings. Yet, the chapters did group, more or less fairly easily, into three equal parts: the first addresses the unconscious in the system, the second focuses on emotion and development, and the third on dialogue and otherness.

However, the boundaries of these sections are quite fluid, and some other interesting themes weave more chaotically through the book. The potential for established psychoanalytic ideas to enrich systemic work is taken up generally by Julia Bland, and specifically by Sebastian Kraemer on countertransference, Deborah Luepnitz on dream interpretation, and Rolf Sundet and Vigdis Wie Torsteinsson on development. Some hitherto unremarked-upon overlaps between systems and psychoanalysis, with possibilities for mutual enrichment, include Mary Donovan's linking of reflecting processes in family systems therapy with reflective function, and Carmel Flaskas's chapter on approaching the realness of experience while holding a sensitivity to dialogical process. A search for integrative solutions to address a number of perceived problems within mainstream contemporary family therapy discourse constitutes possibly the largest strand: holding the tension between universality and difference (Inga-Britt Krause), the concept of emotional system in place of emotion as autonomous *or* socially constructed (Paolo Bertrando and Teresa Arcelloni; David Pocock), and a re-examination of relationship as a means of knowing the other (Jeremy Woodcock, Glenn Larner, and Stephen Frosh).

The chapters

It is now time to introduce the chapters in their own right. Part I, "The unconscious in the system", consists of four chapters addressing unconscious processes from different angles. The first chapter, by Carmel Flaskas, addresses narrative, meaning-making, and the unconscious. Framed by a concern for the limits of languaged narratives in representing social and emotional realities, this chapter explores the complexity of the role of language in meaning-making and the place of unconscious experience in the momentum for narrative. The chapter also brings into play research on attachment narratives, the function of mentalization, and Bion's ideas on the capacity to think as a constellation of theory that extends our understandings of narrative, therapeutic change, and resilience.

The second chapter, by Julia Bland, directly contrasts and compares the cultures of psychoanalysis and systemic therapy in the interests of addressing the practice challenge of working with unconscious processes in family therapy. As someone trained in both modalities, she is able to take an insider–outsider position in thinking about the differences in the theorization of symptom, therapeutic change, and therapeutic style. A tentativeness with respect to the tensions of "mixing" practices allows a discussion of clinical work that, while acknowledging pitfalls, draws on the richness of using psychoanalytic ideas to attend to unconscious meanings in family therapy.

Countertransference is an explicit and implicit theme throughout the book. The spotlight of Chapter Three, "Is there another word for it? Countertransference in family therapy", by Sebastian Kraemer, is on the therapist's subjective experiences in the immediacy of relating to the family, and the question of how to theorize this process. The chapter explores the various ways in which the term "countertransference" has been defined and used in psychoanalysis, and argues the need in family systems therapy for a theory of mind and a theory of suffering. The case discussion underlines the specificity of the therapist's self, and the subtlety and mutuality of the process of influence. Countertransference might be thought of as a primary pathway of connection from clients to therapist. Sebastian Kraemer finds no equivalent concept in family therapy. In the end, if "countertransference" is not used for describing this pathway, we are left with an absence.

Chapter Four completes Part I, and here Deborah Luepnitz describes the development of her own practices in using dreams in psychotherapy with couples as one way of moving between the "upper" (conscious) and the "lower" (unconscious) worlds in the life of the couple. The chapter draws distinctions between dream interpretation in individual psychotherapy and in couple psychotherapy. It also offers descriptions of practice that shine as examples of the use of the therapeutic relationship to allow a creative and safe space for the couple's exploration of their own dream imagery, and of the greater couple intimacy that results from this kind of joint "knowing" of unconscious struggles.

Part II, "Emotion and development", offers a second set of four chapters. The contribution by Paolo Bertrando and Teresa Arcelloni on anger and boredom is pitched towards emotional systems and the reluctance in family therapy to orientate towards "unpleasant" emotions. Every system is seen as an emotional system, and part of the discussion tracks around the territory that the concept of countertransference also seeks to address. Because the focus is on the systemic integrity of emotions (that emotions are relational processes rather than things, that they are part of relational sequences, in turn having relational effects), different aspects of psychoanalytic thinking are called on. Elements of the ideas of Kohut (on anger) and Kernberg (on emptiness/detachment) are drawn into a systemic frame, and ideas of attachment systems are also used to shed light on systemic practices in relation to anger and boredom in the therapeutic system.

Different intersections again with psychoanalytic thinking are used in David Pocock's discussion of working with emotional systems in Chapter Six. Here, four theory maps are introduced to offer a more thorough account of emotional systems. The maps are drawn from developments in attachment theory, contemporary psychoanalytic thinking informed by infant research, and selected aspects of relational psychoanalysis. More specifically, ideas of the emotional ecosystem of attachment, the system of self and interactive regulation, reflective functioning and the work of Fonagy and colleagues, and parental containment and survival in the move from object to subject-relating, are all used to orientate towards the complexity of conscious and unconscious emotional relating in families and in the therapeutic relationship.

Chapter Seven, by Rolf Sundet and Vigdis Wie Torsteinsson, offers a sustained exploration of developmental theory. Drawing particularly on Daniel Stern's work, the developmental domains of relatedness and relating is traced. Turn-taking, shared experience, attunement, and joint attention form the landscape of relating from which self emerges, including the narrative sense of self. These theoretical ideas are brought to life beautifully in the case examples of a young woman with an eating disorder and her family, and the extended work with an eight-year-old boy and his mother, where the boy's lead to do "work" with his therapist is followed. In both these situations, conversation about the problems seemed inaccessible, yet the authors place their engagement with the "unable-to-be-said" within a frame of therapeutic relating and reflective dialogue.

The last chapter of Part II has resonant themes with many of the chapters that have gone before, including the practice challenge of working with unconscious processes, countertransference, the tensions and richness of working from both psychoanalytic and systemic knowledges, strong emotions, and developmental processes. Jeremy Woodcock, in Chapter Eight, unfolds his exploration through the extended discussion of his work with one couple, placing at the centre theory about oedipal thinking and triangles and "thirds". The strong and related emotions of love and hate may be thought about in the context of the experience of being held in mind. The triangular implications of attachment theory and the experience of "thirdness" are brought to bear on understandings of the couple's struggle to know each other. The oedipal configuration is developmental, yet it becomes forever embedded in the capacity to think, which allows an intersubjective space for self and other in the context of thirdness.

The chapters in Part III, "Dialogue and otherness", move across a wide terrain, with dialogues of theory and orientations addressing processes of reflection, universality and difference in culture, and the ethics of otherness. Mary Donovan, in Chapter Nine, explores reflective functioning once again, but here she draws it into proximity with the systemic ideas and practices of reflecting processes. The resonance between the two is highlighted through the careful location of both sets of theory in relation to the challenges of practice. Differences of the intrapsychic and relational slants in theory and practice are still fully acknowledged, and the ethical framing of reflecting processes in systemic therapy is not disputed. However, a strong case is made for also acknowledging reflecting practices as techniques, to call to account the accessibility of psychotherapeutic work with clients and families who are not so easily engaged by mainstream therapeutic practices.

In Chapter Ten, Inga-Britt Krause tackles culture and the elements of cultural universality and difference that lie both within, and outside, consciousness. The chapter argues that systemic ideas have produced understandings of diversity that imply a universality that is then simply left blank, and that while we have theorized the power of social construction to create, we have not theorized the limits of social construction. On the other hand, psychoanalysis has theorized fundamental and universal developmental processes, yet cultural variation remains a largely uncharted territory. The chapter draws on less familiar parts of Bateson's work on culture and emotions, and on Bion's ideas of knowing and thinking. The conclusion is a passionate argument for the need to use both systemic and psychoanalytic understandings to address otherness and sameness, and conscious and non-conscious processes in culture.

The challenge of facing otherness is at the heart of Stephen Frosh's discussion in Chapter Eleven. While reflexivity might offer us practice leverage in approaching difference, the systemic momentum for relational "linking" potentially obscures the irreducible otherness of the other. Three layers of ideas are offered, beginning with the work of Jessica Benjamin, set within relational psychoanalysis. "Enjoyment" of the other becomes possible through the recognition of the other as *different* from self, and there is an extension of Oedipal theory that meets a feminist and political critique. The philosopher Emmanuel Levinas locates ethics as primary; here, intersubjectivity is not forged through recognition of the other, but, rather, created in an ethical relationship of responsibility for the other. Finally, the reflections of Lingis on thirdness and encounter are used to underscore the paradox of the commonality of having nothing in common, and to orientate towards a position in which we might resist a defensive need to feel safe by collapsing the otherness of the other in our knowing.

In Chapter Twelve, Glenn Larner intersects the ideas of Levinas and Bion to produce a fresh casting of the project of psychotherapy. Again, it is Levinas's idea of the ethical relation in the face-to-face encounter with another that is drawn into play. There are also echoes of Sebastian Kraemer's discussion of the intense mutuality of influence in practice. From one angle, therapy becomes what is done to the therapist, as well as an act of responsibility on the part of the therapist in the face of the unknown. Bion's work on thinking is traced again, this time drawing the link between containment and the ethical relation in therapy. In the case material, the experience of a young man and his family resonates with Glenn Larner's own lived experience, and the vulnerability of a therapist's *faux pas*, his lack of knowing, allows a container for the mutual creation of the conditions of thinking and processing emotional experience.

Final comments

We began our journey as editors from positions of similarity and difference with respect to our own relationships to systems and psychoanalysis. One of us (David) has a more even immersion in both systems and psychoanalysis. The other of us (Carmel) is more nomadic, both in terms of her relationship to different ideas and practices within the systemic field, as well as in her relationship to psychoanalysis. This book was forged in our shared desire to gather together the current ideas from a number of systemic therapists who have, in various ways, crossed the systemic/psychoanalytic border, some for many decades. Our thought was that the systemic opposition to psychoanalytic ideas no longer holds the intensity of its historical sway, especially in the context of a postmodern hospitality to the diversity of knowledges. This is not to negate the tensions that exist in attempts at integrations, nor to deny the ambivalence that many systemic practitioners—including contributors to, and editors of, this volume—hold towards aspects of psychoanalytic thinking and practices. Of course, bearing these mixed feelings is not without its complications, but not too dissimilar to managing the ambivalence one might hold towards particular aspects of systemic discourse.

Many kinds of books could be written about the intersections of systems and psychoanalysis, and it is possible that some readers may be disappointed by the absence of a clearer map from us locating these two traditions and their crossovers, for this would be an interesting and very useful project. However, for better or worse, it is not our project here. We are each simply more intrigued by the resonances and possibilities of the different theories and practices and, in particular, we are more engrossed by the common ground of lived experience and therapeutic change.

From start to finish, then, this is not a book with any programmatic aim for a framework integration of psychoanalysis in systemic therapy, nor is it a book offering a definitive map of sameness and difference between the two traditions. Instead, we offer this collection to you as readers to present the potentials of other theory and practice horizons in systemic therapy. We look forward to the further discussion and debates that we trust will follow.

PART I

THE UNCONSCIOUS IN THE SYSTEM

CHAPTER ONE

Narrative, meaning-making, and the unconscious

Carmel Flaskas

I n shaping my contribution to this book, I wanted to tackle some current systemic therapy theory issues. My chapter is, in part, an exploration of the metaphor of narrative, and the liberation and limits of meaning-making through language. It is also about the relationship of conscious and unconscious experience, and the territory that lies between languaged stories on the one hand, and the not-yet-said and the (perhaps) "unsayable" on the other. These topics relate to the process of meaning-making, and the relationship of lived experience to "story", as well as the relationship of the person who is constructing the story to her or his experience. Although this chapter is primarily about theory and ideas, my interest in it has been carved out in the experience of practice, and it rests on layer upon layer of wondering about the experience of therapeutic change and the process of meaning-making in psychotherapeutic work.

The structure of the discussion is quite simple. I begin by sketching the constellation of language, meaning, and the metaphor of narrative in the current context of family therapy theory. The chapter then moves to explore the complexity of the relationship of language to the realness of lived experience, along with the

3

opportunities for meeting realness in the space between unconscious and conscious experience. Tackling narrative and meaning-making from a different angle, the next part of the theory discussion addresses some broad conditions of transformative narratives, drawing on knowledge relating to coherent attachment narratives, and the ideas of mentalization and reflective functioning. Finally, I offer a rather messy piece of practice with a set of reflections on the resonant themes.

Language, meaning, and the metaphor of narrative

Systemic family therapy emerged historically from a psychotherapy landscape of the early 1960s, predominantly marked by intrapsychic theory and the practices of individual therapy. Its project, from the first, was to frame understandings of individual experience within the context of a person's most intimate relationships, and to use the leeway of family relationships directly in therapeutic intervention. Over the past forty-five years there have been many different family therapy practice approaches, and a number of twists and turns in theory emphases. Yet, across this time, the enduring parameters of family therapy have been context and relationship.

Having said this, the practice approaches generated within the first two or so decades look quite different to those generated within the last two decades. A reading confined to the internal development of family therapy knowledge tends to yield a competitive narrative about these changes, with the shape of current theories and practices being positioned as meeting the shortcomings and failures of previous approaches. However, I am more interested here in locating the changing emphases of family therapy knowledge within the broader cultural and intellectual milieu. Oddly enough, the continuity of our core interest in context and relationship is less likely to be lost in this broader reading. It also makes it easier to link, rather than divide, the emphases of the different contemporary approaches in family therapy, which in turn makes it easier to draw out core challenges in current theorizing.

The 1980s was a transitional decade in family therapy, for, during this period, bit by bit, we were significantly influenced by a constellation of ideas that orbited around the broader shift to post-modernism. In 1980, the structural and strategic schools were still very much the mainstream approaches in family therapy. Then, the theory was defined by first order systems ideas, and the inter-actional patterning of behaviour was essentially the main territory of practice focus. By 1990, not only had Milan therapy "arrived" in the English-speaking family therapy world, but it had somehow already managed to become "post-Milan". This approach became mainstream to systemic psychotherapy in the UK context. It sat alongside the beginning elaboration of "collaborative language systems therapy" (which sits now within the broader umbrella of dialogical therapies[1]), as well as the newly named narrative ther-apy, and the newly renamed solution-focused therapy. (Solution-focused therapy had come from the strategic tradition via a rather short-lived use of the label "brief therapy".)

Sixteen years later, this grouping of practice approaches—Milan-systemic, narrative, dialogical, and solution-focused—still occupies the main stage of family therapy, albeit with different levels of popularity in different places, and different levels of merg-ing of ideas from the different approaches. In all of this, the earlier biological and cybernetic systems metaphors have become periph-eral, while social constructionist and narrative ideas inform the theory arena that now assumes postmodernist parameters. Very significantly, the orientation of practices has shifted from patterns of behaviour to patterns of language and meaning.

Social constructionism occupies a pivotal theory position in this turn to meaning in family therapy. In its generic version, social constructionism theorizes a social world that can come to be known only in the context of our relationship to it. We construct knowledge of the world we live in through language and communication, and there can be no knowledge of the social world outside the language we give to it. In a recursive way, the language that we then give to our experience of the social world in turn influences and constructs the world we live in. This generic version of social constructionism effectively addresses the process by which we make sense of the social world and the power of the process of construction in contin-ually mediating that social world.

Some more specific theories of social constructionism take one step further. Here the idea is that it is not just that our knowledge of the social world is constructed in language, but rather that social realities themselves are constructed, and exist, within the domain of language. The work of social psychologist Kenneth Gergen (1991, 1994) has been heavily influential in family therapy (Flaskas, 2002), popularized especially through the work of Harry Goolishian and Harlene Anderson in their early elaboration of collaborative language systems therapy (see Anderson, 1997; Anderson & Goolishian, 1988, 1992). Gergen's theory of social constructionism is an example of this second extension, placing it, as Barbara Held notes, at the extreme end of anti-realism (Held, 1995).[2] In contrast, the generic version of social constructionism occupies a more moderate position, for, while it theorizes the construction of knowledge and its effects, none the less it still allows for the existence of social and emotional realities separate to (and, in this sense, independent of) their languaging.

The metaphor of narrative is linked with the territory of social constructionism. Narrative theory has a life well beyond the social sciences and sits at a strategic crossroad between the humanities and social sciences. One could think of narrative as the languaged pattern of meanings that "tells a story". In dialogical therapy, for example, the core understanding is that we construct our world in language, through narrative, and in dialogue and relationship with others (Anderson, 1997; Rober, 2005). Although Michael White and colleagues draw on somewhat different theory in elaborating narrative therapy, we still see the closely related idea that people live their lives, and understand themselves and their worlds, through narrative, through the stories they come to have of themselves and others, and through the power of the stories others have about them (see, for example, White, 2000, 2002, 2007). Presentations in therapy are framed as situations in which the stories that people have come to have about themselves and their difficulties prevent change. Therapy, then, is a collaborative conversation, and it provides a venue in which new meanings and stories can emerge that allow something different to happen. These last sentences could easily sit as a common description from the contemporary grouping of practice approaches in family therapy.

Now, there are two quite serious challenges that we bump up against if we stay too strictly within this territory of current theorizing. The first challenge, already foreshadowed in the discussion of social constructionist ideas, is the question of "realness". There are many arguments to be found in psychotherapy, and beyond, for not accepting the limits of a forced choice between the ideas of reality being *either* represented *or* constructed in the meanings we give to it. To move to a position that allows for the possibility that language both represents *and* constructs is a helpful step, which brings us to the complexities of the relationship of language to the lived experience of realness.

Second, if the metaphor of narrative is used as the sole anchor point for our practice theory, we run the risk of finding ourselves with an impoverished (and, oddly enough, quite depersonalized) description of the process of meaning-making. Meaning-making has at its centre the person who is trying to create meaning, the realness of her or his lived experience, which is the subject of the meaning-making, and the cultural and emotional conditions of that meaning-making. The content of the narrative itself that emerges is just one part of this process.

These two challenges—how to enrich our understandings of the relationship of language to the experience of realness, and of the location and conditions of narrative in the process of meaning-making—become my point of engagement with psychoanalytic ideas.

Language, realness, and the space between conscious and unconscious experience

The historical reluctance of family therapy to theorize unconscious experience lies partly in its early opposition to psychoanalysis, as well as the behavioural focus of its early practice approaches. I think a number of points of reluctance still hold sway. Included here might be the general lack of fit between the relational circularity of systemic thinking and the assumption that psychoanalysis is still committed to a hierarchical and topographical understanding of unconscious experience, a scepticism about the tendency to privilege unconscious experience as in some way "deeper" and "truer" than conscious experience, a practice distaste for the power the analyst assumes to interpret another's unconscious, and a related suspicion of unadorned practices of interpretation.

There are elements of good challenge in these points of reluctance, and there have been parallel challenges within psychoanalysis in the development of its own theory and practices. Early understandings of the unconscious located it within a hierarchical topography in relation to conscious experience: one could think, for example, of the Freudian schema of id, ego, and superego, or the framing of the main relationship between the conscious and unconscious as being that of repression, so that the content of the unconscious becomes that-which-is-repressed (see Rucker & Lombardi, 1998). However, contemporary understandings now locate the relationship between conscious and unconscious experience very differently. Of course, the cultural shift from modernist to postmodernist parameters was not so selective as to affect only family therapy in the world of psychotherapy. Psychoanalysis has not stood still, and nor have its theory and practices been frozen in time.

Theorizing the unconscious lies at the centre of the psychoanalytic project. Relational understandings began to show themselves most significantly with the work of Melanie Klein, though the strongest momentum builds from post-war in the late 1940s (interestingly enough, around the same time as the development of systems theory). The work of Wilfred Bion (see, for example, 1962, 1967, 1970) provides a watershed in post-Kleinian understandings of the unconscious, moving well beyond any simple understanding of the unconscious as repository of repressed "true" experience. His theory offers understandings of unconscious processes as multi-layered, and existing in complex relationship to emotional experience and the capacity to think. Donald Winnicott's contributions, and the shift from a one-person to a two-person psychology, also show the development of relational understandings (see, for example, 1971, 1989). Meanwhile, more recently, and mainly from North America, there have been the emergence of the intersubjective and relational perspectives in psychoanalysis, which show a location within postmodernist parameters (see, for example, Stolorow, Atwood & Brandchaft, 1994; Mitchell & Aron, 1999).

These sets of psychoanalytic understandings all potentially offer particular ways of thinking about unconscious processes and about the struggle to know and name realities outside our (languaged) conscious knowledge. The need for ways of thinking about experience outside conscious languaged stories is probably greater in the contemporary grouping of family therapy practice approaches. When the focus was primarily on behaviour, it was easier to side-step the unlanguaged, or at least to work around it. With the focus directly on meaning and story, it becomes more pressing to be able to think about what constitutes (in David Pocock's words [1995]) a "better story" in terms of therapeutic change, and how we try to grapple with lived experience through languaging meaning.

Far from experience being held solely within the confines of language, I think one would be very hard pressed to ignore the powerfulness of experience outside language, for better or worse. Both the most sublime and the most painful human experiences are only ever just approached in language. The mysteries of birth and death are never really able to be captured in words, and so much of how we experience intimate relationships is only roughly translatable in language. The pain of mortality, the limits of the body, or threats of physical violation or psychic annihilation find us in territories in which we may feel abandoned by words. Thus, there are times when language can barely represent, let alone construct, lived experience. Sometimes, far from constructing lived experience, language fragments or even dismantles that experience; nowhere is this more striking than in the area of trauma and abuse. In short, language can represent, construct, fragment, dismantle, or at times come nowhere near, lived experience.

When one opts to work in psychotherapy, it is a choice to occupationally engage with lived experience. Yet, language and relationship still remain our basic tools in working with the process of meaning-making in therapy. It is true that there are many ways in which languaged understandings develop and expand emotional and relational potential, and that there are many ways in family therapy that we invite the development of meaning. However, one of the powerful challenges available in the process of developing meaning is the challenge of incongruence between unconscious processes and the limits of a current languaged story. If you like, we are often prompted to change our story, not just because it is causing us problems, but because it is not measuring up to our experience.

For example, a father's desire to parent differently to his own experience of being parented might be challenged by the evidence he notices of the resonance and repetitions of difficulties in his relationship now with his children. A belief that someone might have in the strength of a couple relationship might sit uneasily alongside the experience of nursing a constant anxiety in relation to the other. A woman's story of her specialness, which serves as a nourishing illusion as a way of surviving childhood sexual abuse, could come tumbling down with the birth of her first child, and then living through a time of suicidal thinking might demand a different story and a new set of meanings about the lived experience of abuse. Thus, unconscious processes challenge the limits of languaged conscious stories, and often disrupt the stories we have so far of ourselves in relationship. They provide the opportunity for the development of meanings and stories that more closely meet the realness of lived experience. In this way, the space between conscious and unconscious experience provides fertile ground for re-storying.

Through all this discussion about language and the unconscious, I have perhaps not been emphasizing enough that language is held in relationship, and that language also holds relationship. Very rich, though quite different, understandings are offered here within psychoanalysis, and also within the foundational theorizing of the dialogical therapies. Language both requires and produces relationship. Developmentally, it is simply not possible for language to emerge without a very early sense of "I", and one is forever the first witness to one's own stories. As well, the symbolic representation of language stands in relationship to the experience to which it gives meaning. This is as much the case in situations when the effect of the language is to dismantle the experience so it cannot be known as it is in situations when language is able to represent lived experience in a very rich and full way. Yet, in the territories in which words can come nowhere near lived experience, the attempt to language— however inadequate—can still hold consolation, for language can serve to continue to carry the possibility of human connection. When words themselves may be next to useless, the attempt to language can sometimes still stand as an act of relational hope.

The conditions of transformative narratives in the process of meaning-making

The exploration so far of language, realness, and the unconscious has been part of an argument for expanding thinking about narrative and the process of meaning-making. Along the way, the complexity of the relationship of language to realness has been canvassed, as well as the task of approaching the realness of lived experience, the opportunities provided in the space between conscious and unconscious experience, and the relational context of language itself. Still sticking with the attention to narrative and the process of meaning-making, I shall now take this discussion down a more specific path and consider some of the understandings offered by research into attachment narratives, and by the work of Peter Fonagy and colleagues.

John Byng-Hall (1997) first flagged the significance of the research on narratives of attachment to a family therapy audience, and Rudi Dallos (2006) has recently drawn this research into the integrative practice framework of attachment narrative therapy. I believe that the attachment narratives research deserves far more attention in our field, because it offers understandings of the conditions of transformative narratives in relation to attachment experience. By "transformative narratives", I am referring to the kind of stories that are related to intra- and/or intergenerational change in patterns of relationship. Attachment, of course, is all about patterns of relationship, and it lies in a territory that is both languaged and unlanguaged. The research question in the relevant work of Mary Main and colleagues concerns the role of metacognition in mediating intergenerational attachment patterns (see, for example, Main, 1991). One can think of metacognition as "how you think about your own thinking about something", and metacognition as a process is at the core of how we construct the overarching stories of our own experiences.

The research studies of Main and colleagues (described in Main, 1991) investigated the form of the narratives of those people who had insecure attachment patterns in their own childhood and yet had somehow transformed these patterns in their own parenting so that their children had secure attachment relationships. In essence, a "good" narrative of attachment is not necessarily a happy one in relation to childhood experience, and indeed one can have a very difficult experience of attachment in childhood and still achieve the kind of narrative that offers transformative potential. The research suggests that one important quality here is coherence: the extent to which different parts of the story fit with other parts of the story. A story is coherent if a general description that is given about an important attachment relationship can then be followed up by specific examples that "fit" with the general story; emotional congruence is an integral part of this, for the emotions a person shows in relation to her or his story also needs to "fit" the general story. A coherent narrative in these respects might contrast with a situation in which a person finds it difficult to remember any particular examples, or the examples that are chosen do not really seem to relate to the general description, or may even sound contradictory, or the emotion that is expressed does not seem to make sense in relation to the story that is being told. (See Chapter Three in Dallos, 2006 for a much fuller discussion of narrative congruence.)

A second important quality of a transformative narrative is that it is plausible. Someone hearing the story should be able to relate to the story as believable. This is helped when the person telling the story is able to offer some understandings of the parent's behaviour in terms of the parent's own situation (if you like, the parent's behaviour is understood in a context beyond self, and in a context that is beyond the specifics of the relationship itself). It also seems to be significant that the person is able to tell the story in a way that evokes a connection for the listener with the person and the story. I am inclined to think that the listener's capacity to connect in this way relates to the capacity of the person to hold a sense of self at the centre of the telling of her or his story.

Two conditions, then, of transformative narratives are coherence and plausibility. Yet to simply list these conditions point-blank is potentially misleading, for at first glance it looks as if it is *just* the form of the stories that matters. Yet, even the very brief outline I have just offered belies this misreading, for these narrative conditions reach through to the complexity of the process of meaning-making as a whole. The "internal" coherence of a story relates directly to the extent to which the person's meaning speaks to an experience that is able to be made coherent. Although there is no way we can ever really know about "objective" or "external" reality, there is a way in which an intimate experience of realness can be well met or not well met by the understandings that are constructed around historical experience, and it would seem that this meeting of realness is part of the conditions of transformative narratives.

The condition of plausibility, which effectively relates to how someone else is able to hear the story, is interesting both relationally and psychologically. In the research methodology, plausibility is assessed via the response of another (the listener, the observer) to enter into the story, to find it believable, and to relate to the story and the person telling the story. It is here that the theory and research of Peter Fonagy and colleagues dovetails with attachment research (see, for example, Bateman & Fonagy, 2006; Fonagy, 2001; Fonagy, Steele, Steele, Moran, & Higgitt, 1991). Understandings of the process of mentalization cross both psychoanalytic and attachment theory, and emerged concurrently in both fields (Fonagy, 2001). Mentalization is a symbolic function in human relating: the capacity to interpret the behaviour of self and others in terms of mental states. Fonagy notes that ideas about mental states might relate to beliefs, or attitudes, or hopes, or knowledge, or imagination, or desires, or plans or pretence (Fonagy, 2001, p. 165).

Mentalization is central to the process of meaning-making about self and other, and it links closely to the idea of reflective function that, conceptually, is more related to attachment theory. In an early attachment relationship, reflective function shows in the parents' capacity to wonder about the baby's distress, to try to make some sense of it in terms of the baby's experience, and to respond to the baby from this capacity to think about and "hold" the baby in mind. The third point of this theory triangle is Bion's understanding that the emergence of the capacity to think occurs in the relational context of someone being able to think about us, and the containment and holding of that relationship. Thus, mentalization, reflective function, and Bion's work on the capacity to think provide a triangle of understandings that together speak to the heart of the process of meaning-making and the conditions of transformative narratives.

The empirical research related to mentalization, reflective function, and metacognition and attachment narratives is increasingly overlapping with the research programme on resilience. The capacity to generate what I have been calling "transformative narratives" is now established as a significant factor in relation to the development of resilience (Holmes, 2001; Rutter, 1996; Walsh 2006). This intersection alone should draw our interest in family therapy. But this knowledge is also confirming of, and compatible with, the use of the metaphor of narrative in family therapy. It responds to the limits of our current understandings, offering ways of thinking about the place of narrative in the broader process of meaning-making, and the conditions of the development of meaning which meet the realness of lived experience.

Reflections on a messy piece of work

Let me suspend the theory discussion at this point and reflect on one of the pieces of work that I have been thinking about while I have been working on this chapter.

> The referral was simple enough: a family, two parents and a ten-year-old girl, coming because the girl could still not sleep by herself. She would insist that the mother stay with her until she went to sleep, and then she would wake up and tantrum if the mother tried to leave, leading to the mother sleeping with her daughter most nights. Not surprisingly, the mother felt controlled by her daughter, the father felt excluded from the closeness of the mother–daughter relationship, and the girl was very unhappy and only too aware of how developmentally behind she was.
>
> More surprising was the intensity of feelings in the family in the first session, and there was a desperation and anger that, at least on the face of it, seemed out of proportion to the symptomology. There was also something very messy in the way in which problems in the parents' relationship, and specifically their sexual relationship, were connected to the daughter's demanding behaviour of her mother, and I felt somewhat disturbed by it. Throughout this first session, I was also quite aware of not liking the father, and I often found myself feeling irritated with the mother, whose complaints about her daughter seemed to me to be exaggerated and self-referencing.
>
> Some proportions of the intensity of these feelings unravelled quite quickly in a session with the parents by themselves. The father told me something of his own childhood: that he felt distant from his mother and in fear of his father's physically and emotionally punitive responses. The mother told me of a very painful and abusive childhood, with her mother dying when she was two, her grandmother then physically abusing her from the ages of 2–7, and her father then sexually abusing her from the age of eight until she left home at sixteen. At this point in the session, my negative countertransferences to the parents

began to evaporate, and I felt more able to connect with them both. However, another story is then told that cuts across my tenuous empathic connection, particularly with the father. The couple tell me how they met each other, and the husband becomes angry as he relates that his wife never told him about the sexual abuse. She had become very depressed a year after they were married, and was hospitalized, and the husband only came to know about her abuse when he was told by her psychiatrist. There was a strong and very current sense of the husband's rage and humiliation and betrayal in the telling of this story, which seemed to eclipse any story of his wife's experience of abuse, or even any story she might have to tell of the time of her depression and hospitalization.

The family work continues, and the daughter is quite easy to engage in work around her own growing up. She loves the externalization of her tantrums, and is determined to tackle the sleeping problem. Her parents begin setting some boundaries around her involvement in their relationship, and her initial resentment of this change turns quite quickly to relief. However, as the daughter achieves learning to sleep by herself, the mother finds she cannot sleep. She feels distressed and alone during the night, and begins to write a diary about her feelings and some of the times in her childhood. This diary is initially addressed to me, and she brings it to sessions.

This was an important crossroads in the work. My practice orientation was to help the mother feel supported through the intense pain of separation from her daughter, to try to connect the husband with his wife, and for the two of them to manage the crisis in a way that would allow the daughter to continue to grow and not draw her back into old patterns. For a while, we alternated family sessions with couple sessions. In the family sessions, I would spend some individual time with the daughter, while the husband and wife talked about the wife's diary in a separate room, and then we would all join together for the last fifteen minutes.

There were a number of things about my experience of work with this family that relate to the theory themes of this chapter. First, I note the form and intensity of the mother–daughter attachment, and the very real and very painful barriers for the mother in approaching separation. I also note the "thin-ness" of the narrative that the mother had to language her truly shocking experiences of childhood abuse, and the way in which the husband's narrative of anger towards his wife seemed to take up the emotional space between them.

In challenging my own experience of anger toward the husband, I found it very containing to reflect on the way in which it was the husband who had the narrative of humiliation and rage and betrayal when, of the three of us sitting in the room in that session, it was his wife who might be most expected to have the intensity of this narrative. This thought about projective processes helped me move beyond the clinically not very sophisticated "What a creep!" assessment of the husband towards a sense of the possibility of some unconscious negotiation between the couple. One thought I had was that perhaps the husband had come to carry a languaged narrative of his own experience that related more intensely to his wife's unlanguaged experience. This thought, in turn, helped me take a therapeutic "leap of faith" that the husband might be able to support his wife through this round of her depression and distress in a way that he could not when she had been so depressed the year after they were married. Also, from the other side of the relationship, that the wife might be able to tolerate her husband knowing something more about her experience in the context of her struggle as a mother to allow her daughter to be able to separate from her.

The use of the split dyads in the family sessions was unusual (I have only rarely used this format). It happened in one session on a structural impulse that was informed as much by psychoanalytic thinking as it was by systemic thinking. The beauty and freedom of family therapy is that you can sometimes simply use your own body and presence as "another" and, in this situation, a family of three temporarily became a virtual family of four. The transitional structure during this period of the therapy was useful in keeping some space for the daughter, and it seemed to circumnavigate the potential for the dyad of the mother and myself to exclude the father in the age-old pattern of how threes were managed in the family. At the same time, the combination of the split family sessions and the couple sessions allowed me still to acknowledge the seriousness of the pain for the mother and to invite the couple to know about it together. Through the work as a whole, the mother came to have a narrative about her childhood and her pain as a mother that was richer ("thicker") and more coherent, and her husband was able to find a space to become more of a husband and more of a father. Both parents took responsibility for an explanation to the daughter about some things about the mother's story and their story as a couple. Although this was hard, it allowed the daughter to begin to have some words for why things could be hard for her mother, and why her parents argued, and she began to come to her own understandings about the way in which some things for her parents were quite separate to anything to do with her.

In short, during the therapy, some unconscious processes found their way into more conscious stories, some repetitions were relived in a slightly different way, and the idea that there could be ways of thinking about what might be happening gained some currency among them all. I would like to tell you that the parents took up my referral for couple therapy, and the mother went into psychotherapy for herself. These things did not happen, but the family certainly used the therapy to help the daughter move to another stage developmentally, and as a family they moved to another stage developmentally, with some more coherent and plausible stories and, I would like to think, with a greater capacity for resilience.

Conclusion

This chapter has addressed questions about the boundaries of current theorizing in family therapy. On the one hand, I have appreciated and valued the shift to language and meaning and the metaphor of narrative in our practice theory, and yet, on the other hand, these theory understandings on their own seem limited in addressing the realness of experience, and the richness of the process of meaning-making and the conditions of narrative. The limits led me first to explore the complexity of the relationship of language to realness in lived experience, and the territory of unconscious processes outside conscious languaged meaning. My argument here was that the space between unconscious and conscious experience provides fertile ground for the development of stories that more fully meet the realness of experience. A second layer of discussion about narrative and meaning-making focused on the conditions of transformative narratives, drawing on work on attachment narratives, and sketching the constellation of knowledge emerging about mentalization, reflective functioning, and the capacity to think.

Can you have your cake and eat it too? My discussion in this chapter is not a rejection of current systemic theory. Family therapy can continue to operate well using the metaphor of narrative and social constructionist ideas in a pragmatic way, and can simply put to one side challenges about the limits of our current theory and the practice it describes and generates. At the same time, it seems to me impoverishing of our theory and practice to settle for this. Generally, I subscribe to the idea that there is nothing more useful than a good theory. The conclusion of my chapter, then, is that it is always useful to call on more complex understandings of language and the realness of lived experience, and to have ways of thinking about unconscious experience and the processes of storying, and the conditions of transformative narratives and resilience.

Notes

1. I might well be compressing far too much difference in claiming that a strand of therapeutic frameworks can all fit under an umbrella description of dialogical approaches. However, I do think that "dialogue" is a central organizing theory and practice concept in the (North American) collaborative language systems therapy (Anderson, 1997; Anderson & Goolishian, 1988, 1992), and (from Europe) in the work of Tom Andersen (1987, 1991), Jaako Seikkkula (Seikkula, 2002, 2003; Seikkula & Olson, 2003) and Peter Rober (2002, 2005). In his very recent book, the Italian systemic psychotherapist Paolo Bertrando has melded systemic and dialogical ideas (Bertrando, 2007).

2. See, in this volume, David Pocock's related discussion of critical realism, which theorizes the discursive power of knowledge while still allowing for the existence of a real and complex social world beyond our thinking, against which knowledge can be tested.

References

Anderson, H. (1997). *Conversation, Language and Possibilities: A Postmodern Approach to Therapy*. New York: Basic Books.

Anderson, H., & Goolishian, H. (1988). Human systems as linguistic systems: preliminary and evolving ideas about the implications for clinical theory. *Family Process*, 27: 371–393.

Anderson, H., & Goolishian, H. (1992). The client is the expert: a not-knowing approach to therapy. In: S. McNamee & K. J. Gergen (Eds.), *Therapy as Social Construction* (pp. 25–39). London: Sage.

Andersen, T. (1987). The reflective team: dialogue and meta-dialogues in clinical work. *Family Process, 26*: 415–428.

Andersen, T. (1991). *The Reflecting Team: Dialogues and Dialogues about Dialogues*. New York: Norton.

Bateman, A., & Fonagy, P. (2006). *Mentalization-Based Treatment for Borderline Personality Disorder*. Oxford: Oxford University Press.

Bertrando, P. (2007). *The Dialogical Therapist: Dialogue in Systemic Practice*. London: Karnac.

Bion, W. (1962). *Learning from Experience*. London: Heinemann.

Bion, W. R. (1967). *Second Thoughts: Selected Papers on Psycho-Analysis*. London: Maresfield Library, Karnac.

Bion, W. R. (1970). *Attention and Interpretation*. London: Tavistock.

Byng-Hall, J. (1997). Toward a coherent story about illness and loss. In: R. K. Papadopoulos & J. Byng-Hall (Eds.), *Multiple Voices: Narrative in Systemic Family Psychotherapy* (pp. 103–124). London: Duckworth.

Dallos, R. (2006). *Attachment Narrative Therapy: Integrating Narrative, Systemic and Attachment Therapies*. Maidenhead: Open University Press.

Flaskas, C. (2002). *Family Therapy Beyond Postmodernism: Practice Challenges Theory*. Hove: Brunner-Routledge.

Fonagy, P. (2001). *Attachment Theory and Psychoanalysis*. New York: Other Books.

Fonagy, P., Steele, M., Steele, H., Moran, G., & Higgitt, A. (1991). The capacity for understanding mental states: the reflective self in parent and child and its significance for security of attachment. *Infant Mental Health Journal, 13*: 200–217.

Gergen, K. J. (1991). *The Saturated Self: Dilemmas of Identity in Contemporary Life*. New York: Basic Books.

Gergen, K. J. (1994). *Realities and Relationships: Soundings in Construction*. Cambridge, MA: Harvard University Press.

Held, B. (1994). *Back to Reality: A Critique of Postmodern Theory in Psychotherapy*. New York: Norton.

Holmes, J. (2001). *The Search for a Secure Base: Attachment Theory and Psychotherapy*. London: Brunner-Routledge.

Main, M. (1991). Metacognitive knowledge, metacognitive monitoring, and singular (coherent) vs. multiple (incoherent) model of attachment: findings and directions for further research. In: C. M. Parkes, J. Stevenson-Hinde, & P. Marris (Eds.), *Attachment Across the Life Cycle* (pp. 127–159). London: Routledge.

Mitchell, S., & Aron, L. (Eds.) (1999). *Relational Psychoanalysis: The Emergence of a Tradition*. Hillsdale, NJ: Analytic Press.

Pocock, D. (1995). Searching for a better story: harnessing modern and postmodern positions in family therapy. *Journal of Family Therapy*, 17: 149–174.

Rober, P. (2002). Constructive hypothesizing, dialogic understanding, and the therapist's inner conversation: Some ideas of knowing and not-knowing in the family therapy session. *Journal of Marital and Family Therapy, 28:* 467–478.

Rober, P. (2005). Family therapy as a dialogue of living persons: a perspective inspired by Bakhtin, Volosinov and Shotter. *Journal of Marital and Family Therapy, 31:* 385–397.

Rucker, N. G., & Lombardi, K. L. (1998). Subject relations: unconscious experience and relational psychoanalysis. New York: Routledge.

Rutter, M. (1996). Resilience concepts and findings: implications for family therapy. *Journal of Family Therapy, 21:* 119–144.

Seikkula, J. (2002). Monologue is the crisis: dialogue becomes the aim of therapy. *Journal of Marital and Family Therapy, 28:* 283–284.

Seikkula, J. (2003). Dialogue is the change: understanding psychotherapy as a semiotic process of Bakhtin, Voloshinov, and Vygotsky. *Human Systems, 14:* 83–94.

Seikkula, J., & Olson, M. (2003). The open dialogue approach to acute psychosis: its poetics and micropolitics. *Family Process, 42:* 403–418.

Stolorow, R. D., Atwood, G. E., & Brandchaft, B. (Eds.) (1994). *The Intersubjective Perspective*. Northvale, NJ: Jason Aronson.

Walsh, F. (2006). *Strengthening Family Resilience* (2nd edn). New York: Guilford.

White, M. (2000). *Reflections on Narrative Practice: Essays and Interviews*. Adelaide: Dulwich Centre Publications.

White, M. (2002). *Narrative Practice and Exotic Lives: Resurrecting Diversity in Everyday Life*. Adelaide: Dulwich Centre Publications.

White, M. (2007). *Maps of Narrative Practice*. New York: Norton.

Winnicott, D. W. (1971). *Playing and Reality*. London: Routledge.

Winnicott, D. W. (1989). *Holding and Interpretation: Fragment of an Analysis*. London: Karnac.

CHAPTER TWO

Working with unconscious processes: psychoanalysis and systemic family therapy

Julia Bland

This book addresses not only theoretical integration but also concerns of daily practice: how can we integrate psychoanalytic and systemic therapies, and what do we mean by integration? Working as a clinician trained in both disciplines, I find that there is a tension between the struggle to integrate (or at least hold on to both models) without denying difference, and the wish for clarity and simplicity, a sense of definite anchorage in the clinical sea. My chapter explores challenges in the integration of these two frameworks, addressing theory differences and practice, particularly with respect to working with unconscious processes in family therapy. It moves from a discussion of the cultural differences of psychoanalysis and systemic therapy and their respective contexts of theory to an exploration of their contrasting orientations to symptoms and change, and the differences in therapeutic relationship and style. Finally, clinical examples are used to explore the challenges and possibilities of using psychoanalytic and systemic ideas in working with unconscious processes in family therapy.

Cultural differences

There is a long-standing history of tension and ambivalence between the two cultures of family therapy and psychoanalysis. The "cultural" differences are observable at gatherings of each group. The analytic conference tends to be quite formal and social distance is maintained. As one analyst recently commented, half-jokingly, "It is hardly surprising people are formal, since half the people in the room are analysing the other half or their families . . .". Perhaps it is an appreciation of the intensity of intimacy that characterizes the analytic encounter that makes this group wary of casual social confidences. Or are there pre-existing temperamental differences that draw the more reserved person towards becoming the analyst while a noisier, more extrovert type is drawn to the systemic world? Certainly, the systemic world is more openly confiding, less formal, with immediate use of first names as the norm. Exchanges about the therapists' private life may be woven into conversation more freely, and would be seen as potentially relevant to practice. Some family therapists use their own life experience explicitly when working with families, which is unthinkable for psychoanalytic psychotherapists.

As a family therapist who has trained in psychoanalytic psychotherapy with individuals and spent many years in analysis myself, I find myself in the uncomfortable fence position, the permanently sceptical outsider, potentially regarded with scepticism by both camps as "not really one of us". Another view of the person on the fence—between, but not entirely of, either camp—is that of participant–observer, an embedded anthropologist.

There are real differences between a systemic and an analytic approach. Family therapists tend to see themselves as challengers of the prevailing orthodoxies of power, class, gender, and the medical model, particularly diagnostic labels. In 2005, looking back over thirty years of the Association for Family Therapy, Alan Cooklin wrote,

> We were full of the great challenge to psychiatry, which many of us represented as the inhuman face of "established orthodoxy". In many ways standard psychiatric practice and psychoanalysis, opposed to each other as they were at least in theory, were equally our adversaries. We were shouting from outside the loop. [Cooklin, 2005, p. 2]

This sense of wishing to "join", to position ourselves alongside, or even as champions of, marginalized groups (without patronizing them), still informs the tone of systemic writing and practice. With the embracing of postmodern ideas of relativity of discourses and the social construction of identity through language, the therapist's own cultural baggage demands acknowledgement. We expect ourselves to be aware of where we come from in terms of culture, gender, class, language, colour, assumptions, and experience, and to articulate how these personal particularities might have an impact on our capacity to be useful in the face of difference in the consulting room. All this particular kind of self-scrutiny tends towards the family therapist adopting a tentative and respectful attitude to the family in the room. "Taking the one down position" acknowledges the family, however troubled, as experts on them-selves, and it is one of the most attractive and freeing aspects of this approach. The way is opened to a collaborative style, attending to the family's own use of language, and to overtly acknowledging the limitations that our own experience puts on our capacity really to comprehend the family's experience.

Unlike systemic ideas, the analytic discourse did not arise from the "swinging Sixties", but from a complex and paradoxical man who combined the articulation of extraordinarily provocative ideas such as infantile sexuality with a deeply conventional lifestyle. He visited his mother to play cards every Sunday afternoon until her death. Psychoanalytic work, and the attitude that it demands, rest on the paradox that can be seen in Freud himself: the unacceptable, the unthinkable, the most sexually disinhibited and/or violent, per-verse, and primitive fantasies are not only tolerated, but explored and thought about, with a wish to understand rather than to judge. At the same time, the experimental method, which is indeed the treatment itself, is rigorously disciplined, with the fifty-minute hour, the consistency of time and place, and the reliability and lack of personal disclosure by the analyst. The very freedom that analy-sis offers to the patient—to say anything, however outlandish—is sustained by the disciplined containment and structure.

Psychoanalytic theory makes the claim that some profound aspects of human experience *underlie* cultural difference, such as the experience of rejection, being left out, particularly by the parental couple. One of the most unpalatable, and least accepted, of Freud's ideas is the existence of extreme negative feelings, including murderous hatred and envy, as part of ordinary human emotional experience, which can safely be acknowledged and thought about without increasing (rather *decreasing*) the likelihood of these feelings being enacted in "real life".

The implication of these theoretical ideas is a position of tolerance and acceptance of the aggression and envy that our censorious conscious selves might not acknowledge readily. Many people find it difficult to accept the co-existence of intense, simultaneous and entirely contradictory feelings such as love and hate for the same person at the same time. The analytic process allows the individual in treatment gradually to become reconciled to the creative and destructive aspects of the self, which in turn can result in taking more personal responsibility and being less blaming of the other, with an enhanced capacity for reparation in relationships.

So how different are these approaches? I will look at two specific areas and compare practice ideas emanating from the two theoretical streams, while fully acknowledging that I cannot do justice to the controversies, complexity, and range of ideas *within* each tradition. The areas I will discuss are theory of symptoms and change, and therapeutic relationship and style.

Theory of symptoms and change

The systemic view is that the symptom or presenting problem brought by a family or couple is *in itself* an attempted solution to an intractable state of affairs. "The solution that is the symptom, becomes the problem", wrote Watzlawick in 1974 (Watzlawick, Weakland, & Fisch, 1974, p. 9, quoted in Dare, 1989, p. 4). The presenting problem, often located in one individual within the family, is presupposed to be a reflection of an interpersonal process, which in turn recursively exacerbates the "problem". The therapeutic attitude is non-blaming, anti-scapegoating and tends towards a positive reframing of the symptom itself. Weakland (in Watzlawick, Weakland, & Fisch, 1974, p. 240, quoted in Holmes, 1983) expounds this interactional view of symptoms: ". . . the kinds of problems people bring to therapists *persist* only if they are maintained by the ongoing current behaviour of the patient and others with whom he interacts" (emphasis in original). Dare (1989, p. 25) claims that the search for the meaning of a symptom allows "alternative views as to their predicament which allows for the possibility of increasing self-determination". At a conference in 2006, Paolo Bertrando, a contributor to this book, quoted the English nineteenth century poet and artist William Blake: "a tear is an intellectual thing". This deliberately paradoxical juxtaposition underlines the importance of the capacity to *think* about feelings, a task shared by systemic and analytic work.

The analytic approach to symptoms, those mental experiences that distress patients, is to explain them in terms of a symbolic and unconscious meaning for the individual symptom bearer. While the perpetuating effect of family relationships on the symptom in real time will be understood, the interest is on the unconscious projective mechanisms that might determine why an individual has entered into a relationship with a particular other in the first place. Why does the woman whose early experience of a depressed mother led to a fragile sense of self worth end up with a critical partner who tends to confirm her sense of inadequacy? The analytic view of symptoms includes the assumption of unconscious repetition, which, when understood, can lead into the liberation of freer and less self-destructive choices.

Jeremy Holmes (1983) contrasts the theories of change in this way:

> Family therapy aims to change the state of the system so that the symptom bearer is relieved of his symptoms, and can get on with the normal process of development and change. In psychoanalysis, the analytic relationship is the vehicle of change; in family therapy it is "real life". [*ibid.*, p. 245]

Interestingly, Bertrando (2002) contrasts psychoanalytic and systemic work with individuals, having obviously removed one concrete difference between the two models: the family's physical presence in the room. He writes,

> In a psychoanalytic setting ... the relationships with third parties end up being subsumed by the transferential relationship, of which they become a part ... In systemic work, the therapist metaphorically takes the client by the hand in the therapeutic relationship and

> in this way she "leads him out" of the dual relationship to "visit"
> his present relationships, bringing those relationships . . . to the
> fore. In a way, the scene of the true therapeutic event is what
> happens outside the therapy room. [Bertrando, 2002, p. 364]

An uncontroversial systemic view is that a *change of context* may reinforce change in symptoms. An example of this theory has been given by Peter Steinglass (1987), describing his innovative approach to alcoholism of treating the whole family system, which he sees as organized around the addicted person in a way that reinforces the addiction. Robin Skynner described himself as influenced by the Milan group when they visited the Tavistock Clinic in the 1980s. He makes the point (1989) that an interpretation ideally needs to address the desire for change and fear of change in a single communication. He also attempts to use interpretation to create change, like a Milan-style "injunction" or "prescription".

Skynner (*ibid.*) gave a powerful clinical example of a somatizing husband with a wife in the role of helper, but depressed herself. Skynner's intervention was to suggest to the husband that he is making a big sacrifice by staying ill and distracting his wife from thinking about herself ,which she clearly cannot bear to do. This interpretation recognizes the emotional needs of both to be looked after, and gives a positive reframe to both their unhelpful behaviours. In terms of psychoanalytic thinking, the wife's needs are projected into the husband, so he gets the "double dose" and is "assigned" the sick child role, while she takes on the parental role. As he becomes more incapacitated and demanding, she feels increasingly depleted and deprived, with health professionals subsequently being invited into the projective system to prop it up. The trick is not to join in, but tactfully to point out what is happening, so that the couple can distribute their own needs and resources more helpfully.

This example leads on to the analytic idea of psychic change taking place as a result of the withdrawal of projections, which includes the idea of taking responsibility for one's own mental state and being more able to distinguish which feelings belong to the self and which to another person, who is projecting them into the self. Mutual projection is not theorized as pathology, but is simply part of the way in which we all relate. However, it can become problematic, as described in the couple above. In the consulting room, therapists have a role in tolerating the material projected into them, but ultimately helping patients see what belongs to them. Family members will often not be able to fend off what is projected into them. As Campion and Fry pointed out (1985), the Kleinian idea of projective identification has an explanatory power concerning the interlocking pathologies in a family and intergenerational transmission.

I think that the dialectic set up about the direction of change in the different modalities of psychotherapy is unhelpful and unsystemic. Classically, in psychoanalytic work, interpretation leads to insight, which is supposed to lead to change in affect and (ultimately) behaviour. In behaviour therapy, the change is directed first at the behaviour: getting the agoraphobic person into the supermarket, and hoping the affect and cognitions change later. The cognitive–behavioural approach attacks the symptomatic cycle at a different point, trying to shift rigid cognitive structures and patterns with the hope of allowing emotional relief ("so it's not true that no one likes me"), leading to a wider behavioural repertoire ("perhaps I will accept that invitation"). As Skynner's example neatly illustrates, these different levels—cognition, affect, and behaviour—as well as the unconscious projective processes, all operate simultaneously and recursively on one another. We are simply choosing different modality and language-based contexts from which to describe, define, and intervene in what is a single process: the complexity of human interaction. It is not useful to argue about which is the best point to intervene in a circular process.

Before moving to a consideration of the contrasts in therapeutic relationship and style, I note that there is a massive overlap in terms of the major focus of interest in the therapeutic process. Unsurprisingly, though, processes are languaged very differently in the two traditions. As Holmes (1983) describes, both models are concerned with difference between sexes and generations, with intergenerational boundaries (the Oedipus complex), and with developmental blocks. Systemic therapists talk about separation, generational boundaries, family life cycle, and cultural context, while analytic writers focus on individual psychic development, projective mechanisms, loss, reality testing, giving up of omnipotence, defence mechanisms, and unconscious fantasy. In both modalities, the problematic nature of reality is acknowledged and the aims of treatment are similar. While Minuchin sees therapy as expanding the repertoire of family members in responding to the complexities of life, Freud is alleged to have seen the aim of psychoanalysis to be the conversion of neurotic misery into ordinary unhappiness.

Therapeutic style and relationship

There are a number of points of contrast between the two traditions in terms of therapeutic style and the therapeutic relationship. In broad terms, one could characterize the systemic style as more "modern", more politically correct, quicker, less elitist, more flamboyant, with a more positive attitude to family and individual resources. The therapeutic process is more public, with the one-way screen and reflecting team. Analytic work is more formal in external style, but it could be argued that there is greater freedom in terms of content for both patient and analyst. A greater value is placed on the intellectual power or cleverness of the analytic therapist, the power relationships are unashamedly hierarchical without fear of the "expert" position, and scant attention is paid to political correctness.

Significant differences in style emerge in the use of language and silence. The social constructionist view of language emphasizes the power relationships inherent in the use of language: who has the right to name? In analytic therapy, more emphasis is laid on silence, the meaning beyond words. Many years ago, I heard the analyst Patrick Casement describing being silent for two entire sessions with a woman towards the end of her analysis. She had always had a profound sense of being unbearable to be with and the experience of "being alone in the presence of another", being held in mind, without words, was powerfully affirming and important to her.

This illustration points to another set of differences with respect to the dimensions of "depth" and "breadth" in the therapeutic process, and how this affects (and is affected by) therapeutic style and the therapeutic relationship. To spend 100 minutes in silence with the therapist and find it profoundly valuable is only possible in the context of a long and deep relationship in which patient and analyst have spent countless hours together struggling towards an intimate mental contact, which might often be beyond language. Systemic therapy does not attempt this kind of contact, or at least it is much more fleeting if it occurs. Systemic therapy is intrinsically brief in terms of number of therapeutic hours, even if spread out over more than a year. It is also abstemious (in terms of de-emphasizing the importance of the therapeutic relationship), and there is usually an explicit aim of protecting the family from unnecessary dependence and emphasizing their own resources. Yet, in the analytic view, the intensity of the transferential relationship is not optional—it just happens—and the only question is the extent to which it can be thought about and discussed.

In contrast to the intensity and depth in psychoanalysis, the systemic therapist lays reasonable claim to breadth, taking in a wide range of contexts, social, political, and cultural. The therapeutic effort is directed at widening the repertoire of narratives, and normative assumptions are abhorred. Bertrando (2006) has described several human systems: linguistic, power, relational and emotional systems, and sees the specific task of systemic work to connect the emotional and relational systems: "to give emotions relational sense", evoked by the question "Who is x crying for?"

Self-reflexivity is valued in family therapy training, with trainees doing their own genograms, and being expected to think about how their own family experience impacts on their capacity to work with families. A family therapy training involves personal development, but not at the same depth or intensity as that required in analytic training. However, there is more explicit "showing" of self in the systemic context. Family therapists may demonstrate their self-awareness verbally with a family: "I notice the reflecting team are all women today, and I wonder how that makes you feel?", a comment addressed to a man who is the perpetrator of domestic violence. As Cecchin, Lane, and Ray (1992, p. 9) write: ". . . it is at the moment when the therapist begins to reflect upon the effect of his own attitudes and presumptions that he acquires a position that is both ethical and therapeutic". This stance of self-aware flexibility seems essential to strive for in the work in my clinics with people with long-standing severe mental illness.

Family therapists tend to dislike the analytic hierarchy of knowledge where deep (i.e., the intrapersonal) is good and shallower (i.e., the interpersonal and cultural) is somehow less important. Family therapists also dislike the assumed superiority of the analytic position, with its claim to an esoteric knowledge of the invisible workings of other people's minds. This dislike rests on something of a caricature and leaves out the humility that the best analysts feel in the face of another's experience, yet, at the same time, it also reflects a reality of how *some* analysts write and behave.

In part, the notion of depth is "privileged" in analytic discourse because there is an implicit claim that certain deeply unconscious preoccupations underlie cultural difference and are universal. These would include destructiveness, the oedipal struggle, and the pain of rejection. Psychoanalytic theory certainly does address the negative. Klein's account of the death instinct (1957), whether one subscribes to it or not, is a serious attempt to grasp the nettle: where does human nastiness come from, and why are people so vilely destructive of themselves and others?

Psychoanalytic practice also very directly addresses the negative within the containment of the therapeutic relationship. Psychoanalytic therapists are trained in the survival of being hated, and this toughness may help some patients to master their disappointment in life and therapy. Winnicott (1947) argues for the necessity of hating one's patients and tolerating being hated by them. This capacity—not minding being the bad object—is a real psychic achievement for those of us with a tendency to placate. In orientating to family strengths and resources, the systemic family therapist can want to be liked, and to be seen as helpful and positive. If this therapeutic style becomes too cosy, the therapy is unlikely to be effective and risks being superficial.

A final point in this review concerns the issue of flexibility and fluctuation in therapeutic style. Flaskas (1997) emphasizes that, in comparison with analytic work, in systemic therapy there will be "much greater *fluctuation* in the levels of intimacy and attachment. In this sense there is a *conditional pragmatism* in systemic therapy with respect to intimacy and attachment" (*ibid.*, p. 269, my italics). The term "conditional pragmatism" speaks to an ideal of therapeutic involvement that is highly sensitive to the levels of intimacy and attachment that are most useful to this family at a particular moment. It implies a client-centred approach, and, while not deny-ing the centrality of the therapeutic relationship, demands a modest manoeuvring of the therapist in response to the family's needs.

There is interesting new neuroscientific evidence adduced by Fonagy and Bateman (2006) in relation to the treatment of border-line personality disorder, which could be relevant to Flaskas's idea of fluctuating levels of intimacy and attachment. There is evidence (Bartels & Zeki, 2004) that when the attachment system is highly activated, there is decreased capacity to mentalize, i.e., to think, about the state of mind of self and other. Fonagy and Bateman draw the conclusion that particular caution might be advised with borderline patients who tend to make intense attachments to their therapist. This might in itself be harmful to that same patient's capacity to think, and so there needs to be a careful dose-response curve, with a balance between attachment and mentalization. The advice these authors give to psychiatrists working with borderline patients could suit family therapists just as well. They recommend

> an inquisitive stance rather than an expert role, be flexible rather than set unachievable goals about attendance and behaviour, struc-ture treatment in collaboration with the patient, and develop clear pathways to care in a crisis. (Fonagy & Bateman, 2006, p. 3]

Clinical exploration: working with unconscious processes

Attempting an integrative practice across the different theory and practices of the two traditions also requires the capacity for flexi-bility, especially when working with unconscious processes in family therapy. This final part of the chapter offers two case exam-ples. The first is an example of how *not* to do it: interpretation of unconscious material, while probably accurate, was nevertheless clinically unhelpful. In the second case example, analytic thinking was very helpful in informing therapeutic understanding, yet analytic practices were not used directly.

Mr and Mrs A were a white working class couple in their late sixties whose eldest adult daughter had recently committed suicide. Her suicidal act had put her into intensive care and the agonized family had been forced to witness her dying over two weeks. They had three other adult children, several grandchildren, and many friends. The extended piece of family bereavement work had included discussing ceremonies of remembrance, some of the tensions associated with the suicide (including their question of whether the ex-husband was to blame), and the anniversary of her death. It was harrowing work, made particularly rewarding by the courage and generosity of this elderly couple as they considered their own future together, possibly brief because of the husband's physical frailty.

In a reflecting team, an analytically trained colleague suggested that "Mr and Mrs A must be very angry with their daughter at some level". This comment was experienced by the couple as offensive and hurtful. It provoked a vehement reiteration of their daughter's virtues and temporarily disturbed the good rapport they had established with the therapist and team. My sense is not that my colleague was "wrong": how could there not be "anger at some level" towards a daughter who had effectively ruined their remaining years? But the issue of the gap between insight and technique was forgotten. A judgement was needed about whether this particular couple were able to acknowledge any negative feelings towards their child, and whether any benefit might accrue from such an acknowledgement. In this case, a misjudgement was made. My understanding of the dynamics holds the analytic position, but would have had an opposite clinical application. I thought that the couple's idealization of their daughter was a coping strategy that ironically made her terrible loss more tolerable and they were never going to give up the idealization, which needed to be respected, not challenged.

Here is a contrasting clinical example. Mr and Mrs B were an infertile couple in their fifties who adopted a boy and a girl, three years apart, both late adolescents at the time of referral. The elder child, the boy, had become increasingly wayward, running up debts and stealing from his parents. Then he committed a serious violent offence, and was sectioned for psychiatric reports. Meanwhile, his sister, of a more academic bent, was doing well at college. The parents were distraught about their son, whom they feared would be bullied and incur further psychological damage if sent to prison.

After an initial couple of meetings with the parents, we offered six sessions, to include the parents, both siblings, and staff from the secure unit where the son was held. He presented as a small, stroppy, but jokey young man, who looked younger than his chronological age. It gradually became possible to talk about his experience in the family, with the self-perpetuating split between the good, compliant sibling and the bad, difficult one. He acknowledged feelings of rejection by his birth mother, fantasies of trying to find her, and began to think about how this might affect his adoptive parents.

The mother was able to express her hurt and resentment, and gradually a more relaxed conversation emerged which could include some playful teasing between mother and son. While he was still in the secure unit, his pregnant girlfriend gave birth. He was allowed to visit the baby under escort, and his adoptive mother complimented him on his handling of the baby. By the end of therapy, it appeared likely that ultimately he would be allowed to live with the girlfriend and baby while continuing to receive psychiatric and probation support.

What can a psychoanalytic perspective add to our understanding of this family? At no stage were formal interpretations of unconscious material made to the family, but the understanding informed the work in a number of ways. An assumption would be that, as an adopted child, the young man is likely to have a complex set of feelings and fantasies, conscious and unconscious, about his adoption. Was he so unlovable, even as a newborn baby? Was he so bad he had to be got rid of? This is rejection at its most fundamental, and the resulting hurt and rage will not be dispersed by the knowledge that your birth mother was a sixteen-year-old drug addict who could not manage a baby. This young man was so angry that he committed a violent offence that put other lives at risk.

Splitting is a well described psychological defence mechanism that we all use: us and them, inside or outside. In couples, we often see the splitting and mutual projection whereby an unconscious deal is done and roles are adopted and become entrenched: you be the cautious one worrying about the mortgage repayments and I will be the extravagant, generous one; you be the sick one and I will be the carer; you be the depressed one and I will be the joker. In healthy couples, these roles are not so rigidly assigned that both parties are trapped, unable to be in contact with the projected part of self located in the partner. They can take turns, to some extent, so both have the freedom to adopt a range of roles and positions.

In the B family, the brother and sister had lost any such flexibility. The offender brother was stuck in furious, and ultimately self destructive, acting out behaviour. The younger sister may have been equally stuck in her role, unable to express negative feelings, obliged to conform and please the parents, fulfilling the good sibling role. Alternatively, she may have been a mature young woman who was able to think about and process difficult feelings effectively enough to be able to get on with her education in a productive way. We did not see her often enough to form an opinion about her, but, either way, her external conformity and success would have been experienced by the offending brother as the provocative half of a split. In other words, if she had not behaved so well, he might not have needed to be so bad.

Clinically, these ideas could be used to inform the discussion about how the two siblings differed in character, what this elicited from the parents, the effect of each on each other's behaviour, and so on. The conception and birth of the new baby was also understood by the team to have operated on many levels. There was a powerful unconscious identification of this disturbed young man with the vulnerability of his new baby, and there was also what the team felt to be a reparative urge on his part to take care of his child, and *himself,* represented by the child. Contained within the identification is the touchingly rewritten script: although this child's father was locked up at the time of the birth, he had realistic hopes of getting out and actively taking on the responsible parenting role that his own birth parents could not manage. He was determined that the baby would be cherished as he would have liked to have been himself. From an analytic point of view, this is an avoidance of a repetition, or what John Byng-Hall (1995) called a "corrective script".

There was also a sense of this young man's unconscious triumph, from a humiliating position, over the virtuous (but irritating to him) adoptive parents: "I may be incarcerated in here but I got my girlfriend pregnant, which is more than you two managed". Becoming a father had huge resonance for this young man in terms of maturity, potency, and his capacity to look after the real baby and his own baby needs projected into the new baby. Some of this was conscious, and by the end of therapy he was planning to try and get work as soon as possible to support his new family.

Discussion: what is the status of analytic knowing?

Systemic colleagues might object to these interpretations of the young man's internal world. They are only "tentative assumptions", if that is not a contradiction in terms. The therapy team did not voice these thoughts to the family and they were not "checked" with the family's own experience. This could be described as presumptuous, even dangerous or irrelevant. I would refute those claims: checking with the family would have been clumsy and pointless. Clumsy, because it would have been quite wrong to assume any acceptance of the idea of unconscious mental life on the part of the family, so they could be understandably offended by the suggestion that they had ideas or feelings that they were not even aware of. Pointless, because if we accept that there is such a thing as unconscious mental life, and that it might well be contradictory and even unacceptable to the person concerned, what would the status of the family's rejection of the team's interpretation be? If we had said, "We think this new baby means x to you", and the father or the parents said, "No, that's nonsense", would that have made the interpretation wrong? Not necessarily.

This is one of the nubs of the difficulty family therapists have with analytic theory. It is hard to bear the idea that someone else—the analyst—has the temerity to claim knowledge of the other that is greater than the individual's knowledge of themselves. That claim is experienced as outrageously arrogant and presumptuous, but it cannot be circumvented. Analysts do base their interpretations of other people's experience on generalizations and personal experience, particularly of their own analysis. The analytic literature, a huge body of scholarship, could be seen as its own worst enemy in that it tends to write for an internal audience, for whom unconscious mental life and its determining effect is a given. My point, and its relevance to this book, is that the conviction that underlies analytic theory, that controversial castle of intellectual endeavour, is *experiential*, not intellectual. This is what distinguishes analytic theory from pure science. This is what makes analysts vulnerable to the charge of arrogance: they do indeed sometimes just "know", in the sense of *knowing* that only the human experience of a relationship can give, and that relationship is the therapeutic relationship.

Over years of analysis, analytic therapists have learned just how little they are "in charge" of their own mental life. They submit to the experience of their own conscious and unconscious mental life being subject to challenge and scrutiny. They are invited to join the analyst in this evaluating, sifting, searching process in which the live relationship between the two participants is taken as a central source of information about the internal life of the trainee. This joint, intense scrutiny is, of course, and can only be, ultimately a collaborative process. Nevertheless, at the beginning the trainee has to make what Catholics call "the leap of faith". There is a real hierarchical gap of knowledge and experience between the analytic trainee and the analyst. This gap is not just an intellectual one but, again, an experiential one. The analyst has been on the receiving end as well as having learnt something about what patients have in common via their own clinical work. For the best analysts, this knowledge leads to modesty rather than arrogance, being derived from an appreciation of the complexity of human experience.

Conclusion

Dare (2005, p. 10) wrote that psychoanalysis is "about the continuing influence of intense emotional processes between children and parents on subsequent experiences of intimate interpersonal relationships". The same could be said about family therapy. This chapter has explored the different traditions of psychoanalysis and systemic therapy and the challenges of integrative practice, especially with respect to working with unconscious processes.

Is there any need for a battle about where family therapy is heading? Not in my opinion, with one of its strengths being its broad church aspect, alongside a capacity for self-observation as a group. There is a need for more dialogue, mutual learning and creative intercourse between and across frameworks. Family therapists need have no fear, for they are in the vanguard with the idea of centrality of *relationship*.

In the words of Stephen Frosh (2002), we remain always with "the incorrigibility of otherness". Literature, as well as therapy and biology, addresses human interaction. We may need to reread *What Maisie Knew*, by Henry James, and remember too that "theory is only a metaphor" (Gabbard, 2006, live comment), as we try to tolerate the messy untidiness of the tiny world of therapeutic theory.

> Now that my ladder's gone,
> I must lie down where all the ladders start,
> In the foul rag-and-bone shop of the heart.
> [Yeats, 1940, "The Circus Animals' Desertion"]

References

Bartels, A., & Zeki, S. (2004). The neural correlates of maternal and romantic love. *Neuroimage, 21*(3): 1155–1166.

Bertrando, P. (2002). The presence of the third party: systemic therapy and transference analysis. *Journal of Family Therapy, 24*: 351–367.

Bertrando, P. (2006). Emotional systems: managing emotions in systemic practice. Paper presented to the Institute of Psychiatry, London, April.

Byng-Hall, J. (1995). *Family Scripts: Improvisation and Systems Change*. New York: Guilford.

Campion, J., & Fry, E. (1985). The contribution of Kleinian psychotherapy to the treatment of a disturbed five-year-old and her family. *Journal of Family Therapy, 7*: 341–356.

Casement, P. (1985). *On Learning from the Patient*. London: Tavistock.

Cecchin, G., Lane, G., & Ray, W. A. (1992). *Irreverence: A Strategy for Therapists' Survival*. London: Karnac.

Cooklin, A. (2005). Thirty years on . . . the Chairs. *Context, 80*: 2–3.

Dare, C. (1989). Symptoms and systems: an exploration of anorexia nervosa. *Journal of Family Therapy, 11*: 21–34.

Dare, C. (2005). Thirty years on . . . the Editors. On becoming the editor of an as yet non-existent journal of family therapy. *Context, 80*: 10.

Flaskas, C. (1997). Engagement and the therapeutic relationship in systemic therapy. *Journal of Family Therapy, 19*: 263–282.

Fonagy, P., & Bateman, A. (2006). Progress in the treatment of borderline personality disorder. *British Journal of Psychiatry, 188*: 1–3.

Frosh, S. (2002). *After Words: The Personal in Gender, Culture and Psychotherapy*. London: Palgrave.

Holmes, J. (1983). Psychoanalysis and family therapy: Freud's Dora case reconsidered. *Journal of Family Therapy, 5*: 235–251.

Klein, M. (1957). *Envy and Gratitude*. London: Tavistock.

Skynner, R. (1989). Combining systemic, psychoanalytic and behavioural. *Journal of Family Therapy, 11*: 5–19.

Steinglass, P. (1987). *The Alcoholic Family: Drinking Problems in a Family Context*. New York: Basic Books.

Watzlawick, P., Weakland, J., & Fisch, R. (1974). *Change: Principles of Problem Formation and Problem Resolution*. New York: Norton.

Winnicott, D. W. (1947). Hate in the countertransference. In: *Collected Papers: Through Paediatrics to Psycho-analysis* (pp. 194–203). New York: Basic Books, 1958.

Yeats, W. B. (1940). The Circus Animals' Desertion, from *Last Poems* (1940) in *The Collected Poems of W. B. Yeats*, London: Macmillan, 1967.

CHAPTER THREE

Is there another word for it? Countertransference in family therapy

Sebastian Kraemer

F amily systems therapists are uncomfortable using psycho-analytic terms. This reluctance restricts discussion of thera-peutic process. How does one describe, for example, the therapist's subjective experiences that occur in the presence of the patient or family? Psychoanalysts call this countertransference, yet there is no equivalent word commonly used in systemic prac-tice. Therapists who avoid the word may also avoid the concept, and thereby risk losing sight of fundamental clinical events.

Writing history backwards

"Where does all this stuff come from? How do we decide to say what we say when we work with families . . .?" asks Sigurd Reimers (2006, p. 230). His sources include references to earlier texts by one of the editors of this book (Carmel Flaskas) but no primary psycho-analytic ones at all. The earliest reference in Reimers' paper is to an observation by James Framo that "it is almost impossible not to get caught up in the drama of the family interaction" (Framo, 1965, p. 197) and a candid look at the "cases that touch on a feeling of

'madness' in us" (Reimers, 2006, p. 237). Reimers is thoughtful and observant, but there is something parochial about a paper on the process of therapy that ignores the greatest body of work on the subject.

I did a small "study" in a specialist psychotherapy bookshop some years ago. Looking at the references in a sample of systemic therapy books, I found none before 1956, and rarely any to psychoanalytic texts after that. "As in the Russian revolution existing authorities were simply obliterated, as if they had never been. Even psychology was removed and replaced with philosophy and engineering" (Kraemer, 2002, p. 199). Although there are, besides the contributors to this book and its predecessors, many honourable exceptions,[1] the perception still prevails among systems therapists that psychoanalysts tell patients what they are thinking—"me expert, you dummy"—and that their interventions are focused primarily on past events: "The therapist's narrative becomes the client's reality" (Gergen & Kaye, 1992, p. 172). A psychoanalyst who is disturbed and uncertain in the presence of a patient is rarely described. On both sides of the therapy fence there have been brave efforts to make authentic, non-physical human contact through conversation with clients, but there is little fertilization between discourses. This leaves each open to mutual accusations of mystification and omnipotence, and the poorer for their isolation from each other.

Systemic therapy is rightly regarded as a new paradigm in psychotherapy. In *The Structure of Scientific Revolutions*, Thomas Kuhn (1962) showed how changes in our understanding of the world are not continuous or cumulative, as scientists are inclined to believe. On the contrary, there is a communal conservatism in scholarship and science and it is only from time to time that a new paradigm can emerge. This is not simply a matter of finding new data. "The transfer of allegiance from paradigm to paradigm is a conversion experience that cannot be forced" (*ibid.*, p. 151). Kuhn noted how textbooks "have to be rewritten in the aftermath of each scientific revolution" (*ibid.*, p. 137). "The temptation to write history backwards is both omnipresent and perennial" (*ibid.*, p. 138). The terminology of the old paradigm is discarded, because it has no equivalents in the new. One of Kuhn's examples was "phlogiston", the theoretical construct to explain the phenomenon of combustion, which was not in any way commensurate with oxygen when this gas was discovered in the eighteenth century. Something of this kind seemed to occur in the family therapy revolution, where systemic concepts had no antecedent translations. Yet, the new paradigm did not supersede the old one. Psychoanalysis continued, and developed its own systemic ideas independently. Family therapy barely registered in the psychoanalytical world.

Countertransference

Countertransference was first thought to be an obstacle to psychoanalysis. Sigmund Freud said, "we have become aware of the 'counter-transference', which arises in [the physician] as a result of the patient's influence on his unconscious feelings . . ." (1910d, pp. 144–145). Amnon Issacharoff explains why it had at first been so troublesome:

> It is almost as if [Freud] shied away from public comments on the matter. After all, psychoanalysis was not part of the "establishment" at that time. It was still sensitive and highly vulnerable to its numerous detractors. [Issacharoff, 1979, p. 28]

This vulnerability is the risk of exposing the private and personal feelings that analysts have about their patients. Yet, these are precisely what they learn to notice and take seriously, and from which new understanding arises.

The Second World War changed psychotherapy. The damage done by loss, death, and migration shifted the focus of dynamic psychology from individuals towards relationships.[2] "Psychology and psychopathology have focused attention on the individual often to the exclusion of the social field of which he is a part" (Bion & Rickman, 1943, p. 681). At the same time, sophisticated electronic engineering in guided missiles, and in other equipment using self-correcting feedback, helped to establish the new discipline of cybernetics. Using systems theory, some psychologists and psychiatrists discarded the prevailing paradigm of individual drives and devised new models of family interaction: "the conceptual shift from energy to information" (Watzlawick, Beavin, & Jackson, 1967,

p. 29). Meanwhile, many psychoanalysts, privileging our need for relationship ("the object of desire") over other drives, became more interested in countertransference: their innovations were evolutionary rather than revolutionary. They saw in countertransference a potential source of information, communicated not in words but by the transfer of states of mind or feeling from one to another. Paula Heimann wrote,

> In my view Freud's demand that the analyst must "recognize and master" his counter-transference does not lead to the conclusion that the counter-transference is a disturbing factor and that the analyst should become unfeeling and detached, but that he must use his emotional response as a key to the patient's unconscious. [Heimann, 1950, p. 83]

Margaret Little grasped its elusiveness: ". . . to try to observe and interpret something unconscious in oneself is rather like trying to see the back of one's own head—it is a lot easier to see the back of someone else's" (Little, 1951, p. 33). Countertransference, she said, "is a special kind of identification of the analyst with the patient" (*ibid.*). Psychoanalysts became less censorious of their own mental states. Using different terms, these pioneers were describing systemic processes between patient and analyst.

One of the few psychoanalysts to acknowledge systemic theory was Harold Searles. For many years he worked analytically with schizophrenic patients. He was impressed by the brilliance of the double bind theory and contributed a chapter in a 1965 textbook of family therapy. His work is noted with approval in the classic text of Milan therapy, *Paradox and Counterparadox* (Selvini-Palazzoli, Boscolo, Cecchin, & Prata, 1978, p. 175). Searles' candour in writing about his own states of mind at work is startling.

> In my several-years-long work with a woman who showed a borderline personality organisation at the outset, I found that she recurrently held over my head, mockingly, year after year, the threat that she would become frankly and chronically schizophrenic. . . . In many of the sessions during those years, I felt a strong impulse to tell her ironically that I had felt for years, and still did, that she could become chronically schizophrenic if she would just try a little harder. Essentially I was wanting at such times somehow to convey to her that this was a *choice* she had. . . . In order for

the analyst to help the patient to become able to choose, the former must be able not only to experience, indeed, a passionately tenacious devotion to helping the latter to become free from psychosis, but also to be able to tolerate, to clearly envision, the alternative "choice"—namely that of psychosis for the remainder of the patient's life. [Searles, 1986, p. 217]

[In] my work with patients who have been involved in chronically troubled marital situations wherein there is a chronic, suspense-laden threat of divorce hanging over the marriage ... it has appeared to me no coincidence that, concurrent with especially stressful phases of the analytic work, my own marriage has felt uncharacteristically in jeopardy. [*ibid.*, p. 222]

Searles shows how he is disturbed by his patients. He writes about feelings of romantic love, of intense amusement, and, most powerfully, of alterations in his sense of identity, much more profound than mere changes in feeling. A later paper by the British psychoanalyst, Denis Carpy, notes that change may occur precisely at the point when the patient sees that she has had a powerful impact on the analyst. He presents work with a woman who would talk endlessly about her troubles but wanted nothing to do with her feelings, until the analyst noticed how pleased she was that he was getting nowhere.

... how the patient got under my skin, causing me to act out slightly by making comments which were critical and involved my trying to make her feel something she was unable to feel. What I took to be her triumph at the end resulted, I believe, from her having been able to observe that she had got to me and affected me in this way. [Carpy, 1989, p. 292]

Psychoanalytic therapists are trained to attend to their most private fantasies. They learn this in their own analysis and in one-to-one supervision, where reflecting quite candidly on their mental and bodily states when with a patient is encouraged. Family therapy is less intimate both in practice and in supervision. Of course one can say how one felt (irritated, excited, frightened, bored, amused, baffled, and many other adjectives), but the more fleeting and specific mental or bodily events, which on reflection produce whole sentences with subject, verb, and object in them, might slip through the net and escape recall. Yet, these are often the moments that make a difference in therapy. In supervision, a therapist might say something about how he or she felt while with a patient. The supervisor asks, "Did you say anything about it?" A discussion follows as to why it was so difficult to speak up. One good reason for keeping quiet is that it felt irrelevant, impertinent, or embarrassing, that a personal reaction to the patient should not be revealed. Yet, it *can* be thought about, first in supervision, and then in clinical practice. There is an interesting literature on self-disclosure in therapy (Rober, 1999), but what I am concerned about here is not self-disclosure, but how to use my ruminations and hunches—revealed only to myself—as information.

This is related to the question of training analysis. The requirement to have one's own therapy is an essential condition for any psychoanalytic training, but not for family or systems therapy. Many of the first and second generation family therapists had a psychodynamic training, including personal therapy, before they became family therapists. That is no longer the case, though there are probably more exceptions than most of us think. Lying on a couch with an analyst behind you makes you more familiar with your own freely associated thoughts and fantasies, including those that are not spoken of. The increasing absence of this experience among its practitioners has altered the development of the craft, training, and scholarship of family therapy.

Where do you get your therapeutic ideas from? Gregory Bateson said, "The probe we stick into human material always has another end which sticks into us" (Haley, 1972, p. 26). This means noticing what is happening to you while you work. You might find yourself thinking something and then follow the trail, wondering where that came from, and why it is occurring now. This requires free association. Although some systemic therapists might object to the term, such self-scrutiny is surely the basis of real contact with others in any therapy.

Interviewing a sixteen-year-old boy who had taken a suicidal overdose the previous day, together with his mother, I ask him a question and there is a long pause before he answers. He speaks deliberately and intelligently, so I hang on his every word, as I sense does his mother. I wait, and feel tormented by this young man, who looks quite distressed but he also flashes an enigmatic smile at me from time to time. I said that he seemed a tortured person but that he also tortures others. Mother nods.

The sense of torment I experienced while waiting for words led me to make this comment. Moments like this happen every day in therapy, and most psychoanalysts would regard this vignette as entirely unremarkable. For the rest of us "Where does this stuff come from?" is a question we still have to answer. Reimers (2006) presents an honest and subtle view of family therapists' habitual modes of working and is clearly aware of the processes I am describing here, yet he does not grasp the countertransference nettle. The client–therapist system includes bodies as well as minds, and one source of data, not so available to analysts, is visual. In its purest form, psychoanalysis does not involve face-to-face contact during the session, while family therapy is mobile and active, with elements of spectacle. While listening and talking we are also looking, sometimes only subliminally noticing what we see. In recent years, I have deliberately made an effort to draw attention to this: "Look at the expression on his face as you say that; he doesn't believe a word you say", or "You are fifteen but you look like twenty-five . . ." ". . . is that why she is wearing dark glasses?". The psychoanalyst and psychiatrist Henri Rey, whom I witnessed at work in open clinical presentations at the Maudsley Hospital in the 1970s, was interviewing a man with a very strange face. Others had spoken with him about everything except his face. Rey simply asked, "What do you see when you look in the mirror?"

The development of mind

Looking at faces is what mothers and babies do, the prototype of all intimate human contact. Colwyn Trevarthen compares these interchanges to theatre, demonstrating the "neonates' extraordinary capacities for reactive and evocative imitation" (Trevarthen & Aitken, 2001, p. 3). While focusing on curiosity and communication, prevailing theory in systemic and post-systemic therapy does not relate these to their aesthetic origins in the earliest human relationships. For example, the basic assumption of Harlene Anderson and Harry Goolishian's iconic paper "Human systems as linguistic systems" is that "Therapy is a linguistic event" (1988, p. 371). They

wanted to forge a new paradigm by taking social science out of therapy. Citing the philosophers Ludwig Wittgenstein and Richard
Rorty, they show how conversation creates, rather than discovers,
meaning. "Language does not mirror nature; language creates the
nature we know" (p. 377). "By 'being in language' we refer to the
process of the social creation of the intersubjective realities that we
temporarily share with each other" (p. 376). But they neglect the fact
that language as it is learned in infancy is not simply social. It is a
distillation of the communications that begin as sensuous, musical,
and dramatic qualities: contact with skin, solids, liquids, and gases,
and the apprehension of smells, noises, facial expressions, gestures,
and movements. Anderson and Goolishian have disembodied the
process to produce an omni-competent philosopher–therapist: "a
master conversational artist, an architect of dialogue" (p. 383).
Although no longer the discredited psychoanalytic psychotherapist
who knows best, their therapist must possess acrobatic mental
skills. "The therapist entertains multiple and contradictory ideas
simultaneously" (p. 381). "It is in our questions that we display the
skill of 'worldmaking'" (p. 382). "The therapist maintains a dialogical conversation with himself or herself" (p. 382). They ask this
chapter's key question "How does a therapist choose what to
respond to and in what way?" (p. 381) and in answer acknowledge
the irreducible fact of a personal viewpoint in every therapist:

> As therapists, we all have opinions about people and about how all
> of us should or should not conduct our lives. . . . We cannot be
> blank screens. We think of these prejudgements as opportunities.
> That is, they are the energy to spark curiosity and the drive to
> explore other ideas. . . . In this process the therapist changes . . . the
> only person the therapist changes in the therapy consultation is
> himself or herself. [p. 384]

These words had a powerful impact on family systemic theory.
Aiming for a shift in the therapist rather than the patient is indeed
a radical idea. Change in the therapist that precedes change in
the client was also mentioned in passing by Luigi Boscolo and
colleagues just a year earlier: "While [positive connotation] is often
taken to be similar to the strategy of positive reframing . . . actually
it is much closer to a restructuring of the therapist's consciousness"
(Boscolo, Cecchin, Hoffman, & Penn, 1987, p. 7). Yet analysts had

already, for decades, been struggling to restrain the urge to change patients: "the capacity to forget, the ability to eschew desire and understanding, must be regarded as an essential discipline for the psycho-analyst" (Bion, 1970, p. 51). As early as 1929, Jung wrote "the doctor must change himself if he is to become capable of changing his patient" (Jung, 1954 [1929], p. 73) and described this self transformation as traumatic:

> a good half of every treatment that probes at all deeply consists in the doctor's examining himself, for only what he can put right in himself can he hope to put right in the patient. It is no loss, either, if he feels that the patient is hitting him, or even scoring off him: it is his own hurt that gives the measure of his power to heal. This, and nothing else, is the meaning of the Greek myth of the wounded physician. [*ibid.*, p. 116]

Although Anderson and Goolishian emphasize the risks that the dialogic therapist must take, what is missing from their account is how much anxiety is generated trying to keep an open mind under therapeutic pressure. They are describing a "cool reflection" (Lockyer, 2007, p. 41) rather than sweaty personal engagement.

Resistance to change is a fact of life, not altered by philosophy. In most social encounters we are negotiating with others, often covertly trying to change them rather than ourselves. This is precisely why there is such a sustained endeavour on the part of postmodern therapists to avoid doing so. In order not to impinge too much on other people, many systemic therapists have had to control, even censor, themselves quite carefully. In his work with a patient who had been sexually abused, John Burnham courageously writes "my desire to be respectful had led me to be reluctant to take any risks in the relationship" (2005, p. 17). In pre-postmodern times it was not only analysts who recognized the negative countertransference. Although I can find no published reference to this, the Milan group were famous for the "orgy of linear thinking" they would indulge in behind the screen before coming up with a positive connotation. Jim Wilson sometimes presses colleagues in workshops to tell of an episode that "worked" but which they had "kept to themselves because it would be greeted by colleagues' raised eyebrows as an unusual thing to do" (2007, p. 148).

It is neither possible nor desirable to abandon all therapeutic prejudices, but it is necessary to keep monitoring and questioning them. This is a countertransference task. "Injunctions to take up a position of 'not-knowing' are designed to move our cherished notions aside to make room for the patient's, not to empty our minds entirely" (Kraemer, 2006, p. 243). It is significant that, from the very beginning, systemic therapists relied on philosophers for intellectual inspiration. None of these men (for they are all male) was a therapist, and some, such as Bertrand Russell (whose theory of logical types has a central role in the double-bind hypothesis) and Ludwig Wittgenstein, found in philosophy a refuge from their own personal suffering. The fact that Wittgenstein, Bateson, and Rorty (1986) all acknowledged, with inevitable reservations, the power and depth of Freud's thinking is not noted in systemic texts. Wittgenstein, speaking of *The Interpretation of Dreams*, said, "Here, finally, is a psychologist who has something to say" (Mancia, 2002, pp. 169–170).

Theory and practice do not match here. Anderson and Goolishian's observed clinical work is intimate and embodied. "Instead of a therapist operating on the reality of a person or family from the outside, you had something closer to therapists putting themselves almost bodily into a family's or person's private world" (Hoffman, 2002, p. 138). What were they thinking as they worked like this? Clinical writing cannot describe the real thing accurately, yet there is an opacity in Anderson and Goolishian's text as if they, like the early psychoanalysts, had experienced some resistance to exposing personal contents to public view.

A theory of suffering

The absence of a developmental psychology—of a "theory of suffering" (Hoffman, 2002, p. 110)—leaves family systems therapy too dependent on thinkers whose ideas have come from reflection and scholarship (including mathematics), rather than from observation of people in mental pain or terror, or in helpless states such as childbirth, infancy, and serious or terminal illness. Having begun in revolution, family therapy remains in flight, in a state of restless development from its unacknowledged ancestors. "We tended to ascribe our effectiveness to the fact that we were using a new theory" (Beels, 2002, p. 69). Even its own pioneers, such as Salvador Minuchin and Jay Haley, are routinely discredited. But at the beginning of this story is an emptiness where psychoanalysis should be.

> Working with a translator, I am interviewing a teenage girl, T, and her father. Her mother is in their country of origin and has a serious mental illness. We discuss the mother's condition and the girl, who speaks English fluently, says that neither she nor her father misses her, but she wished she had a different mother to help her now. T is taking dangerous risks and is out of her father's control. He wants me to give her psychiatric treatment to cure that. His voice becomes more shrill and intimidating. I am irritated and frustrated by this man, and say through the translator that I cannot see what the psychiatric problem is. T is insolent and provokes her father with grimaces and evasions. I am disturbed by her coquettishness with him.

> The meeting is not going well, with the translator getting into lengthy discussions of which he gives me only brief summaries. Everyone seems to be talking at once. I am looking at T and say to her, "Can you imagine having an argument with your father in English?" She laughs, with a hint of embarrassment or even mockery, but the father says, almost triumphantly, while raising a fist, and before the question has been translated for him, "Yes!"

Bateson's probe detects a triangle at the back of my head

I came across Gregory Bateson and John Bowlby at around the same time, as a psychiatric trainee in the 1970s. They were almost contemporaries, and both understood human interaction in ethological and systemic terms, yet neither seems to have acknowledged the other in his published work. While my therapeutic knowledge comes from personal development and clinical training, these two polymaths provided me with a scientific basis for a theory of suffering. Bowlby showed that attachment is universal in mammals. An immature individual seeks to be looked after as much as it needs to be fed (attachment is also activated by fear, pain, darkness, tiredness, and any form of helplessness. It is lifelong.). "Looking after", as these simple English words imply, means following the infant's state, trying to make sense of his or her experiences. The human baby, the most immature of all newborn mammals, is programmed to engage with a care-giver immediately.

Although often idealized (especially by male writers), this is a profoundly formative and intimate process, all the more interesting because the couple cannot always understand one another. Small errors are inevitable, and it is these breaks and the repairs that follow (played out in "peekaboo" and later, for some, in psychotherapy) that promote the growth of mind and brain. "Reparation, its experience and extent, is the social interactive mechanism that affects the infant's development" (Tronick, 2007, p. 342). At around the same time as Bowlby first formulated his ideas (Bowlby, 1958), Bateson and his colleagues were observing attachment going badly wrong, where instead of reparation there are "never ending, but always systematic, distortions" (Bateson, Jackson, Haley, & Weakland, 1956, p. 183). This was the double bind of which Bateson later said, "severe pain and maladjustment can be induced by putting a mammal in the wrong regarding its rules for making sense of an important relationship with another mammal" (1973, p. 248). Combining these insights, I understood how the human mammal is, from the very beginning, intensely preoccupied by where he or she stands in relation to others. Human infants have many ways of communicating but no ability to care for themselves. They are, therefore, extremely attentive to the state of the people who do this for them, on whom their lives depend. This works well when the adults can take the lead, but if care-giving is undermined by fear, pain, anxiety, or depression, the infant tries to take over. The more in trouble a care-giver is, the more the offspring's vigilance is used up trying to put it right, at the expense of his or her own development and security. This is a reversal of roles, in which the child becomes parentified (Macfie, McElwain, Houts, & Cox, 2005), becoming an unacknowledged—and hopeless—therapist for a disturbed adult. "[I]nnate among the human being's emotional potentialities, present in the earliest months of postnatal life, is an essentially psychotherapeutic striving" (Searles, 1979, p. 459). To add further complexity to the system, infants are, within weeks of birth, also monitoring not only their own attachments with care-givers, but also the relationships *between* the adults around them (Fivaz-Depeursinge & Favez, 2006), so that when these are in difficulty the child is also attempting systems therapy. Regulating one's place in a three-person system (and multiples of this) is a basic human skill, and lasts a lifetime.

Through theories incorporating ethology and anthropology, I came to understand how self-regulation, curiosity, and social competence evolved in triangular systems. Primate social life depends on alliances that advantage the participating pair but inevitably exclude others (Harcourt & de Waal, 1992). Social bonds among apes are cemented by grooming. This is effective in small groups but, as early humans lived together in larger numbers, such prolonged contact with all one's friends was not possible. According to the anthropologist Robin Dunbar (1996), the functions of grooming were maintained instead by gossip: essentially, two individuals in a coalition to discuss the condition of a third. Dunbar shows how this promoted the development of language itself.

By historical times, the tragic triangle had become the staple setting for stories of passion, murder, and suicide: the rivalry of Cain and Abel, the incest of Oedipus, the jealousy of Othello. Freud added the excitement and conflict aroused by the child's knowledge of the facts of life, the learning of which is not simply a biology lesson but an anthropological achievement, observing the system one is also a part of: "seeing ourselves in interaction with others and . . . entertaining another point of view whilst retaining our own . . . reflecting on ourselves whilst being ourselves" (Britton, 1989, p. 87). The double bind was originally identified in a relationship between two people but, within a few years, some of its authors had added a third, to define the "pathological triad" (Hoffman, 1981). Finally, the revolutionary technique of circular questioning (Selvini-Palazzoli, Boscolo, Cecchin, & Prata, 1980) exposes our compulsive—but not always conscious—interest in differences between individuals and between relationships. In the clinical example above, there was no mother to intervene in a dangerous escalation between father and daughter. I felt like a boxing referee who has to pull the contestants apart, to get them into a healthier relationship; something an effective mother—the one that T wished for—could have done. In retrospect, I see how anxiety about the sexual tension between father and daughter prompted me to take mother's place, to propose another form of intercourse for them that is not secret or perverse, but can instead be celebrated.

These few sentences summarize my theoretical framework. Since we all start off as infants surveying relationships around us, I am hardly unique, but this precise version is mine alone, my particular culture, and the source of my prejudices that, as Anderson and Goolishian say, ignite further exploration. If we do not own, and acknowledge, a clinical theory, there is a risk of idealizing or mystifying our sources, as Lynn Hoffman (2002) tends to do, using poetic metaphors such as the "deep well" to describe where her therapeutic ideas come from. "Inner conversation" (Rober, 1999), "inner movements" (Shotter & Katz, 2007), and similar descriptions refer to the impact on us of our patients and clients. To know where they stand with us, families in therapy need evidence that this impact has occurred; that their probes have got through and made a difference to what we think of them. Countertransference is a primary pathway from client to therapist.

Conclusion

The absence of a developmental theory of mind leaves systemic and post-systemic therapists reliant more on wisdom and intuition and less on reflection of interpersonal process. Because systems therapy saw no use for transference it was thrown out, but countertransference, which is still needed, went with it. I can find no new word for countertransference, a stubborn reminder of the older paradigm's endurance.

Systemic therapies have made possible interventions that could not have taken place in other models: medical, behavioural, cognitive, or psychoanalytic. It was a revolution, after all. My purpose is not to reverse this, but to understand more about what we actually do and to create a richer history of psychotherapy.

Notes

1.   The systems revolution is more evident in retrospect. The original family therapists were familiar with psychoanalysis, many having been trained in it. A systemic/psychoanalytical literature has continued in the background, one of the more recent being Johnsen, Sundet, and Torsteinsson, 2004.

2. "There is no such thing as a baby." This famous statement, never published in these precise words, was first uttered by the psychoanalyst Donald Winnicott at the British Psychoanalytical Society in 1940. He was perhaps the first to note the essentially systemic nature of the baby and mother couple.

References

Anderson, H., & Goolishian, H. (1988). Human systems as linguistic systems: preliminary and evolving ideas about the implications for clinical theory. *Family Process, 27*: 371–393.

Bateson, G. (1973). Double bind 1969. In: *Steps to an Ecology of Mind* (pp. 242–249). St Albans: Paladin.

Bateson, G., Jackson, D. D., Haley, J., & Weakland, J. H. (1956). Towards a theory of schizophrenia. *Behavioral Science, 1*: 251–264 [reprinted in Bateson, G., *Steps to an Ecology of Mind* (pp. 173–198). St Albans: Paladin, 1973].

Beels, C. (2002). Notes for a cultural history of family therapy. *Family Process, 41*: 67–82.

Bion, W. (1970). *Attention and Interpretation*. London: Tavistock.

Bion, W., & Rickman, J. (1943). Intragroup tensions in therapy: their study as the task of the group. *Lancet, 2*: 678–681.

Boscolo, L., Cecchin, G., Hoffman, L., & Penn, P. (1987). *Milan Systemic Therapy: Conversations in Theory and Practice*. New York: Basic Books.

Bowlby, J. (1958). The Nature of the child's tie to his mother. *International Journal of Psychoanalysis, 39*: 350–373.

Britton, R. (1989). The missing link; parental sexuality in the Oedipus complex. In: J. Steiner (Ed.), *The Oedipus Complex Today: Clinical Implications* (pp. 83–101). London: Karnac.

Burnham, J. (2005). Relational reflexivity: a tool for socially constructing therapeutic relationships. In: C. Flaskas, B. Mason, & A. Perlesz (Eds.), *The Space Between: Experience, Context, and Process in The Therapeutic Relationship* (pp. 1–17). London: Karnac.

Carpy, D. (1989). Tolerating the countertransference: a mutative process. *International Journal of Psychoanalysis, 70*: 287–294.

Dunbar, R. (1996). *Grooming, Gossip and the Evolution of Language*. London: Faber and Faber.

Fivaz-Depeursinge, E., & Favez, N. (2006). Exploring triangulation in infancy: two contrasted cases. *Family Process, 45*: 3–18.

Framo, J. (1965). Rationale and techniques of intensive family therapy. In: I. Boszormenyi-Nagy & J. Framo (Eds.), *Intensive Family Therapy* (pp. 143–212). Hagerstown, MD: Harper & Row.

Freud, S. (1910d). The future prospects of psycho-analytic therapy. *S.E.*, 7: 139–152. London: Hogarth.

Gergen, K., & Kaye, J. (1992). Beyond narrative in the negotiation of therapeutic meaning. In: S. McNamee & K Gergen (Eds.) *Social Constructionism as Therapy* (pp. 166–185). London: Sage.

Haley, J. (1972). Critical overview of present status of family interaction research. In: J. Framo (Ed.), *Family Interaction: A Dialogue Between Family Researchers and Family Therapists* (pp. 13–49). New York: Springer.

Harcourt, A., & de Waal, F. (Eds.) (1992). *Coalitions and Alliances in Humans and Other Animals*. Oxford: Oxford University Press.

Heimann, P. (1950). On counter-transference. *International Journal of Psychoanalysis, 31:* 81–84.

Hoffman, L. (1981). *Foundations of Family Therapy*. New York: Basic Books.

Hoffman, L. (2002). *Family Therapy: An Intimate History*, New York: Norton.

Issacharoff, A. (1979). Barriers to knowing. In: L. Epstein & A. Feiner (Eds.) *Countertransference* (pp. 27–43). New York: Jason Aronson.

Johnsen, A., Sundet, R., & Torsteinsson, V. W. (2004). *Self in Relationships: Perspectives on Family Therapy from Developmental Psychology*. London: Karnac.

Jung, C. G. (1954) [1929]. The practice of psychotherapy. *C.W., 16.* R. F. C. Hull (Trans.). London: Routledge & Kegan Paul.

Kraemer, S. (2002). Tribal processes in psychotherapy: the stand off between psychoanalysis and systems. In: P. Nolan & I. Säfvestad-Nolan (Eds.), *Object Relations and Integrative Psychotherapy. Tradition and Innovation in Theory and Practice* (pp. 199–215). London: Whurr.

Kraemer, S. (2006). Something happens; elements of therapeutic change. *Clinical Child Psychology and Psychiatry, 11:* 239–248.

Kuhn, T. (1962). *The Structure of Scientific Revolutions* (2nd edn). Chicago: University of Chicago Press, 1970.

Little, M. (1951). Counter-transference and the patient's response to it. *International Journal of Psychoanalysis, 32:* 32–40.

Lockyer, K. (2007). Being emotionally reflexive in systemic psychotherapy: the case for countertransference. Unpublished MA Dissertation in Systemic Therapy, Tavistock Clinic/University of East London.

Macfie, J., McElwain, N., Houts, R., & Cox, M. (2005). Intergenerational transmission of role reversal between parent and child: dyadic and family systems internal working models. *Attachment & Human Development, 7:* 51–65.

Mancia, M. (2002). Wittgenstein's personality and his relations with Freud's thought. *International Journal of Psychoanalysis, 83*:161–177.

Reimers, S. (2006). Family therapy by default: useful fall-back positions for therapists. *Journal of Family Therapy, 28:* 229–245.

Rober, P. (1999). The therapist's inner conversation in family therapy practice: some ideas about the self of the therapist, therapeutic impasse, and the process of reflection. *Family Process, 38:* 209–228.

Rorty, R. (1986). Freud and moral reflection. In: J. H. Smith & W. Kerrigan (Eds.) *Pragmatism's Freud: The Moral Disposition of Psychoanalysis* (pp. 1–27). Baltimore, MD: Johns Hopkins University Press.

Searles, H. (1986). Countertransference as a path to understanding and helping the patient. In: *My Work with Borderline Patients* (pp. 189–227). Northvale, NJ: Jason Aronson.

Searles, H. F. (1979). The patient as therapist to his analyst. In: *Countertransference and Related Subjects: Selected Papers* (pp. 380–459). New York: International Universities Press.

Selvini-Palazzoli, M., Boscolo, L., Cecchin, G., & Prata, G. (1978). *Paradox and Counterparadox: A New Model in the Therapy of the Family in Schizophrenic Transaction.* New York: Jason Aronson.

Selvini-Palazzoli, M., Boscolo, L., Cecchin, G., & Prata, G. (1980). Hypothesizing–circularity–neutrality: three guidelines for the conductor of the session. *Family Process, 19:* 3–12.

Shotter, J., & Katz, A. (2007). "Reflecting talk", "inner talk", and "outer talk": Tom Andersen's way of being. In: H. Anderson & P. Jensen (Eds.), *Innovations in the Reflecting Process* (pp. 16–32). London: Karnac.

Trevarthen, C., & Aitken, K. (2001). Infant intersubjectivity: research, theory, and clinical applications. *Journal of Child Psychology and Psychiatry, 42:* 3–48.

Tronick, E. (2007). *The Neurobehavioral and Social-Emotional Development of Infants and Children.* New York: Norton.

Watzlawick, P., Beavin, J., & Jackson, D. (1967). *The Pragmatics of Human Communication.* New York: Norton.

Wilson, J. (2007). *The Performance of Practice.* London: Karnac.

CHAPTER FOUR

Interpreting dreams in psychotherapy with couples: moving between the upper and the lower worlds

Deborah A. Luepnitz

D ream interpretation is a highly effective, curiously under-utilized technique in the psychoanalytic treatment of couples, allowing partners to clarify unconscious conflicts, gain compassion for the other, and deepen intimacy.

Freud, who recognized the grave importance of dreams, their role as "royal road to the unconscious" (Freud, 1900a, p. 608), treated individuals only, as have most subsequent analysts. Those analysts who have taken up the work of marital and family therapy have written little, if anything, about dreams. Two recent articles (Nicolo, Norso, & Carratelli, 2003; Scharff & Scharff, 2004) suggest that interest in such work may be growing.

The present author stumbled on new uses of dream interpretation during the treatment of a poor African-American family in the early 1980s. The identified patient, fifteen-year-old Leroy Johnson, had been in trouble since kindergarten, when he ruined the completed art projects of everyone in his class during recess. Years of truancy and vandalism led eventually to a court-ordered psychiatric evaluation on our inpatient unit for thirty days.

Everyone involved with this young man—the caseworkers, previous therapists, and his own mother—seemed resigned to the idea that Leroy was on his way to jail. Working intensively with the family—providing them with possibly the best holding experience of their lives—seemed to make a difference. But, just as the combination of individual, group, and milieu treatment began to have an effect, just as the entire family began moving out of their rigid positions, Leroy relapsed. He spun out of control one night on the unit, and his mother and her partner were called in to assess the damage. Sitting with them in an emergency session, I could feel the heat of their fury, a fury that was sure to give way within hours to a punishing withdrawal. It was obvious that any comment like: "I bet you're all having a lot of feelings right now" would have made everyone erupt in rage.

A beginner therapist at the time, I sat quietly, flummoxed and sad. It was Leroy who broke a long silence with the only comment no one expected, which disarmed us all, and which was to change my analytic/therapeutic practice for life: "I had a strange dream this morning. Could I tell y'all what I dreamt?" He did, and not surprisingly, it revealed what had been avoided and even flatly denied in our sessions: his mix of hatred and longing for his biological father, a man who had both loved and physically abused his mother. The adults began asking Leroy questions about the dream, and then added their own thoughts until it was clear that the dream belonged to the family. It had emerged from their work with me and constituted a means of introducing material that felt too dangerous to engage directly. Our work was set back on track, and the family continued to bring in dreams.

The dream work seemed to intensify the family's positive transference to me through a deepening of the treatment's holding power. The Johnson family had had several bouts of structural and strategic family therapy over the years; this was the first treatment that went beyond issues of authority and behaviour control to the underlying issues of intimacy, mourning, and shared meaning.

At the end of the thirty-day inpatient evaluation, the judge ruled that Leroy could return home. The family continued their therapy with me until Leroy went off to college. (For a full account of this case, see Luepnitz, 1988.)

Family dream interpretation became a mainstay of my work and was especially helpful in an inpatient setting in which the number of sessions was limited. That is, dream work often pointed us in the direction of a conflict or loss that might have taken much longer to surface without it. With families for whom the therapeutic dyad itself was threatening, stimulating fantasies of attack or merger, the dream provided an anchoring third presence. Soon, I began using dream interpretation with couples as well (Luepnitz, 1991).

Freud issued a caveat about assigning dream interpretation to patients, pointing out that if analysts "talked up" dreams, patients would simply resist by bringing in elaborate dreams that would stuff the hour, permitting no time for the important work of free association and interpretation. This can indeed be a problem, but it seems to subside with time, as do other forms of resistance. Not mentioning dreams carries the obverse risk that patients will not understand that dreams are a valued part of the work. I agree with Nancy McWilliams's (2003) view that a bit of education about what psychoanalytic treatment entails can be very helpful, whether one is working with individuals, couples, or families.

Mr and Mrs Wright

In early sessions with couples, I exploit any reference they make to the unconscious, or any comment about wanting "to go deeper than we've gone before" to say, "How would you feel if we talked about dreams?" Typically, one partner will respond enthusiastically, "I love thinking about my dreams", while the other will say, "I rarely remember them," or even, "I don't dream." I then say that my experience is that, during the course of therapy, many people find themselves remembering dreams in a way they had not done before. Some find that making a few notes in the morning keeps them from disappearing.

This does not eliminate the resistance of some adults to remembering dreams, and a certain number will, of course, deride the very notion of unconscious life. Such was the case with Mr and Mrs Wright, a white middle-class couple who had started out in family therapy for their nineteen-year-old son, Mark, after his arrest on a drug charge. After the charges against Mark were dropped, he refused to attend further family sessions, and the parents asked if they could continue to work with me in marital therapy. (Each week, Mark would remind his parents that it was time for their appointment, as though he was relieved to be handing their care over to me.)

> During the first session, Mrs Wright described a dream of trees being blown about by hurricane force winds. While it appeared that they would be pulled up by their roots, they managed to survive. I asked what came to mind about those trees, and she said, "Nothing, really. They were just palm trees like you see in Florida." After a pause she added, "I've only been to Florida once, on our honeymoon."

> She continued, "I don't know if those trees represent me—or maybe both of us. This thing with Mark has strained us both to the breaking point." As she started to cry—for the first time ever in a session—Mr Wright rubbed her arm gently. It seemed he did not know quite what to say to her, but he looked up at me and said, "Mark was conceived during our honeymoon."

> I wondered if Mrs Wright was mourning Mark's departure from our sessions. Was he strong enough to weather new storms on his own? Was the marriage strong enough to survive if the son's troubles, which had kept them together, were not active and present? Mrs Wright decided it was a "good dream" because the trees, although strained, were not destroyed. Mr Wright added nothing further, but I thought that his comment about Mark's conception endorsed the importance of her dream and our work on it. Moreover, it was they—the couple—who had conceived the idea of changing our task from family to marital therapy, and the work they did in this first session felt like an auspicious beginning. However, at the end of the hour, when I mentioned something to Mr Wright about his own dreams being equally welcome, he looked at me as though I had insulted his intelligence. "I don't dream!" he snapped.

> On another occasion when the subject of dream work came up, he offered sarcastically, "What's next—a séance? Shall we dim the lights and hold hands?" I felt belittled, as though taunted by a schoolboy. My second response was a thought that he was communicating a real fear about navigating the dimly lit corridors of the unconscious, and his hostility might hide a wish for me to hold his hand. I also wondered if the word "séance" suggested that the feelings he was afraid of having had to do with someone deceased. I saw my task as one of containing these fears, without yet commenting on them, and certainly without defending dream analysis. That would have placed me unproductively in the position of his mother, whom he had described as extracting compliance from her children. He often heard his wife's requests as

demands, something I had tried to point out to him earlier. To his question, "What's next?!" I replied warmly, "Well, last week you brought several topics to light . . ." and we returned to the upper world.

Over the course of two years, the couple was able to tolerate, even to welcome my interpretations. They realized that they had poured much of their energy into trying to manage their out of control son. Now that he was living with his girlfriend (and doing better than when he had lived at home) they would have to deal with many parts of themselves that had been avoided. I mentioned that without Mark around to carry their anger, they seemed to be feeling more anger at each other. My goal was to help them to express it in more constructive ways. Over a period of months, the "chore wars" were broached, and their sexual relationship gained new life. Whenever Mrs Wright would mention a dream, her husband would comment on it intelligently, but then glare at me as if to say, "I've warned you; don't even ask!"

It was only near the end of our first year of therapy as we were about to stop for a holiday break that he said, as though offering me a slightly shabby gift, "You know, I did have one recurring dream in my life, but it was years ago. Would you be interested in *that*?" He said that for at least a decade he dreamt that he had killed a man with a bow and arrow. He said that the dream was so real he actually used to wonder at times if he had killed someone. I thanked him for bringing this material in, and wondered if he had any associations at all, to the man or the bow and arrow. "No," he said, "That's your department." I turned to his wife, who said, "I don't know, but a bow and arrow makes me think of William Tell. Also, remember she (DL) says a dream is something you wish. Maybe you wished you could kill someone so bad, you thought you had done it."

I said, "If that were true, Mr Wright, who would it be?" He responded swiftly and confidently. "My father. I used to wish he was dead because of the way he treated us." Only then was he willing to talk about his father's contempt for them, his terrifying drunk driving, and an incident in which he shot all the lights off the Christmas tree with a pellet gun, and laughed uncontrollably. (Being left in the dark at age eight with a father wielding a gun must have been frightening indeed.) The work that stemmed from this dream allowed him to see how he had turned his son into his father, and how Mark had unconsciously agreed to play that part.

Some months later, Mr Wright had a positive memory of his father, one of riding atop his father's broad shoulders. "He seemed to like little kids, he had patience for them," he said.

"Your mother still likes to say you were the apple of his eye," added Mrs Wright. Whereupon I said, "The apple of his eye became the target of his rage. That makes me think of Mrs Wright's association of William Tell." Mr Wright, seemingly accepting my comment, asked, "How does it happen? How does love between a parent and child turn to hate?" Clearly, he became able to use that one dream to reflect on the most pressing questions of their life together.

This particular dynamic, involving a partner who claims never to have dreamt, or never to have remembered a dream in life, who then turns out to have had a disturbing recurrent dream, has appeared so often in my practice that I am tempted to offer it as a guiding rule: where there are "no dreams", there has been a disturbing recurrent dream or a nightmare.

Karl and Daphne

In *Schopenhauer's Porcupines* (Luepnitz, 2002) I described a quite different couple whose therapy consisted almost entirely of dream work. Karl and Daphne Loeb began treatment after Daphne had spent a night in the emergency room following a severe panic attack. The couple had been embattled for several months over the question of whether or not to have another child. Daphne, who had recently turned forty, was packing up her three-year-old daughter's baby clothes for a pregnant neighbour when she felt a wave of anxiety pass over her. She knew her husband opposed the idea of more children, and she was gripped by the fear that the best years of her life were therefore over. Who was she, if not a mother? This anxiety mimicked the symptoms of heart failure so closely that she was sent to the emergency room to rule out cardiac trouble.

> In our first session, Daphne outlined her reasons for wanting more children, and Karl—equally passionate on this subject—outlined his. She began to restate a threat she had apparently made at home on several occasions: if he would not agree to another baby "now", she would "go out and get pregnant by another man". Karl was outraged at this, and the two of them proceeded to scream at each other so long and so loud over the course of three sessions, that no thinking could occur. I had to suggest that they put aside the question of a new baby for a while, and

work on other aspects of their relationship. Daphne had mentioned that their three-year-old daughter, who was still not toilet-trained, had been reaching into her nappy and smearing faeces on the walls. I suggested that this was a parenting issue of some urgency, and that we might work on that first, returning to the question of another baby later on. Both partners agreed they needed a break from the fighting, and that a "moratorium" on the baby question would provide some respite. But Daphne also made it known that she was nervous about dropping the subject even temporarily. "I am *obsessed* with this issue, and I'm not entirely comfortable with tabling it. My clock is ticking. How will we know it's time to go back to it? I suppose you'd say it's always there percolating in the unconscious."

The moment the session began, I realized I had dreamt about this couple the previous night. I decided to respond to Daphne's comment about "percolating in the unconscious" with "That's true. I'm thinking we might pay close attention to dreams." Daphne, who, unlike her husband had had several years of individual psychotherapy, said she would love to talk about her dreams, but, turning to him, added, "I don't think you even dream, do you?" To which he replied, "Even asleep, she's gotta be better than me."

They agreed to bring in dreams when possible, and that a first priority would be discussing a plan for toilet training their daughter, who, upset by their fighting, was "creating a stink" of her own. Daphne had been pushing for toilet training for months, while Karl felt it was "torturing" the child because she was not ready. He himself had not been fully trained until age five, whereas Daphne had been trained quite early. This led to some useful reflections on the differences in their general upbringing and family allegiances. In the first month or so of this work, Daphne brought in the following dream:

> I am at a dentist's office and I find out that I need two root canals. I had been eating a sandwich. The hygienist says, "It's a good thing it happened here, or you would have swallowed the filling." They pulled it out of my mouth, and I wondered.

I asked for her thoughts and she said, "There is a void in my life, and I want it filled. I'm glad I'm here in your office." Had she been in individual therapy with me, I would have asked her to tell me all about the dentist's office, about root canals, about *two* root canals, about the hygienist, the sandwich, etc. The associative material plus the day residue would have led us to some interpretation that would have included the transference.

Lacan (1954–1955) emphasized the importance of staying with each word of a dream—of treating the dream text like "Holy Writ" (p. 153). While I find this to be a good guiding principle for individual treatment, with couples my focus is a bit different. After the dreamer free associates and speaks about the dream, I turn to the partner with an open-ended question such as, "What about this dream?" The goal is not to explore each signifier, but to use the dream to address the needs of the relationship at that moment. For example, at a time when two people are having trouble feeling anything but anger for each other, the best use of their dreams might be simply pointing to something that will elicit compassion, such as a dream image of childhood wounds. At a moment when one spouse is feeling particularly starved for attention and recognition from the other, the most important use of his or her dream might be simply to devote the entire session to it.

> In Daphne's "dental dream", I noted the salience of oral dependency and aggression—also evident in the couple's screaming matches. Was I the hygienist, and if so was I pulling something out of her mouth (a dream?) or was I the one she hoped would fill her up? What seemed most important was that she was experiencing a *void in her life*, rather than a right to be impregnated.

> The first dream Karl brought to therapy was simple, and he was a bit embarrassed about it. "I had bought a Walkman." Daphne rolled her eyes and said she had nothing to say. (I wondered if he wanted to "walk, man!" but did not comment.)

> For several months, Daphne would bring in long, complicated dreams, and would enjoy whatever Karl had to say about them. He became more adventuresome in his associations and interpretations, and managed to bring out a great deal of relevant material. During this period, Daphne revealed that she had been disappointed in herself for falling in love with a man who appeared to have no interest in the life of the mind, or what she referred to as "bettering himself". In our sessions, she was seeing a different side of him. She also enjoyed the sheer amount of attention he was paying to her inner life. She had spent many years trying to figure men out, to understand their motives and anticipate their needs. In our sessions, Karl was the sleuth and she the fascinating puzzle, a turning of the tables for which she was very grateful. (I wondered if I had happened on to the ultimate feminist therapeutic technique!)

Karl dreamed:

> I was in my parents' house. There is a lavatory on the second floor. I
> am having sex with a girl from work. It's Gail, who is married to my
> boss. I am worried someone will come in.

When I asked Karl about the dream, he focused on the image of Gail,
his boss's wife, whom he described as attractive in a way totally different from Daphne. All his life, he had wanted beautiful women to chase
him, but Daphne had been the only one. He wondered if he would go
the rest of his life making love to this one person. The dream was just
that, he said: a fantasy of being with someone else. He added, "Daphne
and me, we're happy together in bed. At least we were. But I'm sure
she has thought the same thing." I asked what he thought the lavatory
was doing in the dream, and he said it made the whole thing seem
"secretive and exciting, but also frustrating."

The discussion of the boss's wife led us to talk about Karl's own parents
whom he, as a child, often overheard having sex. His father was a big
man who disparaged Karl as the "little runt", something we imagined
to be an expression of jealousy over Karl's being the mother's favourite.
Daphne said she saw Karl's father as a "castrating" type of man who
wanted to make his son feel like nothing. Karl had apparently told
Daphne that she had a tendency to act the same way, and she had to
agree. "I tear him to shreds, and I feel really bad about it." Karl seemed
very moved to hear her acknowledge this in the session.

Two dreams of Daphne's months later seemed to mark a turning point
for the couple. In the first:

> My daughter was peeing standing up, like a boy.

And in the second:

> I was dressed in a beautiful blue sequinned gown, going to a party or
> perhaps a convention.

Daphne said the first dream was about the fact that they had been talking so much about potty training. I turned to Karl and asked, "What
about this dream?" He replied, "To me, if you take the two dreams
together, it's like the two parts of her mind. She is still of two minds.
She's got kids on the brain, no secret. Maybe she is thinking of having
a boy this time. Maybe she thinks a boy would be easier. And second,
she would also like to be out in the world doing something special, out
there in the public eye."

At that moment, I asked Karl simply to look at his wife. She was thrilled at his attention, his competence, and was moved to tears with gratitude that her "construction worker husband" had become an interpreter of dreams. "I can hardly believe he's doing this! It's so intellectual. And he's good! I told my sister, 'Karl can do what our therapist does!'"

Daphne's idealized and erotic transference to me seemed to change at this time, and she became more sexually interested in Karl. Work on the dreams that followed uncovered something neither had even hinted at earlier: that her main reason for wanting another child was to bear a son who would have the advantages denied her as a girl in a traditional Greek family. And Karl's refusal to even consider another child was a fear that they would indeed have a boy who would grow up and reproduce the father–son relationship he had found so damaging. Openly discussing the possibility of having a boy made these issues less overwhelming. The compromise they reached after a deadlock that had threatened to split them apart was that they would have unprotected sex for a while, but without "trying" deliberately to conceive.

The last three examples have described couples in which the wife was at least initially more comfortable than the husband with the idea of dream work. One woman, familiar with the way I work, told me during our first phone contact that her husband would never go for dream analysis. "He's a very rational man, a problem-solver; he'll tell you dreams are for gypsies and fortune tellers." It turned out that this woman—herself a therapist—was splitting off her own fear of the irrational and projecting it on to her husband, who refused to contain it. He embarked with interest on the dream work and said at the end of therapy that he would miss it. "She has always told me I live in my head, like my intellect had no value. The dream work made me feel I could use my intellect as well as emotions, and maybe sometimes even use intellect to *get* to the emotions."

Whereas his wife had characterized dream analysis as "feminine", others have characterised it as "masculine", associating it with Biblical dream interpreters such as Daniel and Joseph, and modern theorists like Freud and Jung. Discussions of this kind always serve to underscore my own impression that dreams and dream work cannot be accused of being either masculine or feminine. All dreams operate according to the grammar of the unconscious—a grammar we describe with the words *condensation* and *displacement, metaphor* and *metonymy,* as they take part for whole and whole for part (Freud, 1900a). Dreams draw on material from the day's events, and disregard linear time. While sociologists have made much about styles of male and female communication, it would seem that women and men begin to speak the same language when recounting dreams.

If dreams cannot be said to be gendered male or female, are they also unmarked by race and culture? While the unconscious may be the closest thing to a universal structure, ideas about the importance of dreams and their meaning vary enormously by culture and subculture. We know from the Homeric epics that the Greeks believed the gods spoke to mortals in dreams. The Assyrians believed the gods used dreams to communicate with each other (Grotstein, 2000). A patient of mine from northern India was brought up believing that every dream predicts the future. She would recount a dream and then tell me what it portended. On one occasion I mentioned that I found it useful to think of dreams as wish fulfilments; would she be interested in hearing my interpretation of her dream? The patient paused and said at length, "Maybe. But we don't really think of dreams that way." Over the years I made sure to maintain a space for her dream analysis, not impinging upon it with my own perspective.

Students often ask if social class influences a couple's or a family's interest in dreams, assuming that only more educated and affluent patients would be up to the task. In over twenty years of work in this area, the only patients I have treated who have flatly refused to try to remember their dreams have been affluent white adults. During six years working with an inner city population in Philadelphia, and in my current work with formerly homeless people, I have found comparatively little resistance to dream work. (Dream interpretation with a formerly homeless woman is reported in Luepnitz, 2002.)

Cristina and Pam

As for questions of ethnic background, one mixed-race married couple informed me that ethnicity had an enormous influence on the tendency to remember dreams. Cristina, an art history professor born in Chile, married Pam, a WASP lawyer, last year in Boston. Cristina told me in our first session that "WASPs don't dream." Her wife agreed. A bit of practice seemed to make a difference, and soon Cristina assured me Pam was "dreaming like a Latina". They had lived together for fifteen years before being able to legally marry, and had tried therapy together several times without much effect. One month after their wedding, Pam's law firm began a series of lay-offs. For several months they were forced to discuss how they would handle her potential job loss: where they might move, whose career was more important, and how they should manage their finances. They found themselves tense and intolerant with each other in a way they never had been before, and wondered if getting legally married had changed their relationship for the worse.

The first thing that recounting dreams brought to the session was a sense of relief in the sheer pleasure that often accompanies this work. They reported:

A bowl of stones on the piano turned into white roses.

I was eating a new flavour of ice cream called "Cleveland, Ohio". Paul Newman was trying to get in touch with me.

I had ideas about the transformations, excitement and longings represented in their dreams, but added little during this period of time, as they preferred just to recount the dreams and laugh together. As a couple who had been together for so long and who had fallen into the usual emotional ruts, patrolling the paths of the unconscious gave them a feeling of renewal. Cristina began using some of their dream images in her paintings.

Within a few months, the dream work took on a more serious tone. Pam dreamed that she was driving to work with someone who seemed to be the "Flying Nun" from the 1970s television sitcom. Pam assumed at first the nun was doing her a favour, but then it became clear that she was out of control or lost. Pam tried to shout, "I should be driving!" but the sound would not come out. She awakened very upset.

Pam thought the dream was about work, but the figure of the nun baffled her. Cristina looked down nervously and said, "The actress who played the Flying Nun was Sally Field. Your place is being usurped by 'Sally', the name of the woman I had the affair with years ago."

"Yes," Pam continued. "And the car we're driving belonged to my father, well known for cheating on my mother." Pam realized she had had a similar dream the week before, and expressed surprise that she was still dreaming about Cristina's infidelity of a decade ago. While no longer consciously questioning her wife's commitment, she did acknowledge some lingering pain about what had gone on, and the way she had been expected instantly to forget and forgive. Without the unexpected dream, she never would have brought it up again. Cristina was moved to see that this part of the past was still showing up in Pam's dreams, and the two of them were able to talk about the old trauma once more as mature women, reintegrating it at a new level of insight. For example, Pam had never compared her wife's behaviour to her father's. Had she somehow chosen Cristina in part for that amazing seductive quality with which he had charmed the world but also hurt his family? The dream enabled them to talk about these issues without feeling blamed or blaming.

They were feeling quite good about their relationship two years later when Cristina brought in the following nightmare.

> A man—I want to call him the "town crier"—hailed me to say, "It's the Aurora Borealis!" Somehow I knew that meant something dire, like a terrorist attack or the end of the world. All I could think of was "Where is Pam?"

Through tears, Cristina began working on the dream. The beautiful Northern Lights; how could this be attached to something menacing? They had seen them on a cruise to Alaska. It was Pam who recalled that they had had a late night discussion about death on that trip. Both had lost relatives in the previous year, and they found themselves having an honest, if lugubrious, discussion about longevity and loss, about who would die first, and how they would manage.

This couple lived in a suburb thirty minutes south of my office. If the Northern Lights alluded to therapy, it might well have been a dream about termination. The dream might also have pointed to the loss of family members, and/or abandonment by internal objects. What seemed most compelling to the couple at this moment, however, was the issue of mortality itself. This raises an issue highlighted by Jacques Lacan (1979): that psychoanalysis has perhaps emphasized sexuality to the exclusion of that other unfathomable topic, *death*. Any work that can be done in this area in psychotherapy with a couple is truly a gift.

Taking care on the royal road

For insight on the vexed question of feminine sexuality, Freud famously exhorted readers, "Go to your poets . . ." His dream book is alive with literary references, and, of course, begins with a quotation from Virgil's epic poem *The Aeneid*: "*Flectere si nequeo superos Acheronta movebo*": "If I cannot move the upper world, I will move the lower regions" (Freud, 1900a, p. 608).

A short story called "The Wishing Box", by the poet Sylvia Plath (1956), describes a married couple fatally lost on the royal road, touching on a number of issues raised here. Plath names her protagonists Agnes and Harold Higgins, which cannot fail to evoke George Bernard Shaw's *Pygmalion*. Plath's Harold Higgins, however, is not so much a teacher of women as a pure pedant. Agnes envies his highbrow, spectacular dreams in which he trades insights with famous poets. Smearing jam on toast "with vindictive strokes of the butter knife", Agnes asks her husband at breakfast, "What did you dream *last* night?" (p. 48). Only as a young woman did Agnes have vivid dreams like his; now she can report only "I dreamed mother had died", or "I was falling" (p. 49). Harold, unmoved, tries to teach his wife to have better dreams, but his methods fail and she sinks into insomnia and depression. One night he finds her dead of an overdose, but looking triumphant, as though she had finally dreamed of "waltzing with the red-caped prince of her youth" (p. 55).

For this couple, purveying the lower world aroused envy, awe, and dread, but no one was there to contain the flood. The dreams that Agnes devalues as "too simple", such as "I was falling", and "Mother had died", are obviously anything but trivial, but neither she nor Harold knows what to do with them.

In addition to being a rather dire, Plathian parable about marriage, the story serves as a cautionary tale to beginner therapists: dream work is serious; be sure to get good supervision! On the other hand, we are all beginners when it comes to the unconscious, and caution is always advisable when doing this work. Interpretations can be exhilarating, but nowhere is a Winnicottian (1971) distrust of "cleverness" more apt. In the context of a culture that in many ways deplores depth, the power of dream analysis may lie in helping intimate partners to recognize the existence of, and find ways of engaging, the other's inner life.

References

Freud, S. (1900a). *The Interpretation of Dreams. S.E.,* 5. London: Hogarth.

Grotstein, J. (2000). *Who Is the Dreamer? Who Dreams the Dream?* Hillsdale, NJ: Analytic Press.

Lacan, J. (1954–1955). *Seminars of Jacques Lacan. Vol. 2* [reprinted New York: Norton, 1988].

Lacan, J. (1979). The neurotic's individual myth. *Psychoanalytic Quarterly,* 3: 386–425.

Luepnitz, D. A. (1988). *The Family Interpreted: Psychoanalysis, Feminism, and Family Therapy.* New York: Basic Books.

Luepnitz, D. A. (1991). The dream is my co-therapist: working with dreams in psychotherapy with couples. Paper presented at the Harvard/Cambridge Hospital conference on couples: October.

Luepnitz, D. A. (2002). *Schopenhauer's Porcupines: Intimacy and its Dilemmas.* New York: Basic Books.

McWilliams, N. (2004). *Psychoanalytic Psychotherapy: A Practitioner's Guide.* New York: Guilford.

Nicolo, A. M., Norso, D., & Carratelli, T. (2003). Playing with dreams: the introduction of a third party into the transference dynamics of the couple. *Journal of Applied Psychoanalytic Studies,* 5: 283–296.

Plath, S. (1956). The Wishing Box. In: *Johnny Panic and the Bible of Dreams* (pp. 48–55) [reprinted London: Faber and Faber, 1986].

Scharff, D., & Scharff, J. (2004). Using dreams in treating couples' sexual issues. *Psychoanalytic Inquiry,* 24: 468–482.

Winnicott, D. W. (1971). *Playing and Reality.* London: Tavistock.

PART II
EMOTION AND DEVELOPMENT

CHAPTER FIVE

Anger and boredom: unpleasant emotions in systemic therapy

Paolo Bertrando and Teresa Arcelloni

Systemic therapy lacks a proper theory of emotion. In the early days of systemic family therapy, the therapist focused on family interactional patterns, avoiding what the psycho-analytic paradigm had arbitrarily located in a non-observable area—the intrapsychic dimension—where emotions were thought to originate (Bertrando & Toffanetti, 2000). Afterwards, rationalism prevailed within strategic therapies. This saw human interactions as rational contracts between actors who actively sought what they considered the best for themselves (see Haley, 1976; Jackson, 1965). (Kleckner, Frank, Bland, Amendt and duRee Bryant [1992] contend that strategic therapists do not "ignore, avoid or neglect client feelings in treatment" (p. 41), and that such a "myth" is disproved by what strategic therapists actually do in sessions.) When emotions were reconsidered, they were defined as "predispositions for actions" (Maturana, 1988, p. 49) recalling, once again, their prag-matic and developmental function inside a system. Only in later years have emotions begun to find a place within social construc-tionist theorizing and systemic therapy (e.g., Fredman, 2004; Kavner & McNab, 2005; Pocock, 2005).

Like most systemic thinkers, Maturana also emphasizes the positive functions of emotion. Little room is left for what we may define as unpleasant emotions, such as anxiety, anguish, anger, envy, ingratitude, boredom, indifference, disillusion, and disgust. There are many reasons for this. The first, though, is still traceable to the reaction to some key psychoanalytic ideas, from which systemic therapy felt a need to differentiate itself. Second is the optimistic and liberationist ideology intrinsic in the American psychotherapeutic tradition (on which most systemic family therapy was originally based): any individual is fundamentally good, and he or she is made bad only by external constrictions (Cushman, 1995). In this is rooted the tendency to see mostly resources and positive aspects in clients. This tendency was already present in Milton Erickson's work (the celebrated Ericksonian motto, that everyone always does her best, in the situation she is in; Lankton, Lankton, & Matthews, 1991), and brought to its maximum expression by narrative (White, 1995) and conversational (Anderson, 1997) therapists.

Of course, systemic therapists, like all other human beings, experience in their lives the whole range of pleasant and unpleasant emotions. But they behave in therapy as if they had the duty to do something in order to transform, as soon as possible, their clients' feelings into more "positive" ones. ("Positive" and "negative", as used here, is the day-to-day use of these terms. However, relaxed cheerfulness in the face of an imminent threat of death might be less positive from a functional point of view than adrenalin-pumping terror. Conversely, anger in the face of injustice could be considered a very positive emotional achievement.) A good example is the attitude of the original Milan group, aptly defined by Mara Selvini Palazzoli as "my manic team" (see Doherty, 1999, p. 14), which was pervaded by an almost messianic enthusiasm for change. We view this as an almost compulsory "positivization" of emotion, possibly fostered by the technique of positive connotation. In the best of cases, the systemic therapist tolerates the presence of "negative" emotion, but without taking it into consideration. The risk, though, is to put into the background, or, even worse, to completely overlook, everything that may appear negative or unpleasant, thus losing sight of an essential aspect of human relationships. Such acts and emotions are often seminal to understanding and working

through a therapeutic situation. In short, a desire to see only good-
ness might be harmful.

Among the "unpleasant" emotions that we might frequently
find in therapy, anger and boredom are probably the most intense
and difficult to deal with. To describe our way of working with
those two emotions (and also our general considerations about
"unpleasant" emotions in systemic therapy), we would like to start
with two clinical cases.

Anger that bores: the Barbieri family

The family arrived in therapy because of an episode that "made
Patrizia's mother mad". Her fury was sparked when she discovered
that her daughter, the previous week, had not taken her long-
awaited degree even though the mother had already organized
various family celebrations. The daughter had even produced a
fake certificate, which confirmed that she had brilliantly passed her
final exams. The truth finally emerged because of the "casual"
discovery of her student record-book, from which the mother had
learnt that, in the last two years, Patrizia had not passed a single
exam. Like a scene from a cheap novel, the record-book was hidden
under the mattress of her bed, which her mother made every day.

Three women lined up in front of the (woman) therapist, apparently
happy to be there, hoping the therapist could judge one of them the
winner in a match that had been going on for twenty years. Father sat
at one side, a sort of sly imperturbable linesman, always ready to throw
a spanner in the works. The only sign of some agreement was an open
alliance between mother and Paola, the other daughter. Accusations
were raised on two clear-cut fronts, with the father continuously
provocative despite his avowed neutrality. Among reciprocal threats
and ceaseless interruptions, each one of the women tried to recruit the
therapist on to her side. The therapist was silent, with a growing feeling that she should bellow, in order to make herself heard.

Maria, the mother, was a very active fifty-year-old woman, with a
number of "certainties": "Patrizia has been wounding me since she was
three and was attending the nursery school. Even then she was a liar,
and my husband believed her. Now she hates me, and, if she could, she
would kill me—cut me into pieces and put my remains in a plastic bag

. . . At home, we cannot live any more, she attacks me all the time . . . every time an assault or a bad word."

Paola, twenty-two, had "good reasons" for her feelings: "In other families there are discussions, dialogues, but this is not for us: Patrizia yells every time somebody tells her something, and Mum lives in terror" [*Paola cries*]. "She is spoiling my life, too . . . so I tell her . . . [*Paola screams*] 'Go away, if you think you'd be better somewhere else . . . just stop!'"

Patrizia: "Don't believe them! I've always been a Cinderella to them. I've been through all sorts of problems . . . but they're not interested. Do you know that, when I was five, my Mum wanted to shut me in the oven?"

After a heavy pause, the therapist broke the silence to ask, "And . . . was it lit?"

The two sides of boredom: Federica

Federica was young woman of twenty-five; a humanities student at the university. Having lost her mother at eighteen, she lived with her father and a seventeen-year-old sister. She had a difficult relationship with both, as well as with her maternal grandmother, who was a very important member of the family. She lived within the cult of her mother, who died of cancer, and whom she had supported with the utmost care until the end. Federica loved to wear her mother's old clothes, and remembered her with great poignancy. She had been referred by a colleague for bulimia with depressive symptoms. This included at least one or two binges a day for the last few years. The colleague—a male systemic therapist—had worked with her weekly for two years. When invited to speak openly, he acknowledged that the sessions had become somewhat useless and monotonous: in fact, boring. We decided to work with her in a different way: once a month, in a training context, where a male therapist was assisted by a team composed of ten young woman therapists in training, co-ordinated by a woman teacher.

Federica came regularly to each encounter, sad and invariably dressed in black. She often cried while speaking, but her tears seemed vacuous, as if she was acting. She did not succeed in moving to empathy either the male therapist, or the female observation team. Sometimes the therapist openly confessed to the team his boredom with her, despite the fact that her story was truly dramatic and her condition somewhat worrying. Session after session, the situation seemed to be repeated, either identically or with minimal variations that did not change anything. Federica was a young woman trapped in the life of an old person. (Her sense of time appears distorted, slowed down to apparent stillness [see Boscolo & Bertrando, 1993]: *Langweile*, which means "boredom" in German, means, literally, a long extension of time.)

During one of the encounters, Federica appeared to the therapist to be more involved than usual. Her words suggest a deeper participation and the therapist did not feel the self-pity that so often characterized her therapy. When, predictably, tears started running down her cheeks, the therapist could, for the first time, really feel her sadness and grief, and his questions evoked answers that seemed to make some emotional sense.

The therapist came out of the therapy room for a short break feeling an unusual sense of satisfaction. However, entering the observation room felt akin to stepping into a cold shower, since his team were immersed in the deepest state of boredom, listless and apathetic. His tutor said to him, "How tedious, huh? We will have to start from the beginning . . ." The therapist looked at them with dismay, and was speechless.

Unpleasant emotions and emotional systems

Before speaking of anger or boredom specifically, we would like to make clear some of our general ideas about emotions within a systemic framework. Any system, in our opinion, is an emotional system. Or, better, any system can be regarded *also* as an emotional system. Emotions are an essential feature of any human situation, and therefore also of every human system. Our choice is a methodological one: it is the eye of the beholder that enables us see a system as a communication system, or a power system, or a linguistic system, or an emotional system.

Today, after fifty years of systemic therapy, we have some relatively clear ideas about therapists' and clients' world views. We now believe that they do not "belong" solely to any individual: not to me, not to my clients, but rather to our relationships (in the widest meaning of the term, which includes culture). But we seem to find it hard to apply the same thinking to emotions. Such an attitude has a long history. Strategic therapists, as we have seen, even prescribed ignoring emotions (see, for example, Selvini Palazzoli, Boscolo, Cecchin, & Prata, 1978). Emotions, in that reading, were individual phenomena that diverted the therapist from the system. This interdict had a long-standing effect on systemic therapists. Most of them (exceptions include some social constructionist authors, such as Fredman [2004]), to this day still seem convinced that an emotion is an expression of an internal state, belonging solely to the individual's inner world.

In our view, emotions should be considered as processes, rather than things; they are aspects of relating. Emotions do not pre-exist a relationship: such a dichotomy makes no sense in our reasoning, because the individual exists only in relationship. When there is a relationship, there are emotions—and vice versa—whether or not we consider them explicitly (see Bertrando, 2007).

Any emotion is systemic: part of an emotional system. As we think that there is no true self, distinct from a false self, so we believe that there are no superficial emotions, distinct from deeper ones—and therefore more true. Any emotion emerging in inter-action is true within that interaction. If we succeed in having a different understanding of our own position in such a system, our emotional state (the way we experience our emotions) might change. If we do not have an understanding about where we are emotionally, we easily fall prey to emotions that can overwhelm us. If we have a sense of where we stand emotionally, our position does not become less emotional, but we experience it with a higher degree of awareness.

Anger

Psychoanalytic authors provide a diverse range of meanings about anger. Freud hypothesized the existence of a death drive in *Beyond the Pleasure Principle* (Freud, 1920g), and Klein (1948) developed this view and came to see aggressive and destructive drives as intrinsic to the person (a direct expression of the death instinct, externally diverted to diminish anxiety), and apparent from the first few months of life. Other authors see anger as a more contextually responsive emotion. Anger can be the denial of sorrow or anguish, sometimes in the form of its chronic variant, vindictiveness. According to Searles (1956), vindictiveness is a reaction to the grief and anxiety generated by the loss of the other, whereas to Socarides (1966) it is the reparation of an ancient wound through the presumed destruction of a persecutory figure, thus constituting a defence against the anguish generated by severe ego damage experienced in the first years of life.

Anger, however, can also be a (failed) attempt to repair some damage suffered from the other, or a protection from wounds that might come from the other, seen as potentially dangerous. All these are variants of narcissistic anger, theorized by Kohut as disappointment coming from the other, that undermines narcissism. According to Kohut (1971a), anger is provoked by a threat to the integrity of the self, seen as grandiose: an ideal self-object, bound to be perfect. Such anger may also be, according to Kohut, a protection against shame.

Bowlby (1973) maintains that anger and rage are originally reactions to the loss of an attachment figure, elementary attempts to discourage the loved one from going away again. Bowlby paves the way for an interactive conception of anger, which emerges as an effect of a series of desertions and abandonment threats, which consolidates into a pattern: parent threatens abandonment → anxiety → coercive rage in an attempt to prevent a new abandonment → parental guilt. If the pattern is maintained, rage becomes "dysfunctional", producing inside that pattern, estrangement and loosening of the bond. Here, anger is a product of separation anxiety.

Returning to our idea of emotional systems, we must, first of all, consider anger as a property of the system, rather than of individuals or their unconscious. What we have to look for, therefore, is the relational meaning that can be made of anger within an emotional system at a specific moment. In addition, we do not necessarily see anger as a denial of some other individual emotion; we see it as one of the elements in a set of interacting relationships within the system.

Anger may have an important protective systemic effect: its presence makes it difficult to perceive other emotions, especially if these are characterized with a sense of frailty and vulnerability.

Fear, anguish for anticipated hurts, anxiety, pain for a real or imagined loss, are denied; they never appear on the system's horizon. The most relevant and apparent effects of anger are interactional. The presence of anger in one member of the system makes the other members insensitive to other emotions. It generates an emotional system pervaded by hostility, polarizing it in a continuous dialectic of attack, defence, and counter-attack.

Alternatively, anger in the emotional system, revealed in one or more members, can be complemented by contrasting emotions of shame, sadness, discouragement, and desperation. We can say, though, that the most difficult situation (for a therapist, at least) is the one where anger is the prevailing emotion for everybody, which was largely the case in the Barbieri family. Such symmetrical emotional systems not only make it difficult for the therapist to work, but they can easily draw her in, so she too struggles to contain anger towards one, or even all, of the persons involved.

Reflections on the Barbieri family

Let us go back to the Barbieri family. The therapist's spontaneous question, "And . . . was it lit?", has an immediate effect on the family. The unintended and somewhat bizarre humour this brings to the situation changes the emotional system.

> Silence . . . everyone is still.
>
> The three women look intensely at the therapist. Even father stiffens on the chair, which he has previously lounged on as if it were a comfortable seat at the theatre. He speaks: "No, Doctor, you should not have wrong ideas about us . . . we have problems, but we're not that dangerous . . ."

The therapist reflects on the fact that, clearly, it was not the content of her question that made the difference (the story of mother dismembered and put in plastic bag did not create any sensation). The ironic and unintended "joke" produced a change in the therapeutic frame (see Bertrando, 2006), and in this new position the therapist was able to proceed. The therapist and family became part of a new emotional system.

Even after that crucial first meeting, the Barbieris had occasional fights during therapy, but this did not prevent the emergence of new horizons. The parents rediscovered more capacity for being a couple, and the two daughters were able to experiment with different ways of relating. In the final encounter, everyone talked about a future that could include Patrizia's getting her degree and managing to live independently, whereas the assumption for Paola was that she would enter a crisis with panic attacks. When the parents returned the following year asking for couple therapy, we learned that events had, indeed, worked out that way. At the end of the original therapy, Patrizia remembered the therapist's question as a crucial point in the course of the therapy.

When facing the three women with all the dramatic tone and postures of a theatrical scene, the therapist had thought of the Three Furies of ancient Greek theatre. What possibilities for action did she have? Let us try a list.

1. To raise her voice and to add her anger to that of the Three Furies, entering an emotional system where anger was the shareable emotion for all women, with father observing them from his disengaged position. Probably, the session would have then replicated the Barbieris' living room. Or, the emphasis on anger would be consistent with the idea that it is good to show one's emotions, but such a decontextualized expression of emotion would be at odds with the systemic framework of therapy.

2. To get just as bored as the father. That is, to coolly observe the interactions of those around him, maybe reflecting on the predictability of some descriptions: how may times has a therapist heard that somebody is upset because there is no dialogue in the family? This would have confirmed to everyone that the situation could linger on like that forever.

3. To try to find something positive at any cost in the family history, and building upon it a story with a different emotional tuning, according to the principle of Michael White's unique outcome (White, 1989). This might have worked, but at the price of ignoring the most striking emotional feature of the family.

4. To ask questions in order to investigate the meaning of the anger to all those involved. This was the line taken by the

therapist: finding sense in the Barbieris' emotions could allow the emergence of an alternative story.

One fundamental prerequisite when working in an emotional system governed by anger is to decrease the anger. The question is how? In order to change an emotional system it is important, rather than denying or overvaluing anger, to see its possible meanings and work with them. As Kohut (1971a) points out, it is useless to confront anger openly; we need to address the issues that produce it. Probably the best direction for a therapist is to recover the pain, the fear, the sense of actual or potential absence that puts anger in motion. Whether anger is the result of abandonment, or of an excess of presence and pressure from what has been described as symmetrical escalation, there is always an emotional state preceding the explosion of anger. The therapist who is able to concentrate on those aspects may escape the escalation.

In therapy—as in any other situation—anger is a function of one's position in the system. The therapist's potential for anger follows this rule, too. One of us, for example, happens to get angry more easily in triangulating situations. If a client attacks him in individual therapy, he does not get angry, but he does in couple therapy, as if, within a triangle, he could not bear to be attacked from one of the couple members (usually the woman) in front of the other.

Therapy may be more effective with anger if it facilitates a higher degree of mutual acceptance within the system. For this to happen the therapist must, first of all, come to recognize and try to understand her own anger and then to emotionally accept all the members of the system. And acceptance must be sincere rather than simulated, because, in our experience, family members can very easily tell the difference (Ekman, 2002).

Boredom

There is a strong cultural myth among systemic therapists: the therapist must never get bored. Boredom has been even defined as a symptom from a systemic perspective by Cecchin (1987), who maintains that curiosity is necessary to keep an overview of alternative patterns and prevent the therapist from privileging one story. When the therapist gets bored, she is no longer curious; she keeps to a predictable narrative and becomes incapable of seeing any other. Such a situation, however, becomes dangerous when it is adopted as a therapeutic rule. Therapists converted to this notion introduce into the therapeutic system a sort of implicit prescription to clients and to themselves: "I want you to be active, interesting, lively, and eccentric". This risks clients feeling unacceptable if they do not perform in these ways. Therapy is often an interesting and enjoyable activity, for sure, but experience tells us that it also includes anxiety, fatigue, fear, insecurity, headache, feelings of inadequacy, a sense of one's limits ... and boredom. One of the preferred metaphors for systemic therapy is "dance". Dancing may certainly be fun, but it also involves a hard tiresome training, failures, and a range of difficulties that are not necessarily symptoms.

Boredom has been banned from the systemic therapy room and perhaps this is why, behind the one-way mirror, team members often feel it and speak about it. It is comparatively frequent for an observation team to find a session boring, and, true to the imperative "do not get bored", they try to get the therapist to enliven things without disclosing to clients the boredom within the team. This happens frequently when the group behind the mirror is made up of young therapists in training, who feel more sharply the difference between what can be shown to clients and what is better kept secret (see also Bertrando & Arcelloni, 2006).

In our view, yawns and sleepiness behind the mirror are part of the therapy since they are part of the relationship. The therapist does not decide to let boredom emerge or to hide it, she rather simply lives a relational situation where boredom is one of the elements that define her position in that moment. This is why, in the encounter with Federica, the therapist feels emotions that are in sharp contrast with his observation team.

Reflections on Federica

Confronted with the colleagues' observations, the therapist is dumbfounded and disappointed. He also feels irritated and bewildered by their reaction. His colleagues, in turn, do not understand his attitude; he should be grateful because they have brought ideas that can liven up all that deadness, and he is instead nervous and unco-operative. Some analysis of the situation is necessary.

Taking the client, first of all: is she bored by her life? For several sessions, she has been describing an unchangeable situation: the conflicts with her father, the lack of progress in working on her doctoral dissertation, the instability of her love relationships, and the painful memory of her dead mother. Everything is repeated, described with the same heartbreaking tone, the same tears, and the same monotonous speech. Maybe what she likes to call depression is nothing but boredom, the deadness of endless repetition.

However, there must have been something else going on, since we also need to account for the differing perceptions of the therapist and his team. Here, the dialectic authentic/inauthentic emotion plays a part. To the therapist, the client emerged, perhaps for the first time, from her existential boredom, finding in a session a truthful, convinced tone. To the team, her contribution was not authentic; it was a simulation, or at least a partial simulation. But, if the client was not authentic, then not only all her actions, but also all those of the therapist become fake to the team. The team finds no meaning in the session and boredom sets in. (Sometimes boredom behind the mirror may also include a kind of frustrated disengagement born out of the rivalrous feeling that those watching could be doing the therapy job better: "Why isn't he exploring *that* issue?")

From the first session onwards, many team members had constructed an explanation for Federica's "simulation": she had been trying to seduce the therapist. The seduction issue, perceived in the female team as an essential part of the gender relationships in the therapy room, coloured for them the entire therapeutic interaction. In such a reading, seduction produces simultaneously a (flattered) interest in the therapist, and a (irritated) boredom in the team members.

It is interesting how boredom in one part of the therapeutic system becomes useful information about an inconsistency: the therapist questions himself about his own reaction, the team members become curious about their assumption. This reciprocal questioning generates hypotheses about Federica. Maybe she lives in boredom (that she calls depression), maybe she produces boredom in the persons around her (and this contributes to her inability to enter into a genuine encounter and to become properly considered in the minds of others).

The therapist returns to the therapy room, and shares openly with the client the issue of boredom and seduction raised in the team reflections. She listens attentively, sometimes surprised, sometimes disagreeing; by the end, she is almost grateful. From the next session onwards she begins to report changes in her life.

Following her therapy, which, in all, lasted for thirteen sessions, Federica had changed: she got her degree (not as a direct effect of therapy, but there was some acceleration in the process), she became involved in a stable relationship, she was studying for a doctorate and searching for a job. The relationship with her family was not much improved, but she was able to manage this with greater detachment and less anxiety. When reflecting on her therapy at follow-up, she explained that one of the most important sessions to her was the one we have just described. The perception of boredom allowed the therapist to face, with her, some crucial themes: the possible seduction, her existential boredom, her difficulties in communicating to others her emotional life, and accepting the feelings of others.

To give boredom back its dignity does not mean, of course, that we should fall asleep in front of our clients. Even if we overlook the ethical side, such behaviour would be a way of privileging one emotional position, an idealization of the exhibited bored feeling. Such a feeling of void and helplessness might, however, be essential information on the state of an emotional system.

Kernberg (1975), referring to the experience of emptiness as a detachment of the self from its internal objects and a corresponding loss of the sense of belonging to a network of human relations, says that the sense of emptiness by a patient might induce in the therapist a reaction marked by that very emptiness. Kernberg's analyst experiences the same sense of emptiness and extraneousness he finds in his patients, becomes uninterested in persons that he perceives as inanimate, mechanic objects. Kernberg, coherently with his approach, sees this phenomenon as a sort of emotional contagion (or, better, the result of projective identification) that relocates the patient's emotion in the analyst. We prefer to see this as the establishment of an emotional system characterized by a sense of emptiness. The analyst in Kernberg's article, anyway, reacts very much like a systemic therapist, making a comment (we perhaps would have asked a question about the patient's state of mind).

Kernberg, however, shows us that an analyst does not appear worried by boredom. If an analyst gets bored, Kohut (1971b) proposes the idea of a defensive boredom, a therapist's reaction to the patient's attempts at seduction, but nothing to be feared. The average systemic therapist, however, abhors boredom. Why? Let us go back to our previous observations. Boredom emerges confronting what is predictable. Cecchin (1987) says that playing cards with a little boy is boring because his moves are predictable. If the therapist aims at creating turmoil in the system, she will have difficulty in accepting predictability, which is a kind of stillness. Stillness is alien to the systemic therapist. It causes an epistemological contrast with her way of knowing, based on difference. If I think that everything I see is predictable, I cannot catch the unavoidable differences between the reality I see and my own picture of reality. I feel useless, and boredom tells me I am not working properly.

We are defining boredom as an absence of activity, both actual and potential. Of course, in this perspective, careful listening is an activity too. When the therapist becomes passive, she renounces the possibility of active listening. The more she feels passive, the more she is bored, and so on. If I have the feeling of being just a sponge, I cannot help being bored. But the feeling of not being listened to is my problem if clients talk to me and I feel as if I am not there. What I can do is to change the dialogue; any activity can bring me out of boredom, including reflecting upon my sense of boredom. Phenomenologically, if the client says something that relates to what I can do, I listen attentively and participate. (Tears and laments do not protect from boredom, either, unless they are embedded in a system where they make some emotional difference. The more Federica cried, the more the team behind the screen pleaded: "That's enough—do something different!")

Infants who get the right amount of physical care, but not enough maternal care, become apathetic (see Bowlby, 1969). In a therapeutic relationship, if therapist and clients receive enough emotional understanding, they cannot become apathetic or bored. Of course, what, for the newborn is warm maternal care, for therapists and clients is the acknowledgement of the relational (emotional) system in which they are embedded.

Although boredom was a central theme in discussions behind the mirror, nobody—therapist included—thought about asking Federica whether she felt bored. We often take for granted that our clients do not feel the burden of repetition, probably unavoidable to some extent in the ritualized frame of therapy. Sometimes we ask our clients if what we say makes sense (Boscolo & Bertrando, 1996), but the question "How do you feel?" is rather infrequent, although it is usually the first question the team asks the therapist when she enters the observation room for a team discussion. Actually, we have a wide experience of clients saying, on their own initiative, that therapy is useless or even damaging, but we never had a person tell us that therapy is boring. Sometimes, though, we have thought that some instances of dropping out from therapy were caused by the clients' unspoken boredom.

To try to find an answer to this question, we have begun asking our clients whether they feel bored in our conversations. This question tends to activate them. It is an open question (the therapist does not know the answer), and it generates information on the emotional system as it emerges in the therapeutic encounter. It often produces amazement ("Can I really say that?"), and, at the same time, it restores boredom as one of the legitimate subjects of the therapy. Reflecting on boredom takes repetition and immobility out of the conversation, creating a new emotional system enabling the therapist and clients set off on unexplored paths.

Closing remarks

One possible objection to our position is that, by theorizing the emotional system, we deny the very possibility of individual states of mind. We are not saying, however, that a person's emotion is determined by the emotional system she is embedded in. Instead, our view is that this person's emotion is deeply influenced by the prevailing emotional system she finds herself a part of at any given moment. We accept, here, a relational definition of emotion of the kind theorized, among others, by Manghi (1998), Dumouchel (2000), and Gross (2006). This does not mean, though, that a person, within an emotional system characterized, for example, by anger, will perforce become angry. Sometimes, we see situations of what might be called emotional complementarity, when one person is very angry and blaming and the other person seems to have accommodated within this emotional field and is passive and self-blaming. We see self-harming teenagers who seem to self-regulate their hate to avoid upsetting their otherwise vulnerable or retaliatory parents (see also Pocock, Chapter Six, this volume). All the same, at the relational level, anger is the emotion all participants are responding to, at least to an extent: there is a two-way relationship between the interactional emotional system and the individual awareness and feeling of each participant.

In the end, what is essential in working with unpleasant emotions, according to our view, can be reduced to a few points: not to fear them; to be free to speak openly about them; recognizing them as legitimate aspects of the therapeutic relationship; and to consider them as elements of an emotional system. Such ideas guide our practice, and allow us to operate with unpleasant emotions while maintaining our systemic perspective.

References

Anderson, H. (1997). *Conversation, Language and Possibilities*. New York: Basic Books.

Bertrando, P. (2006). Cornici che collassano: umorismo, psicoterapia. In: P. A. Rovatti & D. Zoletto (Eds.), *L'umorismo nella comunicazione umana* (pp. 157–182). Milan: Raffaello Cortina Editore.

Bertrando, P. (2007). *The Dialogical Therapist: Dialogue in Systemic Practice*. London: Karnac.

Bertrando, P., & Arcelloni, T. (2006). Hypotheses are dialogues: sharing hypotheses with clients. *Journal of Family Therapy, 28*: 370–387.

Bertrando, P., & Toffanetti, D. (2000). *Storia Della Terapia Familiare: Le persone, le Idee*. Milano: Raffaello Cortina Editore.

Boscolo, L., & Bertrando, P. (1993). *The Times of Time: A New Perspective for Systemic Therapy and Consultation*. New York: Norton.

Boscolo, L., & Bertrando, P. (1996). *Systemic Therapy with Individuals*. London: Karnac.

Bowlby, J. (1969). *Attachment and Loss, Vol. 1, Attachment*. London: Hogarth.

Bowlby, J. (1973). *Attachment and Loss, Vol. 2, Separation, Anxiety and Anger*. London: Hogarth.

Cecchin, G. (1987). Hypothesizing, circularity, and neutrality revisited: an invitation to curiosity. *Family Process, 26*: 405–413.

Cushman, P. (1995). *Constructing the Self, Constructing America: A Cultural History of Psychotherapy*. Reading, MA: Addison-Wesley.

Doherty, W. J. (1999). Il dissenso e la curiosità. Intervista con Mara Selvini Palazzoli, *Terapia Familiare, 61*: 11–24.

Dumouchel, P. (2000). Le corps et la coordination sociale ou les émotions In: N. Paquin (Ed.), *Réseau. Les Ancrages du Corps Propre* (pp. 149–190). Montréal: XYZ Éditeur.

Ekman, P. (2002). *Telling Lies: Clues to Deceit in the Marketplace, Marriage, and Politics* (3rd edn). New York: Norton.

Fredman, G. (2004). *Transforming Emotion: Conversations in Counselling and Psychotherapy*. London: Wiley.

Freud, S. (1920g). Beyond the pleasure principle. *S.E. 18*: pp. 1–64. London: Hogarth.

Gross, D. M. (2006). *The Secret History of Emotion: From Aristotle's Rhetoric to Modern Brain Science*. Chicago, IL: The University of Chicago Press.

Haley, J. (1976). *Problem-Solving Therapy*. San Francisco, CA: Jossey-Bass.

Jackson, D. D. (1965). Family rules, the marital quid pro quo. *Archives of General Psychiatry, 12*: 589–594.

Kavner, E., & McNab, S. (2005). Shame and the therapeutic relationship. In: C. Flaskas, B. Mason, & A. Perlesz (Eds.), *The Space Between: Experience, Context, and Process in the Therapeutic Relationship* (pp. 141–155). London: Karnac.

Kernberg, O. F. (1975). *Borderline Conditions and Pathological Narcissism*. New York: Jason Aronson.

Kleckner, T., Frank, L., Bland, C., Amendt, J. H., & duRee Bryant, R. (1992). The myth of the unfeeling strategic therapists. *Journal of Marital and Family Therapy, 18*: 41–51.

Klein, M. (1948). A contribution to the theory of anxiety and guilt. *International Journal of Psychoanalysis, 29*: 114–123.

Kohut, H. (1971a). Thoughts on narcissism and narcissistic rage. *The Psychoanalytic Study of the Child, 27*: 360–400.

Kohut, H. (1971b). *The Analysis of the Self*. London: Hogarth.

Lankton, S. R., Lankton, C. H., & Matthews, W. J. (1991). Ericksonian family therapy. In: A. S. Gurman & D. P. Kniskern (Eds.), *Handbook of Family Therapy, Vol. II* (pp. 240–274). New York: Brunner/Mazel.

Manghi, S. (1998). La tana del cuore: appunti sulla natura sociale delle emozioni. *Pluriverso, 2*: 32–43.

Maturana, H. R. (1988). Reality: the search for objectivity or the quest for a compelling argument. *The Irish Journal of Psychology, 9*: 25–82.

Pocock, D. (2005). Systems of the heart: evoking the feeling self in family therapy. In: C. Flaskas, B. Mason, & A. Perlesz (Eds.), *The Space Between: Experience, Context, and Process in the Therapeutic Relationship* (pp. 127–139). London: Karnac.

Searles, H. F. (1956). The psychodynamics of vengefulness. *Psychiatry, 19*: 31–39.

Selvini Palazzoli, M., Boscolo, L., Cecchin, G., & Prata, G. (1978). *Paradox and Counterparadox*. New York: Jason Aronson.

Socarides, C. W. (1966). On vengeance: the desire to "get even". *Journal of the American Psychoanalytic Association, 14*: 356–375.

White, M. (1989). The externalizing of the problem and the re-authoring of lives and relationship. *Dulwich Centre Newsletter, Summer*: 3–21.

White, M. (1995). Behaviour and its determinants or action and its sense: systemic and narrative metaphors. In: *Re-authoring Lives: Interviews and Essays* (pp. 214–221). Adelaide: Dulwich Centre Publications.

CHAPTER SIX

Working with emotional systems: four new maps

David Pocock

T he worst dentist I ever had was a Scotsman with terrible breath who engaged in the sort of institutionalized lying that was common, I suspect, in the dentistry of children in the early 1960s. The phrase "It will'na hurt laddie", I soon came to realize, heralded the onset of unavoidable squirming agony . . . or so I remember it. And "Never mind laddie, just a wee bit more" was a sure sign that whatever he was doing to me would not be finished this side of lunch-time. My best strategy, apart from simultaneously tensing every part of my body, was to dig my nails into my palms to try to spread the pain around as much as possible.

The best dentist I ever had, about ten years ago, was a Home Counties woman who, whenever I flinched, said, "Ooh", as if I were a baby, which, of course, in some ways, I am. Her "Ooh" was not a direct reflection of my feeling but an acknowledgment that it hurt, plus a small modification of that hurt. The modification was a little pantomime that showed, quite unconsciously, that while she recognized the pain, she was not feeling it as I was (it would be no good for us both to squeal) but it was a compassionate acknowledgment of my discomfort and her part in causing it. Sadly, she left the practice after five comparatively painless years, presumably to become a saint.

I have no idea whether dental training includes specific work on the management and understanding of feelings, but my guess is that the space for emotional understanding on a dental curriculum is similar to that in most family therapy training. Within the culture of family therapy, work with emotions is, with some notable exceptions (e.g., Bertrando & Arcelloni, 2009, this volume; Dallos, 2006; Fredman, 2004; Kavner & McNab, 2005), still strongly identified with psychoanalysis and accordingly—given the schizmogenic development of family therapy (Pocock, 2006)—not a high priority. This is not to say that family therapists are not careful with the feelings of those they work with. The great majority of family therapists that I have met are compassionate people with an above average capacity for empathy. The problem is that emotional systems are complex and not obvious. Empathy is always necessary, but not always sufficient. I believe that a more adequate account of emotional systems requires aspects of what is currently mainstream in both family therapy *and* psychoanalysis together, with some bridging of the space between them.

But, if family therapy has got along reasonably well without specifically addressing emotion, then why bother with it? There are several possible answers to this. One of the most pressing is the sheer ubiquity of bad feelings at the point when help is sought. In my National Health Service (NHS) work, I read about twenty referral letters per week, covering a disparate range of presenting problems, but what is common to all is that at least one person feels really bad and cannot carry on with things as they are. One or more feelings of anxiety, fury, hopelessness, guilt, shame, rejection, and blame are in the text or sub-text of every referral. I think these emotionally laden presentations need to be met with an understanding of the way relationships can help and hinder in their management.

So far, I have used the words "feelings", "emotions", and "affect" interchangeably, and this is commonly the case. However, there are good reasons to specify the meanings of these terms (Siegel, 1999), and from now on in this chapter I use "feeling" to refer to an emotion that has been consciously experienced, and "affect" as emotion in one person as observed and described by another. The statement "I am angry" is a declaration of a feeling, whereas the statement "You seem angry" is a declaration of observed affect. More controversially, perhaps, I use "emotion" to describe an interchange of energy operating at both conscious and unconscious levels between the mind and body of an individual *and* between the minds and bodies of individuals in relationship.

Readers with more than a passing interest in social constructionism might experience some unease at the idea of emotions operating at an unconscious level, and might be more comfortable with the idea of feelings as co-constructed through discourse. What we feel consciously, and certainly what feelings we express to others, does involve a process of evaluation that is highly influenced by culture. (However, it has been found cross-culturally that, at the age of six months, all babies show the basic categorical emotions of joy, disgust, anger, surprise, distress, and sadness [Ekman, 1983; Izard, 1979]. This is not surprising, given that all humans are members of a single, closely related, species. Cultural variation builds on, and is likely to be constrained by, genetic inheritance.) As Glenda Fredman (2004) writes, we learn to do feelings through participation in cultures, and these have their own local emotional grammars. In this chapter, I do not seek to challenge that view. If anything, I want to extend the definition of culture to apply not just to very large groupings, but also to small ones. Even a relationship of two people develops its own set of procedures (ethos) about what emotions will be felt and expressed as feeling and how other emotions will be managed (Pocock, 2005).

Psychoanalysis is, of course, at ease with the idea of unconscious processes, but scientific evidence that emotion is primarily non-conscious also comes from neurobiology through the use of EEGs. These show patterns of energy within the brain which activate and arouse us—and those we are in relationship with— primarily through non-verbal communication via the face, posture, and tone of voice. Emotion, then, is the energy that connects us with ourselves and others at the level of body and mind (Gerhardt, 2004; Siegel, 1999), and this is the case even if such emotions are not experienced as feelings. For example, children who are classified as avoidantly attached are able to deactivate their attachment behaviour when reunited with their attachment figure during the Strange Situation test (Ainsworth, Blehar, Waters, & Wall, 1978). They appear emotionally switched off when the parent returns, but studies have shown high levels of bodily arousal as measured through elevated heart rate (Kobak, 1999; Spangler & Grossman, 1993). For such children, emotional arousal seems not to have become experienced as feeling. They have come to anticipate rejection and misattunement from their care-givers, so feeling pleased or relieved to see the parent again (as a securely attached child would) might have been removed from their range of feelings to avoid further hurt. This kind of emotional adaptation is a key aspect of what I want to say about emotional systems.

The value of social constructionism to family therapy has been its highlighting of the social determinants of knowledge. But this has come at a price. Social constructionism is a relativist epistemology and can give no help in evaluating whether one set of ideas is a better description of the external world than another. Most social constructionists, when pushed, do believe in an external reality, and not all forms of constructionism are anti-realist (Burr, 1995), but social constructionism will always favour the social creation of knowledge over the social discovery of knowledge. There are many knotty arguments about this that I can simply step over, since there is now a new epistemological–ontological kid on the block called "critical realism" (see López & Potter [2001], and Pocock [2008] for an introduction), which transcends some of the bleak and irresolvable debates of realism *vs.* constructionism.

Essentially, critical realism conceives of a complex—but structured and ordered—world in which things are always going on, even if we cannot perceive them, measure them, or talk about them. Knowledge is seen as socially created through discourse but, nevertheless, and unlike social constructionism, critical realism also recognizes that some knowledge claims can give a better representational account than others of the world beyond our ideas. I think this is a more encompassing epistemology and ontology, and means that culture, science, and theory building do not have to be continuously at war with each other. Some consider that critical realism might replace postmodernism (López & Potter, 2001). That remains to be seen, but, for the moment, it seems a useful playground in which a variety of theories, which might otherwise have been corralled in separate categories, can be allowed to run around together.

I will shortly outline four theories, emerging in the last five to ten years, which have helped me to bridge my systemic family therapy training and my, fairly traditional, individual psychoanalytic train-ing. This bridge—made up of developments in attachment theory, contemporary psychoanalysis informed by infant research, and other aspects of relational psychoanalysis—allows a more thorough account of emotional systems. These ideas do not integrate into one neat, joined up meta-theory; linkage points can be found, but theoretical ideas have their own social traditions that cannot easily be transcended. However, theories can be "layered" to give a richer view and provide more clinical options. (See Goldner, Penn, Sheinberg, & Walker [1990] for a fine example of layering.)

Having mapped out the components of this bridge, I will try to illustrate these ideas through two case examples. The four theories are Patricia Crittenden's dynamic–maturational model of attach-ment, Beatrice Beebe and Frank Lachmann's theory of self and inter-active regulation, Peter Fonagy and colleagues' work on reflective function, and Jessica Benjamin's version of intersubjectivity theory.

The dynamic–maturational model of attachment

Attachment theory, originally developed by John Bowlby (Bowlby, 1953), has long been available as a link between psychoanalysis and systems but has been, somewhat inconsistently, taken up within both therapy cultures. The basic attachment patterns described by Mary Ainsworth and her colleagues (Ainsworth, Blehar, Waters, & Wall, 1978): A (avoidant), B (secure), and C (ambivalent), and, more recently, D (disorganized), have been validated cross-culturally, although the basic types seem to vary in proportions between cul-tures. One difficulty with attachment theory is that the infant patterns of attachment are somewhat crude distinctions and diffi-cult to use clinically. Despite Bowlby's advice to Ainsworth to call the three original types A, B, and C until more was understood about them, it is the "avoidant", "secure", and "ambivalent" labels that have stuck. "Avoidant" and "ambivalent" tend to stand out as dysfunctional categories, as distinct from the desirable "secure" category, but what attachment researchers consistently make clear is that these are adaptive emotional strategies on the part of the infant. In other words, these need to be understood as *infant strategies within the context of an emotional system.*

This is not to say that all strategies are benign; that is clearly not the case, but they need to be seen as the best ecosystemic fit within the available resources of their care-givers, who, themselves, are simultaneously trying to adapt to the infant. For example, an infant classified as ambivalently attached, who becomes excessively distressed when reunited in the Strange Situation, might well have found a behaviour that is a congruent fit to a care-giver who is preoccupied with his own upset feelings. Conversely, an infant classified as type A (avoidant) will understandably suppress all upset if she has learned that revealing this will lead to rejection from an emotionally dismissive parent.

There has been a tendency to assume that these early categories might be valid through the life-span but, as Crittenden (2000) points out, when children mature they are capable of a much more elaborate range of affective responses and operate within a wider relational field of parents, siblings, and peers. In older children, affect can be consciously or unconsciously denied, exaggerated, or falsified in order to elicit certain responses from care-givers. Crittenden elaborates the basic Ainsworth A, B, C model, incorporating new adaptive strategies within the existing broad categories, identifying nine sub-categories at pre-school age and thirteen by adulthood. She outlines the way in which the pattern of a child may become opposite, but complementary, to the parent. For example, a feigned helpless (C4) pattern in a parent creates a context in which one or more children within a family might develop a compulsive care-giving (A3) strategy. Or a compulsive compliant (A4) parent might become complementary to an aggressive (C3) child.

I will not elaborate further on her model, partly because I am aware that the culture of family therapy has only a limited tolerance for typologies. The main idea that I wish to carry forward is Crittenden's theme that the affective range in one person may be understood as a specific adaptation within the emotional ecosystem of significant relationships.

A system of self and interactive regulation

Beatrice Beebe and Frank Lachmann (2002) use general systems theory to draw together their thirty years' experience of infant research and adult psychotherapy. Through painstaking examination of videotaped face-to-face interaction between mothers and infants, they show that interactions—of face, voice, and bodily orientation—are co-constructed. They identify their work with much of the current thinking in relational psychoanalysis, in which the mind is seen as inherently social, interactional, and interpersonal (Aron, 1996). Beebe and Lachmann show not only how caregiver and infant regulate emotion through engagement (which they call interactive regulation), but also how each separately regulates his or her own state of attention or arousal (which they call self-regulation). Three issues are underlined: first, that interactive and self-regulation are each themselves part of a system; second, that optimal systems have a *balance* of self and interactive regulation; and third, that sub-optimal systems rely on an excessive use of self-regulation to manage arousal.

My boyhood dentist offered no soothing or containment through interactive regulation: quite the opposite, I could not trust his words, so I relied entirely on crude self-regulatory methods of tensing my body and digging my nails into my hand to manage the arousal, and this remained the pattern until well into adulthood. My best dentist, through a process of empathic emotional acknowledgment (well-timed "Oohs"), was frequently available to allow soothing through interactional regulation. However, there were still times when she was, quite understandably, preoccupied with my teeth rather than my emotions, and I then fell back on milder forms of self-regulation (such as concentrating on the end of my toes) until she was more available and interactive regulation was again possible. This dynamic, shifting back and forward between self and interactive regulation to manage emotional arousal, is, in the view of Beebe and Lachmann, a life-long human feature and forms the theoretical basis of their adult psychotherapy practice.

A securely attached child is free to express a wide range of feelings (within a given cultural context), knowing, from experience, that she will remain acceptable. Children with fragile or retaliatory parents often learn that their anger and rejection is not acceptable, and any expression of these feelings will further undermine their security. Beebe and Lachmann's account sheds light on the non-reflective self-regulatory strategy of self-hatred as an adaptive response in these circumstances. (There is a link here with Ronald

Fairbairn's [1952] notion of "moral defence", in which the child exonerates the parent by blaming herself to preserve something good in the relationship.) This may take the form of depressive self-hating cognitions (low self-esteem), or more ruthless and concrete uses of the body such as those found in eating disorders, substance abuse, self-harm, somatic illness, and attempted suicide.

Reflective function

Donald Winnicott (1971) writes of the mother giving back to the baby the baby's own self. What feels real to the infant about himself is dependent on what the care-giver reflects back through his or her responsiveness. There are links here with Wilfred Bion's (1962) notion of containment: his theory that the mind of the parent can, through reverie, take in bad feelings projected by the infant and give back a sense of understanding and tolerance that the infant takes in and that eventually allows self-containment through thinking. Peter Fonagy and colleagues (Fonagy, Gergely, Jurist, & Target, 2004) build on these ideas and suggest that, through repeated interactions with an attuned parent, the child establishes a capacity to know her own emotional states of mind as well as the states of mind of another. They refer to this, variously, as the capacity for reflective function, or an ability to mentalize, or to develop a theory of mind. Some of the most seriously disturbed patients in adult psychotherapy (e.g., those with a diagnosis of borderline personality disorder) have little capacity to reflect on their emotional states, which are consequently highly labile and overwhelming, and this is strongly associated with chronic early misattunement by care-givers.

Fonagy and colleagues' detailed account of affect mirroring suggests that when a care-giver's response is appropriate, well timed, and marked, this gives the infant—through a process they describe as social biofeedback—a representation of his emotional state combined with a secondary representation of the care-giver's response, which can be internalized. Over time, the infant and child can use these internalized representations to think about feelings for himself. By "marked", they refer to that particular aspect of care-givers' affective response which shows that, while they have registered the emotional state of the child, they are not feeling it in the same way themselves. An attuned parent may respond to an angry infant with "Oh you're very cross!" but in a slightly jokey, fond way, making a cross face that is also partially smiley. (My good dentist marked her response to me with *pantomimed* "Oohs".) An unmarked response would be where the parent really is just as angry as the child.

Britt Krause (2002) uses the ideas of Fonagy and co-authors to explain how culture influences the development of self. What feels authentic to a child about herself is dependent on how she sees herself represented in the responses, first of parents, then siblings, peers, and other adults. These responses will be contingent on the affective repertoire of these significant others which, in turn, will be highly influenced by culture.

As previously implied, the work of Fonagy and colleagues can be used to expand on the system of self and interactive regulation of Beebe and Lachmann. Affective attunement during interactive regulation can lead to a different form of self-regulation in the child, one in which the infant can regulate her own emotions through reflective function.

From object relating to subject relating

So far, the emphasis has been on parental attunement and recognition of the emotional state of mind of the child, and an understanding of the adaptations available to the child when things do not go well. However, this can slip into a one-way account that leaves out the possibility of the child's recognition of the care-giver as a separate subject with an equivalent centre of self. A sizeable proportion of the children (mostly boys) seen in our CAMHS service are referred for omnipotent, out-of-control, raging behaviour, for whom parents (more usually mothers) have become objects to control rather than subjects with whom mutual recognition is possible. Such boys may grow into dominating or abusive men for whom women remain objects rather than persons.

I think it is true that early and/or long-term parental misattunement, trauma, and loss can play a part in this. Instead of continuing to communicate his emotional needs, the child may pursue an omnipotent ideal of getting what he wants when he wants it. However, omnipotence can also thrive on parents giving in to the insistent demands of the child, and this seems often to be underpinned by a fear of the child withholding love, becoming upset, or hating the parent if deprived of what he wants. The feminist and relational psychoanalyst Jessica Benjamin (1999) develops Winnicott's idea (1971) that to achieve recognition of the mother as a separate person in her own right the child needs to attack and destroy her *as an object*: that is, to destroy the internal representation he has of her, with which he strives to force her to comply. It is through destruction that he can discover something of what she is really like as a person. What is crucial here is not just attunement, but *survival as a parent* in the face of these attacks.

Traditionally, psychoanalysis has seen resolution as occurring through integrating good and bad object representations of the mother, and later, in the case of a boy, of the oedipal father claiming the mother and the child identifying with him. For Benjamin, this sets the developmental bar too low, leaving out the discovery of the mother as a real person with a separate centre of self. Maternal survival in the face of destruction is, for Benjamin, the main pathway to mutual recognition and subject-to-subject relating.

Survival in the face of destruction sounds dramatic, and some presentations of out of control aggressive teenagers are very intimidating indeed. But the process of destruction and recognition that Benjamin has in mind more usually proceeds in small frequent doses, such as the toddler who is absolutely enraged that his mother will not let him eat chocolate for breakfast, or run in the road, or hold the cat up by its back legs, and so on, for a couple of hundred thousand times. What is needed from the care-giver is not to collapse and give in and become just what the child wants, or to retaliate destructively, or to confuse the child's destructive aggression with an internal object of her own, such as an abusive or rejecting parent or partner, but *simply to hold on to the idea of him or herself as a parent and the child as a child*. Each time the destructiveness is survived, the parent emerges a little further as a real, separate subject in whom, eventually, there can be genuine delight in mutual recognition.

Benjamin's theory sheds additional light on the problems when care-givers undermine each other's parental authority. In the child's mind, the parents can be immediately split into the good (giving-in) object and the bad (withholding) object, with no progress made towards mutual recognition of child and parent as subjects. The parent setting limits is always defined as bad in this split, and even benign forms of control can then feel mean and depriving to the child.

Case examples

Self-regulating a feared disaster

Misha, aged thirteen, the only child of separated Black-Caribbean British parents—was referred with a range of obsessive–compulsive behaviours. She repeatedly cleaned all kitchen utensils and surfaces with antibacterial spray for fear of getting an illness that would make her vomit. She quite often drew her mother into her sterilizing rituals. She was especially worried about school assembly, since, in her mind, she might catch flu viruses from other children, and that would also make her sick.

Her parents had separated when she was aged six, and she saw her father very occasionally but "only when he wanted". He would turn up every couple of years and demand to see her. Both joked, rather nervously, that he was a hard man to say "No" to. On further exploration, it became clear that Misha's mother was terrified of him, since, although not physically violent, he had "put her down" throughout their relationship. She lived in fear of him coming back again, although she had not previously discussed this with Misha. The mother had felt put down throughout her life, and felt her parents had not allowed her to stand up for herself. Her fear seemed to be what *might* happen if she ever stood up to anyone.

Misha, herself, seemed quite unconcerned about seeing her father, but had no answer to the question of whether she wanted to see him or not. The idea of having any choice in the matter was simply inconceivable. In the absence of feelings, I inquired about dreams (sometimes a useful approach, since emotions that do not reach consciousness seem often to be processed through dreaming). She rather dismissively told me about recurring dreams of Viking raids. In some of these dreams, everyone was killed apart from her. I pointed out that the Vikings were a frightening force that came every couple of years that no one could stand up to, just like her mother said about her father. I asked her if she ever feared her father would take her away from her mother against her will. She said that she did, which seemed a small breakthrough, but she rather surprised me by then saying in a challenging way that she thought neither the dreams nor her rituals had anything to do with her father. She persisted with this over several sessions. However, her symptoms lessened considerably because, she said challengingly, she had decided to change them herself. Her mother agreed to be referred for individual counselling to help with her fear of standing up for herself, which was also a problem for her at work, where she was experiencing some bullying.

I think mother's fear of the father—based partly on her experiences with him but also on her internal parental objects—was communicated to Misha even though mother "didn't talk about it". Rather than be flooded further with mother's anxiety, I think Misha developed a closed self-regulatory system where she could attempt total omnipotent control over the threatening aspects of her environment represented by the viruses. (Towards the end of the therapy the mother told me that the first time Misha felt scared of being sick was when they were both in the car with the father, who was angry and drove very fast, refusing to hear the increasingly desperate pleas of both of them to slow down.)

Although the work did not obviously evoke conscious feelings in Misha about her father, nevertheless, something seemed to change and the OCD based self-regulation became less needed. She seemed to relish disagreeing with me and not accepting my ideas, instead choosing to autonomously pursue her own solution, which I encouraged. It might be that this new experience of disagreeing and successfully standing up to me (partly representing her father object in her transference) helped to modify the feared disaster (Bentovim & Kinston, 1991) of standing up to father that seemed to be shared unconsciously by both mother and daughter at the level of family myth (Byng-Hall, 1995).

Self-regulating murderous rage

Michael, aged twelve, was referred urgently following a serious suicide attempt. His mother had found him with the ligature round his neck, but had been able to release him in time. She was understandably terrified that he would do it again, but, when I met them, Michael mostly seemed ashamed by the incident, which he just wanted to cover up. He said he did it "just to see what it might feel like". He was an only child in a white British working-class family. His father had an affair when Michael was three years old and, following its discovery by Michael's mother, the father left the family to live with his girlfriend. The father had felt guilty about leaving Michael—whom he loved—and had kept in very regular contact with him. As a teenager, he had lost contact with his own father through divorce and, I believe, his corrective script (Byng-Hall, 1995) was to avoid this, at all costs, with Michael.

Michael's father told Michael that he would always keep a place in his new home for him. (This, I think, was partly out of guilt for leaving Michael and partly to attack Michael's mother.) Michael's mother was badly hurt by her husband's affair and any mention of him by Michael would make her upset and angry. In the absence of any interactive processing of his loss, Michael nurtured a private fantasy that one day either his father would come back so that they could be together again, or that he would live with his father and have him to himself.

A month before the referral, Michael had discovered by accident that his father was getting married and was expecting a baby son. Michael immediately refused to have anything more to do with his father. He had borrowed some of his father's DVDs, and, that day, smashed them to pieces. Unwisely, this was communicated to the father by Michael's mother. (At some level, I think she was quite gratified by Michael's hatred of the father, since this was synchronous with some of her feelings about him.) Eventually, Michael was persuaded to meet his father again, but on the understanding that father's fiancée was not to be present. As Michael reached the door, he realized that the fiancée was also in the house, and refused to go in. His infuriated father brought out the new camera he had bought for Michael's birthday, unwrapped it in front of Michael, and then crushed it under his foot. The following day, Michael attempted to hang himself.

I think Michael had lost his father from the family at a crucial point in his oedipal development, leaving Michael and his mother alone. This loss meant that Michael was not easily able to manage relationships with more than one person. His fantasy was of having his mother to himself *and* his father to himself. The real loss of father from the family was neither available to be processed through interactive regulation with father, because of father's guilt in relation to Michael and father's corrective script in relation to his own father, nor with the mother, because of her hurt and antagonism given the circumstances of the break-up. I think Michael's careful fantasy, that he would one day have both parents to himself again, was constructed to avoid all sense of loss and was sustained intact through nine years. It was shattered at the moment when Michael accidentally discovered that he would lose his exclusive relationship with his father both to the girlfriend (who had previously been dismissed from Michael's mind and whom he merely tolerated) and, perhaps even worse, to a replacement future baby brother who would occupy the space in the house that Michael believed had always been reserved for him alone.

During the work, Michael was, in the presence of his mother, able to put into words how hurt he had felt that his father had not personally told him about his marriage and the new baby. His mother was able to acknowledge this empathically, and very helpfully said that perhaps his father was really worried about finding the right time to tell him because he was aware how difficult it would be for Michael. He seemed able to accept this from his mother, and her attempt to find both father and son emotionally understandable allowed Michael to begin to turn to her to manage more of his feelings.

Michael's smashing of his father's DVDs and rejection of him were, I think, attempts to communicate to father, through projective identification, his own sense of rage and rejection; in other words to force the father to feel what he felt. Outside the front door of the house, father, I believe, lost touch both with himself as a father and with Michael as his son, and the parental relationship did not, in that moment, survive. Instead, in father's mind, I think Michael became confused with his own internal rejecting father-object, leading to serious retaliation. Michael's rage and rejection were not contained by his father but pushed straight back at him, together with all the rage and rejection of the father doubling the arousal in Michael. All Michael could do with such a murderous intensity of rage and rejection was to enact the most serious form of self-regulation, which is to murder one's body.

When I met with the father on his own, I soon told him that I thought he had been an exceptionally good father to Michael, since I felt he expected me to judge him for crushing the camera. (He was, I think, very ashamed of his retaliatory behaviour.) After a while, he was able to accept that Michael was not rejecting him, but powerfully communicating to him Michael's own sense of rejection born out of his three-year-old wish not to share his father with anyone. Within a few days, contact between father and son was restored, and over the following months Michael became more settled and, significantly, was eventually able to attend his father's wedding and involve himself with his new half-brother.

Summary

When the therapist joins the relational system, a new emotional culture is created through which previous emotional adaptations can be explored and re-evaluated (Pocock, 2005). The collaborative discovery of new emotional understanding can tilt systems relying on excessive self regulation back towards interactive regulation and the longer-term possibilities of increased reflective functioning. Parents can be helped mindfully to hold firm (rather than collapse or retaliate) when the emotional arousal wrecking their parental state of mind has been understood and held, allowing the beginnings of new security and loving recognition. Where this can be achieved in family therapy, it need not be a lengthy process, as it frequently must be in individual therapy.

The family systems therapist's capacity to be affected and to think about her countertransference experiences is an essential part of this process, although beyond the scope of this paper. However, I hope that it has been possible to provide some meaningful account of the availability of new maps to help explore this uncertain, difficult, but worthwhile territory.

References

Ainsworth, M., Blehar, M., Waters, E., & Wall, S. (1978). *Patterns of Attachment: A Psychological Study of the Strange Situation*. Hillsdale, NJ: Erlbaum.

Aron, L. (1996). *A Meeting of Minds*. Hillsdale, NJ: Analytic Press.

Beebe, B., & Lachmann, F. (2002). *Infant Research and Adult Treatment: Co-constructing Interactions*. London: Analytic Press.

Benjamin, J. (1999). Recognition and destruction: An outline of inter-subjectivity. In: S. Mitchell & L. Aron (Eds.), *Relational Psychoanalysis: The Emergence of a Tradition* (pp. 183–200). Hillsdale NJ: The Analytic Press.

Bentovim, A., & Kinston, W. (1991). Focal family therapy: joining systems theory with psychodynamic understanding. In: A. Gurman & D. Kniskern (Eds.), *Handbook of Family Therapy, Volume II* (pp. 284–324). New York: Brunner/Mazel.

Bertrando, P., & Arcelloni, T. (2009). In: C. Flaskas & D. Pocock (Eds.), see Chapter 5 this publication (pp. 75–92). London: Karnac.

Bion, W. (1962). *Learning from Experience*. London: Heinemann.

Bowlby, J. (1953). *Child Care and the Growth of Love*. Harmondsworth: Penguin.

Burr, V. (1995). *An Introduction to Social Constructionism*. London: Routledge.

Byng-Hall, J. (1995). *Rewriting Family Scripts: Improvisation and Systems Change*. London: Guilford.

Crittenden, P. (2000). A dynamic–maturational approach to continuity and change in pattern of attachment. In: P. Crittenden & A. Claussen (Eds.), *The Organisation of Attachment Relationships: Maturation, Culture and Context* (pp. 343–357). Cambridge: Cambridge University Press.

Dallos, R. (2006). *Attachment Narrative Therapy: Integrating Narrative, Systemic and Attachment Therapies*. New York: Open University Press.

Ekman, P. (1983). Autonomic nervous system activity distinguishes among emotions. *Science*, 221: 1208–1210.

Fairbairn, R. (1952). *Psychoanalytic Studies of the Personality*. London: Routledge and Kegan Paul.

Fonagy, P., Gergely, G., Jurist, E., & Target, M. (2004). *Affect Regulation, Mentalization, and the Development of the Self*. London: Karnac.

Fredman, G. (2004). *Transforming Emotion: Conversations in Counselling and Psychotherapy*. London: Whurr.

Gerhardt, S. (2004). *Why Love Matters: How Affection Shapes a Baby's Brain*. London: Routledge.

Goldner, V., Penn, P., Sheinberg, M., & Walker, G. (1990). Love and violence: gender paradoxes in volatile attachments. *Family Process*, 29: 343–364.

Izard, C. (1979). *The Maximally Discriminative Facial Action Coding System (MAX)*. Newark, NJ: University of Delaware Instructional Resources Centre.

Kavner, E., & McNab, S. (2005). Shame and the therapeutic relationship. In: C. Flaskas, B. Mason, & A. Perlesz (Eds.), *The Space Between: Experience, Context, and Process in the Therapeutic Relationship* (pp. 141–155). London: Karnac.

Kobak, R. (1999). The emotional dynamics of disruptions in attachment relationships: implications for theory, research and clinical applications. In: J. Cassidy and P. Shaver (Eds.), *Handbook of Attachment* (pp. 21–43). London: Guilford.

Krause, I.-B. (2002). *Culture and System in Family Therapy*. London: Karnac.

López, J., & Potter, G. (2001). After postmodernism: the new millennium. In: J. López & G. Potter (Eds.), *After Postmodernism: An Introduction to Critical Realism* (pp. 3–16). London: Athlone.

Pocock, D. (2005). Systems of the heart: evoking the feeling self in family therapy. In: C. Flaskas, B. Mason, & A. Perlesz (Eds.), *The Space Between: Experience, Context and Process in the Therapeutic Relationship* (pp. 127–139). London: Karnac.

Pocock, D. (2006). Six things worth understanding about psychoanalytic psychotherapy. *Journal of Family Therapy, 28*: 349–366.

Pocock, D. (2008). Be dragons here? Why family systems therapy needs a new operating system. *Context, 97*: 20–23.

Siegel, D. (1999). *The Developing Mind: How Relationships and the Brain Interact to Shape Who We Are*. London: Guilford Press.

Spangler, G., & Grossmann, K. (1993). Biobehavioral organisation in securely and insecurely attached infants. *Child Development, 64*: 1439–1450.

Winnicott, D. W. (1971). The use of an object and relating through identifications. In: *Playing and Reality*. Harmondsworth: Penguin.

CHAPTER SEVEN

Thinking through togetherness: developmental metaphors and systemic thinking

Rolf Sundet and Vigdis Wie Torsteinsson

T he field of systemic family therapy, usually with good reason, has been sceptical towards expert knowledge in every form. Instead of acting as someone who knows better, the family therapist has generally recognized the client's expertise, and the co-operation and reciprocity between family and therapist as the "gold standard" of therapeutic practice. Critical voices have, however, cautioned against a disavowal of therapeutic expertise, since this might prevent the therapist from making his/her professional knowledge useful to the family (Minuchin, 1998). In this chapter, we discuss concepts drawn from the knowledge base of developmental psychology, with an extended focus on the basics of human relating (Johnsen, Sundet, & Torsteinsson, 2004). Our main purpose is to outline how these concepts can enable the therapist to work collaboratively in ways that enrich the family therapy paradigm.

Much contemporary family therapy revolves around language: the generation of change through promoting new descriptions and co-authoring new stories. While social constructionist family therapy literature insists on the basic significance of language in the generation of meaning and meaning-making processes, the understanding of how language connects with non-linguistic interplay, or even how relational processes contribute to bringing about new linguistic expressions and new stories is sparse. When a parent says that he "understands", but his seventeen-year-old daughter responds as if he has said just the opposite, then how do *we* understand and react to what is happening between them? When a boy of eight enters therapy with his mother, but refuses point-blank to talk about difficult things, how do we handle this as part of a therapeutic process where we want everybody to be involved?

In this chapter we look at clinical work through a lens of developmental theory, with a particular interest in situations where words are not enough, or where talking about problems is not acceptable to the client. The girl of seventeen and the boy of eight will be presented in a more detailed way to exemplify three themes that are central to our understanding: emotions, subjectivity, and language.

To understand language you also have to attend to emotional exchanges. These exchanges have to be understood first as turn-taking, then the establishing of a common focus and joint attention: in short, the experience of sharing. The theories and concepts of Daniel Stern will be our main point of reference (Stern, 1985, 1995, 2000).

Lost intersubjectivity: the case of Catherine

Catherine is a seventeen-year-old girl who was referred to a specialist inpatient service at the age of fifteen. At that point, it also became clear that she was suffering from a serious eating disorder. This problem had been a part of her life since she was twelve, without anybody really noticing. The psychologist who referred her said that, despite difficulties with motivation to change, they had been able to co-operate with her in several ways, but the biggest worry on the part of her therapists was that they had not been able to address the eating disorder. She would not be weighed or agree to blood tests, and would only occasionally talk about her relationship with food.

Her parents were so defeated by worries about her health that they wanted someone else to take charge of their daughter's life. They had been very involved in the former attempts to break the circles of dysfunctional starvation, overeating, and vomiting but they had not succeeded. They readily admitted that their daughter had been too stubborn, insisting on holding tightly to her patterns of starving, eating, and exercising, and they could no longer handle her. Her father partly blamed himself; he was suffering from a chronic somatic illness that had started when Catherine was a very small child. He was then in pain for much of the time, and often was demanding and angry with the children. Catherine has an older brother who had been in psychiatric treatments for several years. Her father had also spent some time in a psychiatric unit due to serious depression. At some time during her childhood, Catherine had appointed herself the one child who was going to be the pride and joy of her parents; the one who would not be a problem. When this venture broke down, she concluded that she could never succeed in anything again.

Catherine's communication with her parents is mostly concentrated around them trying to convince her that she has a problem, and her insisting on the necessity of following her own mind. She says that she will not even consider trying to change her destructive eating patterns until her parents understand her. To her parents and even to her therapists, who in every way tried to convey that they really wanted her to have a mind of her own and that they understood her point of view, her complaints about not being understood were a mystery. The following excerpt from a conversation can illustrate the dilemma:

Father (to therapist): "Catherine is always complaining that nobody understands how she feels and thinks. I can't understand this: I keep saying to her that I understand her every day. I can even feel her stress and the necessity of her compulsive strategies. I use them myself from time to time to feel that I have control over my own illness."

Catherine: "I know, I know; in one way I know that you understand, but there is something missing—I don't know what it is; I really don't know!!!"

Therapist (to mother): "What do you think about what is going on between these two people? Does this make sense to you?"

Mother: "I had an idea while I listened to them talking. I'll try to put it into words, but I don't know how successful it will be. I also hear my husband telling Catherine that he understands her way of thinking, and in some ways I think he really does. They have quite a lot in common, these two. But when I think about the conversations they have, when he is trying to get across his understanding . . . he says it with a lot of emotion . . . and Catherine goes all quiet . . . perhaps she is waiting for something more . . . "

Therapist: "What could that something more be?"

Mother: "I don't know, really . . . maybe that the understanding would change him in some way, that the continuation of the conversation would be different in some way. That him seeing her point of view would change him in some way . . . or even change her. But he goes on saying the same things he always says, about what *he* thinks she should do . . . I don't know if this makes sense, really, but this is the only way I can put it into words . . ."

There are several ways to explain what is going on in this conversation. But this is a difficult situation to handle using traditional family therapy theory and interventions. There is no conflict, no disagreement in this dialogue, just a subtle problem of reaching each other. Even though the father says "the right thing"—the very words Catherine is waiting for and wants to hear—there is something missing between them, something that stops the words from making an impression on Catherine. In our understanding, this is a problem about intersubjectivity. They both attend to the same feeling, but not in a way that makes it possible for either of them to feel that they are emotionally sharing something. Instead, they both continue to feel alienated from the other. There is a gap between the expression of *feeling the same* and the actual experience of *sharing a feeling* that words are unable to bridge. We will try to explain the theoretical base for this as we go along. But first let us take a detour through another concept that has come to the fore in the therapeutic community in recent years, that of mentalization.

Mentalization and the reflective position

The development of a capacity to see ourselves (and others) as intentional beings, with minds of our own, is still a mystery to us in many ways. The concept of mentalizing (or reflective function) is fast developing as an important concept in many therapeutic and theoretical contexts. Mentalization "is the process by which we realize that having a mind mediates our experience of the world" (Fonagy, Gergely, Jurist, & Target, 2004, p. 3). The infant is conceptualized as initially unable to distinguish between inner and outer reality. (The inability to make this distinction is also known as psychic equivalence.) The preliminary phase of development of mentalizing requires a parent who can mirror the infant's mental state in an accurate, contingent, and marked way (see Bateman & Fonagy, 2006)

The next phase is the pretend mode. Here the mental world is decoupled from the external world; the child can experiment with different ways of being, gradually developing both a sense of personal agency ("I am aware that I both want to—and can do—this") as well as the appreciation of the mind of the other ("I am aware that you as a separate person both want to—and can do—that") (Fonagy, 2006). The as-if mode is a prerequisite for symbolization: the capacity to play with reality, to see it in different versions. But, at this stage, play with reality presupposes a decoupling that allows the imagination to flourish.

There are several similarities between these formulations and important aspects of family therapy practice. Ideas of the multiverse (Maturana, 1988) and reflecting processes (Andersen, 2006) endorse a creative play with different meanings, without the necessity to commit oneself to any specific interpretation in the here-and-now. These methods underline the importance of play in contemporary family therapy. (The connection between reflecting practices and theories of mentalizing are explored by Mary Donovan in Chapter Nine.)

One building block in the concept of mentalizing is the bridging of difference between the infant and parent in order for the infant to become capable of seeing and handling himself as a contributor to the relationship as a separate self. The theoretical base of attachment theory partly explains this; the infant seeks security, the grown-up provides it. However, the feelings have to be picked up and mirrored by the parent in a manner that provides information to the infant that *the infant's* feelings have been recognized. To feel recognized in this way allows the infant to construct a "theory of mind" and to recognize, in turn, the independent mind of the other. This mirroring makes it possible for the child to come to know herself as a separate person.

Through these ideas, psychodynamic theory and practice have become increasingly attentive to new aspects of the parent–child relationship. But both family therapy and the developmental psychology of Daniel Stern additionally emphasize the systemic and reciprocal features of this relationship. While Fonagy, Gergely, Jurist, and Target (2004) emphasize the *difference* in positions and contributions for the participants in communication, in our view they underplay the *reciprocity* of communication. For Stern (2000), the experience of sharing is crucially important. We will return to this point.

Expanding the base of developmental knowledge

Since the systems slogan, "the whole is more than the sum of its parts" (Bertalanffy, 1968), was formulated, family therapy has maintained a sceptical attitude towards the individual as the basis for understanding human relationships. The turn to language in family therapy changed our ideas about wholeness, in that the important focus shifted from a predefined "family" to those who were in dialogue about the problem, no matter which, or how many, persons were involved. The perspective from developmental psychology is mainly concerned with dyads, but it offers a way of seeing both the individual subjective aspect and the systemic relational aspect at the same time.

The emotionality of the relational exchange is crucial. How do we create meaningful exchanges prior to the use of words, and what is our vehicle of communication? Stern's answer is that we exchange emotions, but emotions defined in a much wider manner than we are used to. As we have seen, mentalization is preceded by emotional exchanges between infant and parent in a finely tuned reciprocity, but what makes these exchanges the glue of relationships is what Stern calls "vitality affects". This term refers not to discrete categories of emotion, such as disgust or sadness, but rather to the rhythm of energy and intensity in the patterns of emotional expression of both infant and care-giver. So, for example, the emotions of anger or happiness (which Stern calls "categorical affects") can each be expressed with great differences in intensity and vigour (vitality affects).

Daniel Stern also maintains that to understand meaning-creating relationships, we need to see them as consisting of both an individual and a relational aspect. Turn-taking as a complicated co-ordination of action would be impossible without both the subjective and the relational perspective. In this view, a sense of self is presupposed from the start, before self-consciousness or language. A sense of self can be seen in the intentional acts of the infant (agency), and in the phenomenon of joint attention: having a shared attentional focus. He theorizes development as consisting of five "domains of related-ness", corresponding to five "senses of self". Both the domains of relatedness and the senses of self are realized through the interplay of infant and care-giver. This interplay is an intersubjective system of mutual influence: a dance of turn-taking.

The domains of relatedness can be seen as increasingly complex versions of this turn-taking. For the newborn baby, regulation and co-ordination of physiology, affect and stimulation is the central issue. Regulating the infant's cycles of rest and activity, sleep and eating, is vital to the first weeks and months of life. Anyone who has seen a baby crying itself into complete chaos knows the impor-tance of this regulatory activity for the infant's well being. It is achieved through the innate capacity of the baby for social interplay and turn-taking and the availability of an attuned and containing care-giver. For the rest of our lives we continue to build on and expand the behaviours that help us to regulate physiological stress such as anxiety, frustration, or restlessness through co-ordinated regulatory activity with another person. The emergent self is the experience of organizing processes, as well as the product of these processes.

The next developmental line is the domain of relatedness, char-acterized by imitative actions, and its accompanying sense of a core self. The infant's capacity for imitation is well documented (Meltzoff & Brooks, 2007). The interplay between infant and care-giver is characterized by repeated themes conducted in a varied form (e.g., the game of peek-a-boo). From interplay with a regulat-ing other, we internalize interactions that, at all times thereafter, make up our expectations of what will happen when we are together with other people. This is a constructive process; from every experience we build expectations as to what will happen next and, in so doing, we make the world familiar. Agency, self-coher-ence, self-affectivity, and self-history all characterize this experien-tial state. The turn-taking is transformed into an experiential state where category affects and their vitality aspects can be generated by the infant, eliciting behavioural responses that are much wider and richer than the simple regulation of physiology and affect. This increased complexity and richness is the core of the continuous construction model of development. Feeding an infant is a similar, but also a very different, experience from sharing a meal with a one-year-old child!

The next layer of development is experientially characterized by joint attention, joint intentionality, and joint affectivity. Stern names the relational exchanges "affect attunement" and the accompanying self-experience "the subjective self" (Stern 1985, p. 138). This layer implies a qualitative change in the child's relationship to himself and his partners in interchange. We see a movement from concern with outer behaviour to the sharing of inner states. The question of "how do I know what other people really mean" is born. This implies the recognition that inner states can be expressed in multiple ways, and that the necessary translation processes become more complex, but also richer and more varied.

So far, these layers of development are non-verbal, and dominated by the immediacy of experience. Affect attunement, with its implications of both sameness and difference, and joint attention form a central step towards language. The ability of the care-giver to attune to the states of mind of the infant, builds upon the infant's capacity to let a set of behaviour stand for an inner affective state. To let something stand for something else is a core capacity in language. The central experience of the sense of a verbal self is that the absent can be given a presence by letting something present, a word, stand for something even when it is absent. The word "mama" can evoke experiences of some of the interplay and related affects that are shared with the mother in "real life". Words also relate to other words, and partially obtain meaning from the connotations of the different verbal contexts. "Father", "papa", "daddy", and '"dada" all refer to the same person, but with a very different nexus of associations. Relationally, this opens a whole world of negotiation of meanings. It is the start of a doubling where we not only meet the world through the immediacy of our experiences, but also can relate to it through giving our experiences meaning. All this is fulfilled in the last developmental layer, called "a sense of a narrative self".

Narrative implies the experience of creating connections and coherence in one's life through stories. By doing this, we create our lives, but also become observers to our own lives. By creating a distance to one's immediately lived life we can open new ways of relating to it (White, 2007). The relational theme here is co-construction. The generation of distance and meaning happens through the verbal turn-taking between child and parent. But the affective sharing of experience is a necessary presupposition for this to happen.

Stories are first mostly told by parents, often on cues from the child as in the following example:

Child: "Pu pu!!"
Parent: "Pu pu??"
Child: "Pu pu!!!"
Parent: "Oh, do you mean the pussycat we met at granny's house yesterday?"
Child: "Pu!"
Parent: "You wanted to say 'Hello' to the pussycat, didn't you?"
Child [*looks at his hand*]: "Ow!"
Parent [*caresses the child's hand*]: "And the pussycat scratched your hand, didn't he! And it hurt!"
Child: "Pu! Ow!"

This exchange is a typical example of how we get started as storytellers. It would not be possible without the sensitive tuning in to the affective aspect of communicating, establishing a joint focus of attention, and of sharing an experience.

Continuous development means that all these senses of self and domains of relatedness are present throughout a person's life. All five layers continue to be important in relating to other people and to all other aspects of our world. At each age and in each new important relationship, a reshaping of each layer can be seen. Affect regulation will need to deal with new developmental challenges at different ages. Loss or the threat of breakdown of an important relationship can result in world-shaking anxiety (dysregulation) as well as a profound experience of losing the one person who understands (loss of intersubjectivity). The same applies to agency, intersubjectivity, and giving experience a new presence through words and stories. Development is continuous; life always presents new challenges and opportunities for change.

Now we will look again at Catherine's dialogue with her father in the light of these developmental concepts. At first sight it appears that Catherine's father is reflecting his daughter's emotions back to her. He believes, and indeed states, that he knows and understands what she is talking about. In a mentalizing language, we could see their problem as an unmarked way of giving emotions back to Catherine: her father is lost in his own anxiety and only makes his daughter even more confused and desperate. But Catherine's mother points us in another direction; there was something missing in the area of reciprocity. To share a feeling in the context of inter-subjectivity is, at the same time, to recognize the difference between the persons involved, and thereby expand one's own perspective; intersubjective sharing of a feeling is not the same as becoming alike. For Catherine and father this difference was clearly stated when they talked about another important aspect of their lives: their common love for dogs. Here they could recognize both their shared feelings, and the difference between them in the ways they expressed and handled these feelings. Father knew that Catherine's engagement gave increased depth and complexity to his own experience. Catherine declared that their dogs made her understand both herself and her father in a better way. We did a lot of work outlining the difference between the *sharing* they experienced in this situation, and *feeling the same* as they described in relation to the need for control. They could use their common but implicit knowledge of important developmental aspects of their relationship to get back on track.

Joint attention

Something important happens after the age of four years, when children can understand that people they observe may be misled, have irrelevant information, or plainly not know as much as they know themselves about a particular situation. This is the logic of the false belief studies that theories of mentalization are based upon (Ainsworth, Blehar, Waters, & Wall, 1978). But developmental psychology also tells us that this is not all there is to say about knowing other people's minds. As Naomi Eilan puts it, "There is something utterly simple and basic about the transparency of our minds to each other in the case of joint attention which this whole kind of account misses" (Eilan, 2005, p. 3). And we miss it because we presume too much of a basic opacity in the mind-to-mind relationship. What is there, in the absence of the subject's capacity to deploy the distinction between true and false belief, to show us how we understand other people's minds?

We can glimpse the processes involved by looking at imitation and affect attunement. In imitation, expressions of affect by the infant are responded to with a corresponding or similar expression by the parent. The child also smiles as a response to the smile on the other's face (Hobson, 2002). But the smile is not a pure copy; to produce a similar expression, the infant has to translate what she sees into something that fits her own position in space in relation to her communication partner (Kugiumetziakis, 1999). Even imitation is a complex, co-ordinated activity that presupposes a recognition of the difference between the communication partners. Imitations of facial expressions reflect an openness towards expressions of affect and imply mutual affect regulation. In intersubjectivity, an outer focus of attention is included, and the dyad becomes a triangle. A smile or a frown can be an emotional reaction to a phenomenon in the world, a commentary on the world, or an evaluation of it. At the same time it is a tool for directing the attention of the other towards something happening in the world. The recognition of intentionality lies in a checking of the other person's attention focus, and the recognition of the other person's attention to your attention. Joint attention is not just about having the same visual focus. It is also recognizing that the focus is important, that it has value in some way or another. Peter Hobson (2002) describes joint attention as the cause of "the momentous leap" (p. 108) into understanding that the world can be seen from different perspectives. These capacities, which imply an understanding of other people's intentions, and of their view of the world being different from the infants' own, are present in infants' co-ordinated activity in relating to other people from the first weeks of life. It surely cannot be ignored in trying to understand the building blocks of how we construct the internal worlds of our communication partners?

Language development requires, among other things, a joint attention to aspects of the world, an awareness of the collaborative processes involved in interacting, and a willingness and ability to negotiate and co-ordinate meaning (Bruner, 1995). Parents need to shape their contributions to adjust to their children's level of development, but there still has to be a co-ordinating effort from both sides of the relationship.

The difference between the concepts of intersubjectivity and mentalization also becomes more pronounced. The communicative sequence in intersubjectivity underlines a shared experience, or a shared focus of attention. This sharing presupposes difference, whereas the processes that precede mentalization provide a linear account of the care-giver communicating back an emotional content that belongs to the infant. The systemic experience of wholeness being more than the sum of its parts is lost.

Psychotherapy without problems: the case of Espen

Espen was a boy of eight years of age. He lived with his mother and was referred with a diagnosis of ADHD. He was medicated with Ritalin, and both his hyperactivity and his attention problems had been reduced to a manageable level, at least within the school context. The main problem was, according to his mother, his behaviour towards her. He was angry, had a "foul mouth", and refused to follow her instructions. Inviting Espen to comment on this, he simply refused to talk, except for stating that there was no problem. Instead, he asked the therapist what kind of car he had.

This meeting took place in a combined day-care and outpatient unit, with the possibility of working intensively for three weeks. Espen and his mother stayed in the unit for three weeks, working with the therapists Trude (Clinical Social Worker, Trude Finseth) and Rolf. From day one, as indicated above, Espen both denied that there was a problem and refused to talk about any areas of difficulty. Instead, there were a lot of other things he wanted to talk about, especially if he could be the one to ask the questions. He was a very verbal and inquisitive young man! The situation was completely different for his mother. She was exhausted by the struggle between them. In this situation the two therapists split up. Mother and Rolf talked together; Espen and Trude went their own way.

During the first week, mother and Rolf talked a lot about the problems she experienced at home. They met Espen and Trude two or three times during the day. One day, Espen impatiently asked Trude, "Can we stop this and start working instead?" Leaving the unit in the afternoon, Rolf asked Trude what this "work" was. Trude explained that Espen was playing in one of the offices, spending time organizing papers and office equipment. "Organizing" meant moving all this material around in a more or less haphazard fashion. Next week his demand was the same: "Let's start work." Trude explained that he then acted out some characters from a TV show and they had started to dress up as those characters. They had even started to make video recordings of each other in their new roles, and Espen had concluded that they should make a movie which, during the last week of the stay, started to take shape. Parallel to Espen's work with Trude, mother and Rolf continued talking about, and working on, problems as mother was experiencing them. In the last week of the stay, there were sessions together with Espen on doing homework and how to manage this without ending up quarrelling with his mother. He attended and tolerated this, but demanded regularly that he wanted to work with Trude.

After a three-week period of inpatient treatment, a regular outpatient contact followed. Espen and Trude, and mother and Rolf, met regularly, first once a fortnight, and then, after eighteen months, once per month. In total, the collaboration lasted three years. During the first year, Espen and Trude made three videos: one crime story and two documentaries. The two couples worked separately, but also with joint meetings, although Espen quickly demanded to start "working". After getting used to this parallel way of working, there was no problem in having no problems in a health institution that traditionally works with problems.

The family therapeutic practice in this unit is inspired by Anderson and Goolishian (1988), Andersen (2006), and White (2007). Conversation and dialogue, collaboration and transparency, are central ideas in this work. In addition, the unit has found that using measures of process and outcome as tools for conversations, and changing our practice in response to this feedback, are in accordance with these ideas of conversation and collaboration (Lambert et al., 2001; Miller, Duncan, & Hubble, 2004).

During the three years of contact, the measure of outcome was gradually but slowly moving from an area depicted as "dysfunctional" into one described as "functional" (Lambert et al., 2001). Conversations with mother confirmed this picture as an adequate representation of the development of Espen, of their relationship, and the status of problems in their life. For the therapists, the most fascinating part was that the focus of the therapy with Espen was not on problems but on his "work". How can we understand this?

One interpretation is that he always knew they had problems, but just could not—or would not—talk about them. One way of looking at development is that it is a process of work. We believe that Espen was working on his own developmental processes. For any individual, comparison with norms is not meaningful for development. Only comparison with one's own development of skills and abilities are relevant. "Are things happening with me in my life that give me more opportunities and choices and ways of adapting to my environment?" People develop from where they are and not according to an external standard.

Espen started his work with Trude by moving paper. A simple turn-taking situation established a regulatory process between him and his therapist that was clearly enjoyable to Espen. Having established this particular activity, called "organizing the office", a second area of interest arose: some TV characters gave opportunities for more elaborate forms of turn-taking activity. The sense of a core self (Stern, 1985) points to the generation and stabilization of self-invariants, the things I know about myself and my world that do not change. Self-invariants are established from a theme-with-variations format (Stern, 1985). Self-agency is characterized by senses of volition and mastery. The work of Espen and Trude encompassed collaborative themes of creating structure and dealing with being different persons and being in different positions. One way of understanding this is that a relational and interactional domain of turn-taking was created that became stabilized around these themes. Again, using Stern´s concepts, regulation of affect, stimulation, and activity, and work on self invariant—especially volition and mastery—were the central components in creating this domain.

From the bystander position, intense experiences of sharing were observed in the way Espen and Trude worked together. The sense of a subjective self is characterized by sharing of joint attention, intention, and affective states. Standing on the sideline, one could observe conversations that included both descriptions and reflections on what they where doing and what kind of importance this had in their life. Conversation and dialogue—the use of language—became a natural and fitting part of this work. Regulatory experiences, joint turn-taking around themes with interactional variations, sharing and affect attunement, and conversational processes could all be seen in the creative task of movie-making.

At the same time, there were conversations and interactions between the three couples: Espen and Trude, mother and Rolf, and certainly Espen and mother. This was not, therefore, two separate individual therapies but an interlocking set of conversations and interactions where events in one couple could be seen as creating a context for consequences occurring in the other couples and, as such, the primary perspective on the totality of the therapeutic work was that of a family therapy perspective.

Concluding remarks

The story of Espen illustrates a way of thinking about psychotherapy: that therapeutic action must be tailored to the client´s presuppositions, preferences, intentions, and skills. Using the model of development as continuous construction, we can perceive that Catherine and her parents were caught in a struggle to find a conversational format that allowed joint attention and mutual sharing to arise. A dialogue about the eating disorder had to be grounded in the experience of sharing. Catherine and her father could not share the experience of controlling emotions through rituals, even though they had parallel experiences, but it was possible to work from other areas, including their common interest in dogs.

The story of Espen exemplifies another possibility, even if it can be seen as a paradoxical way within a psychotherapeutic context. The main point was to move attention away from conversations about problems—and what is wrong, dangerous, or difficult—to let actual interplay develop around a joint area of interest. We moved the attention away from talking about a particular situation to creating situations where language and linguistic activity had another function; that is, to support the chosen means of interaction (in this case, initially, the "work") and allowing meaning and understanding of this particular situation to arise as something belonging to this context. All this is caught within Espen's phrase: "Let's start working". Stated differently, Espen is saying, "I am not doing therapy, I am developing"; or "My way of doing therapy is to do development."

To participate in a relationship in a way that makes change possible, it is necessary to understand how relationships work. But this knowledge is not acquired in order that therapists can tell other people how to live their lives. Instead, it enhances sensitivity to different aspects of the therapeutic relationships and opens possibilities of expanding the range of ordinary developmental processes within both family and individual therapy. This view of development has given us an opportunity to reconcile important aspects of our experience as therapists in collaborating with children, adolescents, and their parents. Non-verbal interplay and the generation of experience in the immediacy of the moment, together with verbal interplay and the generation of meaning and reflection in dialogue, are central aspects of creating opportunities for change within the therapeutic context. The necessary starting points for therapy are the establishment of turn-taking and responding to each other's responses. The next necessary step is the establishment of joint attention. Turn-taking and joint attention are, in our view, the decisive windows of opportunity for establishing a relationship that provides an opportunity to generate descriptions, meaning, and reflections that can lead to new relationships and behavioural forms. Psychotherapy then becomes an activity that is characterized by change, both through what Stern (2000) calls "moments of meeting", and through reflective dialogue.

References

Ainsworth, M. D. S., Blehar, M. C., Waters, E., & Wall, S. (1978). *Patterns of Attachment: A Psychological Study of the Strange Situation.* Hillsdale, NJ: Erlbaum.

Andersen, T. (2006). The network context of network therapy: a story from the European Nordic North. In: A. Lightburn & P. Sessions (Eds.), *Handbook of Community Based Clinical Practice* (pp. 177–190). New York: Oxford University Press.

Anderson, H., & Goolishian, H. A. (1988). Human systems as linguistic systems: preliminary and evolving ideas about the implications for clinical theory. *Family Process, 27:* 371–393.

Bateman, A., & Fonagy, P. (2006). Mentalization and borderline personality disorder. In: J. G. Allen & P. Fonagy (Eds.), *Handbook of Mentalization-Based Treatment* (pp. 185–200). Chichester: Wiley.

Bertalanffy, L. V. (1968). *General System Theory: Foundations, Development, Applications.* New York: George Braziller.

Bruner, J. (1995). From joint attention to the meeting of minds. In: C. Moore & P. J. Dunham (Eds.), *Joint Attention: Its Origins and Role in Development* (pp. 1–14). Hillsdale, NJ: Erlbaum.

Eilan, N. (2005). Joint attention, communication, and mind. In: N. Eilan, C. Hoerl, T. McCormack, & J. Roessler (Eds.), *Joint Attention: Communication and Other Minds* (pp. 1–33). Oxford: Clarendon.

Fonagy, P. (2006). The mentalization-focused approach to social development. In: J. G. Allen & P. Fonagy (Eds.), *Handbook of Mentalization-Based Treatment* (pp. 53–99). Chichester: Wiley.

Fonagy, P., Gergely, G., Jurist, E. L., & Target, M. (2004). *Affect Regulation, Mentalization, and the Development of the Self*. London: Karnac.

Hobson, P. (2002). *The Cradle of Thought. Exploring the Origins of Thinking*. London: Pan.

Johnsen, A., Sundet, R., & Torsteinsson, V. W. (2004). *Self in Relationships: Perspectives on Family Therapy from Developmental Psychology*. London: Karnac.

Kugiumetziakis, G. (1999). Neonatal imitation in the intersubjective companion space. In: S. Braten (Ed.), *Intersubjective Communication and Emotion in Early Ontogeny* (pp. 63–88). Cambridge: Cambridge University Press.

Lambert, M. J., Whipple, J. L., Smart, D. W., Vermeersch, D. A., Nielsen, S. L., & Hawkins, E. J. (2001). The effects of providing therapists with feedback on patient progress during psychotherapy: are outcomes enhanced? *Psychotherapy Research*, 11: 49–68.

Maturana, H. (1988). Reality: the search for objectivity or the quest for a compelling argument? *The Irish Journal of Psychology Special Issue*, 9: 144–172.

Meltzoff, A. N., & Brooks, R. (2007). Intersubjectivity before language. In: S. Bråten, (Ed.), *On Being Moved: From Mirror Neurons to Empathy* (pp. 149–173). Philadelphia, PA: Benjamin.

Miller, S. D., Duncan, B. L., & Hubble, M. A. (2004). Beyond integration: the triumph of outcome over process in clinical practice. *Psychotherapy in Australia*, 10: 20–37.

Minuchin, S. (1998). Where is the family in narrative family therapy? *Journal of Marital and Family Therapy*, 24: 397–403.

Stern, D. N. (1985). *The Interpersonal World of the Infant: A View from Psychoanalysis and Developmental Psychology*. New York: Basic Books.

Stern, D. N. (1995). *The Motherhood Constellation: A Unified View of Parent–Infant Psychotherapy*. New York: Basic Books.

Stern, D. N. (2000). *The Present Moment in Psychotherapy and Everyday Life*. New York: Norton.

White, M. (2007). *Maps of Narrative Practice*. London: Norton.

CHAPTER EIGHT

Love and hate and the oedipal myth: the perfect bridge between the systemic and the psychoanalytic

Jeremy Woodcock

S o, who are you, reading these introductory thoughts? Can you imagine me, the writer? Can you also bring into your mind, however vaguely, an impression of the ideas we may think about in this chapter? If so, I would conjecture that your entry into thoughts about what is being written, and the flowing together of your mind and my own, stands on ground described in psychoanalytic theory as arising from our joint resolution of the oedipal situation. The oedipal myth, as used by Freud, is often reacted to by systemic therapists as an example of the quaint absurdity of much of Freud's foundational thinking. It is also sometimes read as indicative of regressive attitudes and paradigmatic of the failure of psychoanalysis to get to grips with a balanced, gendered account of human development. The notion of the oedipal triangle was initiated by Freud, and developed by later psychoanalytic thinkers such as Klein and Winnicott, the self psychologists such as Kohut, as well as within the intersubjective psychotherapy tradition. This rich development of theory offers a powerful way for thinking about the basic building blocks of emotional life.

In this chapter, an account of the oedipal situation will be given that offers a bridge between the systemic and psychoanalytic.

Through a case discussion, the chapter will trace the development of oedipal ideas within psychoanalysis. It will go on to reveal how the notion of the oedipal triangle—a three-way relationship invested with powerful positive and negative emotions—can illuminate some of the deeper dynamics of family life and the therapeutic relationship. Furthermore, the chapter will explore how psychoanalysis, with its roots in some of the darker moments of the Western psyche, understands hate as a potential complement and precursor to love. When theory is held lightly, the oedipal struggle can feature as an illuminating myth rather than a blueprint of the grand design of the human mind.

Theory as metaphor; theory as hypothesis

What the seemingly colliding worlds of the systemic and psychoanalytic illustrate is how potentially split the two approaches can be unless one has the capacity to hold the theoretical implications of each paradigm lightly (Orange, 1995). My own predilection is to attempt to be rigorous in the understanding of any theory, but always to see theory as metaphor. Metaphor has the facility to hold perspectives in tension, while simultaneously pointing up the temporary, contingent, even illusory, nature of our grip on reality. Metaphor enables theories to illuminate each other without being judgemental. It also permissively acknowledges the reflexivity of the observer and places one in a socially constructed frame. This being so, I also think of any theory as hypothesis, affirming some of my prejudices about being in the world, and lightly holding them up to affirmation or disconfirmation.

The point about this in practice is that it allows one to hold potentially contradictory thoughts about the patient, and the therapeutic relationship, and what emerges in work with different levels of engagement and complexity. Human life is far too complex to push into a box, and so, the more we can make our thinking flexible, the better. If theories are held lightly there is a greater chance of meeting the patient authentically in a looser, more humane place, rather than in a theoretical corner. Furthermore, the capacity to do this can be conceived as a developmental achievement. It requires the ruthlessness to contain and acknowledge the true measure of what one knows, and the necessity of giving up omnipotent and narcissistic wishes that impel us to exceed the limitations of our knowledge. It means we appreciate that knowledge is a subjective achievement and that the position of the other confronts us with the possibililty that what we experience emotionally and intellectually will always be limited and at the same time open to change (Hoggett, 2001).

The struggle to be seen

Let us begin with a case of therapeutic work with a couple that illustrates their struggle to be seen or not seen in the relationship. It is the therapist's grasp of the implications of the oedipal dynamics that can draw out the revealed and hidden in a helpfully connected way.

> Hermione and Bruce came into therapy after nineteen years in a relationship in which they struggled hugely to trust each other and to be emotionally satisfied. For long periods their union hovered close to dissolution and they started therapy during an extended period of crisis. Each wanted the relationship to work, yet both doubted their individual capacity to trust the other to allow their relationship to work in an emotionally satisfying way. In their first years together, when they had quickly produced three children, Bruce had spent many evenings with his former partner and his first child, seemingly being unable to refashion the tie of those relationships. Latterly, he was extremely jealous of Hermione, to the extent that she was cautious about wearing anything that hinted of glamour or independence, regardless of whether she was on her way to work or making rare forays out in the evening on her own. Hermione revealed that she stifled her feelings, suffered excruciating migraine headaches, and that she held Bruce at arm's length sexually. Neither, it seemed, was able to see the other in their full personhood nor to show their full personhood to the other.

> It was difficult to hold the middle ground with this couple, and the triangle between the three of us felt intense. From an external point of view, it might have appeared that I held the ground well, but internally I was pulled first one way, then the other. For Hermione, I appeared at times to represent the ideal therapist who cautiously challenged

Bruce's controlling and jealous behaviour. She registered stifled pleasure as I teased away at Bruce's hidden beliefs about why she should
not go out on her own. Bruce actually despised his own controlling
behaviour and wanted to hide it from view. Hermione, in turn, was
cautious about turning him off therapy by over-exposing things that
made him ashamed, and I had to guard against the gratification of
being the well-regarded male in alliance with Hermione. At other
times, I had to be aware of the risk of over-identifying with Bruce as I
made interventions about the way "us males" sometimes behaved.

The key to this case for me was the absence of the oedipal resolution.
In their families of origin, the three-way fight had long since been
settled to their respective disadvantage. Hermione described her
mother as having been sharp-tongued and cruel. As a little girl, she was
dressed up like a doll, but threatened if she revealed strong feelings,
acted spontaneously, or got herself dirty. Her father was kindly but
ineffectual, and, in the final instance, he was likely to side with her
mother, who cowed both Hermione and her father. Bruce described his
parents as mostly being either emotionally absent or cruel: "I was a
street child, the butt of my elder brothers' jokes, and their violence . . .
mother was feisty, discontented in her marriage . . . a poor cook, and a
reluctant mother . . ." What was apparent was that neither Bruce nor
Hermione had much of a satisfactory identification with either parent.
Hermione longed for her father to rescue her, but he was crushed by
her mother. Bruce longed for his mother and family to look after him
as a child. He acknowledged his nascent sexual feelings toward his
mother as a pubescent boy, but she brushed him aside peremptorily in
much the same way as he imagined she brushed his father's sexual
advances away. Both Bruce and Hermione felt overlooked and
emotionally abandoned to struggle alone with passionate feelings. As
therapist, I was pulled into the tide as the representative parent who
might perhaps struggle passionately over them both.

Being held in mind

What neither Bruce nor Hermione experienced in their childhood
recall was a sense of a benign parent holding them in mind in a
continuous way across the years and through the inevitable
vagaries and challenges of their development. Hermione spoke of
her father as seemingly wishing to reach out, but these times felt
intermittent and rare. Bruce had no recollection of being held in

mind at home, and life was represented to him by both his parents as tough and uncompromising in its deprivation. Brief pleasure was won at some personal cost. For instance, he identified his mother dressing up to go out to the local political party meeting, where she might have been a formidable leader if her life chances had been different.

It was not that either Hermione or Bruce had actually been invisible to their parents, but their inner world had little or no recognition. According to Heinz Kohut (1976), who developed the tradition of self psychology, every child has a need to identify with an idealized parental figure. If this positive identification is achieved, then the child has the experience of having self-worth mirrored back in an empathic manner by the primary care-giver. These empathic experiences allow the child to learn the conscious and unconscious skills of emotional regulation that are necessary for the development of a coherent, vigorous, and healthy sense of self. For Kohut, psychotherapy is therapeutic in so far as it allows the patient to replay processes that are parallel to her (or his) child-hood experience and allows the therapist to take the role of a care-giver who is attuned and responsive to the patient's inner world (*ibid.*). Although Kohut's theoretical position is quite anodyne, systemic therapists might nevertheless baulk at its vital corollary that the therapist represents a parental figure in the transference.

Transference

The relationship of Hermione and Bruce called forth many layers of emotional development in each other. In psychoanalytic work, these layers are thought of as transference phenomena, which can be understood as the manifestation of emotional states acquired in relationship to others at earlier periods of one's development that are played out in the presence of current relationships. Transference phenomena are most often conceived of as occurring in the patient in relation to the therapist. However, in work with couples, trans-ference phenomena are more complex, and are likely to be three-way, towards the therapist as well as between the couple.

I was interested in understanding both the layers of transference towards me and the transferences they evoked in each other. For instance, as different manifestations of Bruce's anger were evoked in therapy, I wondered if Bruce and Hermione could identify the early origins of the anger and, in doing so, if they were freed to be more understanding and playful of the complexity between them. Could Hermione recognize through her mothering of their sons that Bruce's anger was more often like that of a frustrated little boy rather than the enraged and belittling adult he appeared to be, and did this shift in her perception enable her to attune and respond to Bruce in a different way? Equally, could Bruce recognize the currents that arose in him, be reflective, and put his vulnerability into words instead of acting-out like a withdrawn curmudgeon? For Hermione, as she lost her fear of her own and Bruce's anger, could she let fly with more emotional freedom, stand up to Bruce, and meet him in his state of arousal and equally be aroused in her own terms with him?

The triangular implications of attachment theory

One of the most significant bridges between the systemic and psychoanalytic has been attachment theory (Woodcock, 2000). However, apart from some outstanding exponents in both camps (Byng-Hall, 1995, 1999; Fonagy, Gergely, Jurist, & Target, 2002; Holmes, 1996), generally systemic and psychoanalytic practitioners have had quite an ambivalent relationship with attachment research, although this has changed over recent years (Clulow, 2001; Dallos, 2006; Pooley, 2004). The dilemma for systemic practitioners has been that attachment theory concentrates on the dyadic relationship between care-giver and child rather than the complexity of whole family relationships. Also, in contrast to systemic practitioners who prioritize the external relationship patterns between family members, attachment theory has developed conclusions about internal working models of relationship between self and others. Meanwhile, psychoanalytic psychotherapists have had problems with Bowlby and attachment theory because, although Bowlby was a psychoanalyst, he was, none the less, persuaded that environmental explanations for children's separation anxiety were at least as convincing as psychoanalytic assertions about the primacy of phantasy in shaping the developing child's world.

Bowlby's ideas in this respect were similar in many ways to Stern's current thinking (Stern, 1998, 2004).

So, it would seem that experimentally driven attachment theory sits rather uneasily with purist therapeutic models, whether systemic or psychoanalytic. By contrast, however, attachment theory can very helpfully inform applied psychotherapy practice, and its ideas have a powerful clinical valence because they are based upon observable modes of relational behaviour. Furthermore, although dyadic in origin, models of attachment behaviour assume that an optimal attachment carries with it the ability to have a dialogue with an internalized other, which is one of the key features in the resolution of the oedipal situation. In essence, in order to internalize the other in a mature way, one has to be able to conceive of the other as having relationships that are separate from oneself. This oedipal assumption is deeply embedded in attachment theory.

In the case of Hermione and Bruce, it was apparent that Bruce had an ambivalent attachment to Hermione, predicated on the ambivalent attachment between himself and his mother, who had been uncertainly available as his primary care-giver. What such an attachment suggests is that in the face of intimacy and distance Bruce experienced arousal, which he then sought to modulate by creating a watchful distance. The systemic part of me wondered if his disappointment and anger about Hermione could be a behavioural trope that emerged from his confusions and discomfort in the face of intimacy, which then generated in Hermione a reciprocal confusion, discomfort, and distance. The psychoanalytic part of me wondered if the hatred that I sensed Bruce felt toward Hermione was amplified by his experience of her unattainable desirability and predicated on the hatred and desire he experienced toward his own mother. These feelings had lacked opportunities for being resolved in childhood, because his typical infantile phantasies had been amplified by the experience of his mother directing him to play on the street, rather than being ameliorated by being nurtured at home where his sensations might have been contained, and worked through, by the natural processes of projective identification available between children and their parents. We see in this clinical example how Bruce's attachment experience of his ambivalent mother was forged through his awareness of her attachment to other situations seemingly more important than him: as a result, he always carried a sense of himself as at the outside edge of a triangular emotional system.

Mentalization as a bridge between the psychoanalytic and the systemic

The bridge between the psychoanalytic and the systemic that is being built in this discussion becomes easier to negotiate, if more complex, with the addition of the fascinating thinking developed by Fonagy and his colleagues about the evolution of our capacity for mentalization (Fonagy, Gergely, Jurist, & Target, 2002). One could think of mentalization as the capacity to reflectively participate in one's feelings as they arise, and this process is specifically described as *mentalized affectivity*. Critical to mentalized affectivity is the capacity to be reflectively immersed in one's own feelings in a way that allows those feelings to be simultaneously appreciated, nuanced, and modulated. This thinking chimes in with the psychoanalytic theory of change, which conceptualizes that change is most likely to occur through gains of insight that most naturally involve the simultaneous capacity to have an emotional experience of one's cognitive process. In some ways, mentalization goes a step beyond this idea in suggesting that the full capacity to be emotionally free and insightful allows one to "swim" confidently and reflectively and relationally in one's feelings. The reflective capacity is not necessarily grounded in the dualistic cognitive *a priori* of "I think, therefore I am", but instead lies in an appreciation of the contingent depth of one's felt history of relational emotional experience.

In the systemic paradigm, change has most often been theorized as arising from insight that has emerged from the cognitive appreciation of new meanings emerging from relational work. Indeed, it is through the portal of emergent new meaning that change is most denoted as occurring in the systemic paradigm. Meaning is hugely significant in the process of mentalization, but it is not given the same pivotal significance. In mentalization, meaning is contingent on the flowing together of emotional and cognitive experience in a relational process. For instance, conflicts between differing emotional, relational, and cognitive domains no longer impede each of these domains of experience being appreciated. Conflict might still be there, but it can be borne, and what can be borne naturally takes on new meanings. New meanings have equal emotional and intellectual resonance and what is meant is also felt.

A return to the case study may help to draw out the clinical significance of these ideas while adding depth to the descriptions of attachment behaviour, which, unalloyed, can seem "clunky" and deterministic. One of the key emotional themes that emerged frequently in my countertransference was a sense of the hatred between the couple that was conveyed as being quite unacceptable as an openly expressed emotion. Bruce seemed to hate Hermione if she so much as intimated an emotional connection with anyone outside the family. His ambivalent childhood attachments made him very watchful of her and fired him up to be both deeply suspicious and anxious, and in control of any of her attachments beyond himself. He also hated her apparent unattainability, for he felt he could not "inhabit" her sexually and emotionally. He had the experience that he could not understand the emotional rules that would let him in, much as he never understood why his mother would not let him in. His processes of feeling and thought were constantly split. He could not put the hateful feelings this aroused into words for fear of rejection, nor could he mentalize his feelings and bring them into his consciousness, and so his powerful emotions were confused and muted in their internal manifestations and their outward expression. In the grip of powerful internal currents, he merely sulked or behaved with a curmudgeonly bad temper.

Countertransference, empathy, and circularity

My countertransference to this emotional experience developed over time as the conversation in sessions criss-crossed this territory and the couple resisted attempts to draw feelings out into the open. I was continually bemused that they would not respond to my invitation to guess at each other's thoughts, fantasies, or feelings. I had to deal with evidence in me that something was going on, the hunch that there was something that they were not putting into words: for example, that Hermione's timidity was not merely the product of her early experience but was being taken up, and reinforced by, the covert struggle of huge emotions of rejection and control. I guessed that Hermione hated Bruce's intransigence, his seemingly unmovable lack of ability to share her experience. Yet, she also could not quite bear him close, because he might spoil her fragile sense of self, which had little affirmation from her parents, and in particular from her father, the most significant male figure in her early life. She hated both Bruce and her father for not rising to the occasion, and was prone to blame herself for not being sufficiently bold and attractive to make that happen.

What seemed to flow together in this couple was a fear of putting into words the inner world of the other and a fear of the power of hatred. The issue that preoccupied me was how to flush out into the open what my countertransference seemed to be telling me might be going on between the three of us. My own countertransference was not merely "sitting" in the cognitive space of my head; rather, it was felt in my apprehension, consciousness, and body, and was attentive to the currents that arose. The key task during these moments was to use my experience imaginatively to enter the mind of both Hermione and Bruce, to empathically deduce what was going on: in short, to make use of my oedipal experience in the service of empathically encountering their subjectivity.

The *sine qua non* of family or couple psychotherapy is that the couple will serve as informants of their own and their family members' experience, emotions, behaviour, and states of mind. In systemic therapy, circular questioning was discovered to be a superb way of enabling families to reveal their submerged assumptions and feelings. Circular epistemology relies on a belief that there is sufficient empathic knowledge and experience for this to happen. Empathy denotes that we are able to guess fairly accurately the feelings of others through a shared assumptive framework and the mapping backwards and forwards of emotions and behaviour. It seemed incredible that Hermione and Bruce lacked this ability to such a degree. My theoretical hunch was that the potential for empathy was pretty intact, but what was absent was a safe experience of hatred and thereby a severe limitation in their capacity for encountering the full subjectivity of each other.

Hatred as a precursor to love

Hatred has been considered in the systemic paradigm (Dell, 1982; Framo, 1962; Shamai, 1998), but it has never had a thorough systemic formulation. It has relied heavily on ideas disputed and borrowed from psychoanalysis or received into the literature from common cultural usage. By contrast, hatred has had a thorough development within the psychoanalytic tradition, particularly by Kleinians (Mann, 2002). In Kleinian thought, hatred is a more fundamental and primitive state of mind than love; it precedes love, and is a way-station on the developmental pathway to love (Hinshelwood, 1989). This idea that hatred is an essential prerequisite to love might at first seem to be astonishing. The implication that follows is that the couple or family that come into therapy hating may be in a better position to make progress than a couple or family where hatred has never reared its ugly head. How might this be so?

Klein believed the infant hates the sufficiency of the breast; the fact that the breast is separate, the fact that it can be withdrawn or that it is insufficient, the fact that it cannot be possessed (Spillius, 1988), and the fact that it is not "mine". To properly understand the implications here, we might say that these are metaphors for primitive states of mind (Bronstein, 2001). These states of mind can come upon us in their full force or as attenuated, more worked-through versions, at any time in our life. For instance, discovering that our new lover is indeed separate, individuated, and not all enfolding; or finding that our new supervisor cannot give us everything we feel we need to handle a difficult case within a particular hour. However, when we "pause to consider" our state of mind in relation to the other's apparent insufficiency, we realize that our phantasy, that is, our unconscious inner dynamic which shapes our experience of being in the world, has wanted to turn our lover or supervisor into the sufficient breast. Our "pause to consider" is a developmental achievement. It means we have acquired the capacity to understand that the feelings and thoughts that flow into us do not necessarily represent reality, but a version of it shaped by our unconscious mental life and the subjectivity of others. Furthermore, it means we have acquired the capacity to think in the face of very powerful primitive emotions.

Thinking, thought Bion, arises out of the frustration. It is the infant's frustration with the inevitable incapacity of the mother that generates the healthy necessity for thought (Bion, 1962). In essence, the first proto-thought is the realization that the mother is not I. By contrast, hating tends to divide things from each other in the mind. Hatred that is uncontained attacks the links a mind might make; it splits other people into things that are hated and rejected (Bion, 1957). It attacks the links between different objects in the mind and emotional states, whereas love makes links and suffers differences and allows emotional complexity to co-exist.

The oedipal struggle

The capacity for reflective thinking is enhanced by the infant's safe and contained experience that the mother is not entirely preoccupied by them but has other concerns. In classic psychoanalytical literature, this is represented by the oedipal struggle. Here, the notion is that the mother has another erotic pull on her that is separate from the child, and the male child's fear is that the father will castrate him because of his illicit longings. Conceived in concrete terms, this story of the male child's development toward selfhood seems absurd. But, understood as a metaphor for the triangulation between the child's world and the adult world, it potentially provides a wealth of clinical insight.

Furthermore, it provides a potential bridge between the world of systemic theory, rooted in notions of relational interdependence and psychoanalytic thinking, where the relational world is primarily conceived in terms of the internal landscape of object relations. Thus, in psychoanalytic thinking, the interdependent relational world is an internal world coloured and shaped by phantasy. This difference in conception shapes the different clinical approaches. The psychoanalytic therapist attempts to represent an invariant relational experience to the patient, against which she or he plays out an internal landscape. By contrast, the systemic therapist works interactively with the actual relationships in the room and the layers of these relationships through time. The systemic therapist also holds in mind absent family members and their relational qualities, interactional impacts, history, and beliefs. In each of these therapeutic settings, the network of relational triangles is essential to understanding relationships in the individual or family and the therapeutic relationship.

In classic triadic circular questioning, the therapist attempts to draw this self-knowledge out in conversation with the family, hoping to expand their experiences of overt, covert, and subjugated beliefs, so that family members are able to make more informed and conscious decisions about the ways they conduct their relationships (Cecchin, 1987). In doing so, the systemic therapist is making use of the oedipal situation, the capacity of family members to conceive of each other's minds. When fully developed, the oedipal mind is able to conceive of the mind of another, to deduce mood, intention, humour, playfulness. It is the inherent capacity for growth rooted in these creative qualities that therapy attempts to uncover, develop, and make use of.

However, in the developmental trajectory of therapy (which somewhat mimics that of life), the therapist has to be able to withstand being hated and attacked because he or she is bound to fail. The therapist needs also to be able to withstand being loved and idealized. The therapist will have relations with others about whom the patient might be overwhelmingly curious. These "others" might not be people, but could be a theoretical orientation, a professional identity quite separate from the patient, a professional community, or, indeed, a "real life" outside the therapy. The therapist will bring these outside influences to bear in the life of his or her thinking. This thinking itself represents a third place, which the patient gets to grips with through the therapist's observations, interventions, and interpretations, becoming yet another oedipal triangle in which patient and therapist mutually influence each other.

The other as a foreign country

What gradually became apparent with Hermione and Bruce was that both struggled to enter the mind of the other. It was as if the other was a foreign country. Naturally, this did not apply to every aspect of their relationship, but it was a key feature of these areas in which they clashed and miscommunicated. The force of this dawned on me gradually. For instance, I wondered with Hermione if she could imagine what was making Bruce angry. No, she said, she just couldn't for one moment start to imagine what was going on inside him. Both Bruce and Hermione offered this as the default response. How could they know what was going on in the other, that would be impossible, wouldn't it? Bruce sometimes suggested

that to do so was tantamount to controlling Hermione in a domi-
neering and sexist manner. "Even if you do so tentatively and
compassionately?", I wondered.

Gradually, I pressed Hermione to conceive the visceral and emotional quality of Bruce's anger. She said she could not, anger was a
massively negative emotion, and the experience of her mother
would not let her go there, it was dangerous. That being so, I asked
if she could notice it without making a judgement about it, just
being as purely curious she was able to be about Bruce's anger.
When she tentatively allowed it to fully register without judgement,
she said it made her feel furious. Furious and strong, I wondered?
Cautious and stronger, she said. Slowly what emerged was her own
freedom to feel angry and, in the same process, her ability to imagine the origins of Bruce's anger within himself: the frustrated boy,
the rueful young adult, the cautious and curmudgeonly grown
adult he could so often be now.

Most striking, though, was that neither Hermione nor Bruce
could tolerate the consciousness of hatred either in themselves or
others, and yet both hated in various ways. My task was to see if it
was possible for them to tolerate their hatred. I wondered with
Bruce, at a relevant moment in therapy, about who he thought I
was, and what my feelings towards him might be. He said, rather
shyly and tentatively, "Well you're just a therapist who I pay to
listen." Perhaps he was aware that in saying this there was some
hatred in it. After all, it was true that I was paid to listen, but his
reply annihilated the emotionally engaged and caring part of me.
By contrast, Hermione, who laughed at Bruce's reply, wanted me to
care for her. Bruce did not mind me caring for her if I was his
neutral, paid-for therapist, but he showed more vital signs of hating
me if I was a feeling therapist.

I eased myself carefully into the oedipal space between them,
which kept opening up and then disappearing, because it just could
not be tolerated. It seemed to me that there was a developmental
trajectory to this process, and that the two of them first of all had to
be able to identify, and tolerate, the powerful negative currents
within themselves. As they did so, they were able to conceive, and
put into words, a sense of each other's internal world. They began
to know that their hatred could not annihilate either me or each
other, and this allowed space for more loving feelings to emerge. In

doing so, their emotional attunement to each other developed, and they were able to tolerate the differences and varieties in their internal worlds.

Systemic, psychoanalytic, or intersubjective?

It is difficult to determine entirely in what paradigm I worked with this couple. The systemic frame was there in a number of ways: in my engaged curiosity; in my awareness of their geneogram, reliably enquired after and held in mind, rather than literally sketched out; through my sense of a socially constructed, gendered account of their relationship, equal, at least, and complementary, to the transference relationship; and in the triadic "what if" questions addressed to each other, which flowed more smoothly in the final stages of our work together, once the couple had worked through the seized-up pre-oedipal patterns they were locked into.

The psychoanalytic was also there in a number of ways: in the attention I paid to the therapeutic relationship and the shifting emotional currents; in the use of my countertransference as an indicator of the emotional life of the couple; in the way I conceived of the unfolding relationship as a developmental process; in the work done in the here and now, which primarily focused on what they brought minute by minute in the session, in relation to each other and to me, rather than in my curiosity about what had transpired between them in the week, or between them and others; and, finally, in the weekly regularity of the sessions and the invariance of the setting, and in the way I left them to lead, sat with silence, and was minimally self-disclosing.

Yet, the intersubjective tradition was also present in the way I conceived of the relationship as contextually embedded in our uniquely subjective attachment histories, and in my attention to the developmental unfolding of self as a subject of curiosity and relatedness (Aron, 1996).

The oedipal as a way of thinking

In the oedipal configuration, the young child learns that his or her care-giver's preoccupation with "another" means that the care-giver has an independent emotional life. If the child can tolerate looking in on that relationship, and appreciating that two people can think, love, struggle, and compromise over this third emotional object in their lives, then the child can develop a picture of an internal world that is benign and understandable. Crucially, there will be a space for the child to be held in mind in the semi-private, but nevertheless public, arena of the life between a couple. Even more crucially, the child's ability to appreciate being held in mind by a second *and* a third person gives the child the sense of an expanded inner world, which can be thought about and negotiated. This provides a primary experience of being held in mind by a tolerant, mutually influencing couple. At best, this experience of looking in on loving and thinking provides a direct appreciation of the empathic thinking space.

The "couple" the child looks in on does not necessarily need to be an actual couple, and it can be represented by a single mother and her relationships with adult others, and, indeed, other forms of relationships. What is critical is the mutuality of relationship that enables the child's tolerance of other intrusions into the intimate life between self and care-giver, and for the space to be created in a way in which the child can be held in mind in a negotiable way.

You can think of me writing this chapter because you have had those experiences. Probably in childhood you let in a third and opened yourself up to real thought. Real thought is open to the incredibly different and negotiable textures of the reality we inhabit. It allows the flowing together of thought and feeling in the here and now; it does not split thought and feeling but allows them to coincide; it does not seek to extinguish experience; and nor, at its best, is it afraid of what it might find.

References

Aron, L. (1996). *A Meeting of Minds: Mutuality in Psychoanalysis*. New York: The Analytic Press.

Bion, W. (1957). Attacks on linking. *International Journal of Psychoanalysis*, 40: 308–315. Reprinted in E. Bott Spillius (1988) (Ed.), *Melanie Klein Today, Volume 1: Mainly Theory* (pp. 87–101). London: Brunner-Routledge.

Bion, W. (1962). A theory of thinking. *International Journal of Psychoanalysis, 43*: 306–310. Reprinted in E. Bott Spillius (1988) (Ed.), *Melanie Klein Today, Volume 1: Mainly Theory* (pp. 178–186). London: Brunner-Routledge.

Byng-Hall, J. (1995). *Rewriting Family Scripts: Improvisation and System Change*. New York: Guilford.

Byng-Hall, J. (1999). Family and couple therapy: toward greater security. In: J. Cassidy & P. Shaver (Eds.), *Handbook of Attachment: Theory, Research and Clinical Applications* (pp. 625–645). New York: Guilford.

Bronstein, C. (Ed.) (2001). *Kleinian Theory: A Contemporary Perspective*. London: Whurr.

Cecchin, G. (1987). Hypothesizing, circularity, and neutrality revisited: an invitation to curiosity. *Family Process, 26*: 405–413.

Clulow, C. (2001). *Adult Attachment and Couple Psychotherapy*. London: Brunner-Routledge.

Dallos, R. (2006). *Attachment Narrative Therapy*. Maidenhead: Open University Press.

Dell, P. (1982). Beyond homeostasis: toward a concept of coherence. *Family Process, 21*: 21–41.

Fonagy, P., Gergely, G., Jurist, E., & Target, M. (2002). *Affect Regulation, Mentalization and the Development of Self*. New York: Other Press.

Framo, J. (1962). The theory of the technique of family treatment of schizophrenia. *Family Process, 1*: 119–131.

Hinshelwood, R. (1989). *A Dictionary of Kleinian Thought*. London: Free Association.

Hoggett, P. (2001). The love that thinks. *Free Associations, 9*: 1–23.

Holmes, J. (1996). *Attachment, Intimacy, Autonomy: Using Attachment Theory in Adult Psychotherapy*. Northvale, NJ: Aronson.

Kohut, H. (1976). *The Restoration of the Self*. New York: International Universities Press.

Mann, D. (2002). The desire for love and hate. Is this? In: D. Mann (Ed.), *Love and Hate: Psychoanalytic Perspectives* (pp. 1–27). London: Brunner-Routledge.

Orange, D. (1995). *Emotional Understanding: Studies in Psychoanalytic Epistemology*. Hillsdale, NJ: Analytic Press.

Pooley, J. (2004). Layers of meaning: a coaching journey. In: C. Huffington, D. Armstrong, W. Halton, L. Hoyle, & J. Pooley (Eds.), *Working Below the Surface: The Emotional Life of Contemporary Organizations* (pp. 171–190). London: Karnac.

Shamai, M. (1998). Therapist in distress: team-supervision of social workers and family therapists who work and live under political uncertainty. *Family Process, 37*: 245–259.

Spillius, E. (Ed.) (1988). General introduction (pp. 1–7). *Melanie Klein Today: Developments in Theory and Practice, Volume 1*. London: Brunner-Routledge.

Stern, D. (1998). *The Interpersonal World of the Infant*. London: Karnac.

Stern, D. (2004). *The Present Moment in Psychotherapy and Everday Life*. New York: Norton.

Woodcock, J. (2000). Refugee children and families: theoretical and clinical approaches. In: K. Dwivedi (Ed.), *Post Traumatic Stress Disorder in Children and Adolescents* (pp. 213–239). London: Whurr.

PART III
DIALOGUE AND OTHERNESS

Reflecting processes and reflective functioning: shared concerns and challenges in systemic and psychoanalytic therapeutic practice

Mary Donovan

H istorically, systemic psychotherapy evolved in contexts of making sense of the difficulties of families and individuals not readily amenable to a classical psychoanalytic, insight-orientated approach. They sought relief for their suffering, but did not necessarily view the interpretation of intrapsychic conflict as part of this focus. Over the years, systemic family therapy has constructed an impressive repertoire of alternative styles of practice for engaging and helping people to develop their capacity to stand back and reflect on their presenting difficulties as part of the change process. Circular and reflexive questioning, as well as reflecting teams, are notable examples of this rich legacy (e.g., Andersen, 1990; Brown, 1997; Tomm, 1987a,b).

Contemporary psychoanalysis demonstrates a similar preoccupation with exploring ways of engaging and working with people not readily responsive to a traditional interpretive approach. "We no longer practice in an era in which interpretation is viewed as the exclusive therapeutic arrow in the analyst's quiver" (Gabbard & Weston, 2003, p. 823). In psychoanalytic discourse, Fonagy and Target's theory of mentalization or reflective functioning (e.g., Fonagy & Target, 1996, 2003; Fonagy, Moran, Edgcumbe, Kennedy, & Target,

1993; Fonagy, Steele, Moran, Steele, & Higgitt, 1991) is a notable example of this project to broaden the repertoire of psychoanalytic practice. This chapter explores shared ground between systemic and psychoanalytic orientations that this highlights, and specifically teases out connections between the systemic perspective on reflexivity and reflecting processes and the psychoanalytic perspective on reflective functioning. It concludes that the truly innovative nature of integrative thinking across the different therapeutic orientations is most clearly demonstrated in the endeavour to increase the range of those engaged and helped by psychotherapy.

A personal perspective on the systemic/psychoanalytic debate

My interest in the subject of this chapter dates back to experience as a social worker in the 1980s. During my training, I had been introduced to the principles of both systemic and psychoanalytic theory and practice. I recall being fascinated by both, and assumed, perhaps naïvely, that I could draw on these models in my work. Once practising as a social worker, I found that the disjuncture between the circumstances and expectations that my clients brought to our encounters and the expectations that I brought, drawing on the therapeutic models to which I had been introduced, became painfully obvious. Many of my clients seemed unfamiliar with—or disinterested in—talking as a route to solving their problems. For those who welcomed my involvement, their interest was often in the practical resources that I might access on their behalf. The therapy text books to which I had been introduced had little to say on this subject, and books that did were mainly from the radical, Marxist-influenced literature that permeated social work at that time. By and large, this literature had little interest in developing therapeutic models and was much more interested in community action that explicitly addressed material deprivation.

One notable exception within the therapy literature that I encountered was the writings of Salvador Minuchin (e.g., Minuchin, 1974; Minuchin, Montalvo, Guerney, Rosman, & Schumer, 1967). His work represented something of a breath of fresh air in terms of its therapeutic engagement with families living in acute material deprivation, albeit in a cultural context that was very different from the world in which I worked. I have a hazy recollection of stumbling attempts to apply some of Minuchin's ideas during home visits to families who seemed bemused by my efforts and that of a colleague. I can only hope they felt thought about, at least. It was during these early days in my career that I also came across the diagnosis of "personality disorder", which seemed to be applied to a number of parents on my child protection caseload. When asked what it meant, a senior colleague joked that it meant they could not be helped. His joke reflected the lack of effective therapeutic services for many of the parents I encountered with deeply troubling mental health problems that had an impact on their children. These were not the clients I read about very much in the therapy literature. I wondered if I was working with the "wrong" client group for such therapeutic intervention.

Later, on my moving to London, a world of therapeutic training opportunities presented itself to me. Perhaps the "right" training might connect me with client groups who were amenable to psychotherapy. I undertook training in once-weekly psychodynamic intervention and began the long journey of personal analysis. By now I had read Mattinson and Sinclair's classic text, *Mate and Stalemate* (1979), and was greatly impressed by the manner in which they addressed the problems of social work clients from a perspective informed by attachment theory and psychoanalytic theory. However, my psychodynamic training also showed me that contributions of this calibre from within the psychoanalytic fold were rare. Much of the literature informing my training was drawn from a model of intensive psychoanalytic intervention and, while theoretically rich, seemed technically limited in relation to my work context. My own interest in psychoanalysis deepened, but it seemed a long way from the world of the families in my social work practice. Here, I noticed that colleagues with systemic training appeared more adept at making the leap between the formulations of their training and the circumstances and difficulties of the families with whom we worked. I was introduced to circular questioning and other systemic techniques, and my interest in this orientation was rekindled, subsequently leading to a clinical training in systemic psychotherapy.

Both my trainings have had a profound impact on how I think and practise. When I consider each in isolation, it is easy to describe that influence. When I think about the intersections between the two, I enter a much more complex place. Writing on the subject has become an important part of my efforts to make sense of this place of integration and of difference (Donovan, 2003a). More than anything else, my therapeutic trainings have taught me that the "right" clients are an elusive breed, even if these are the cases we prefer to discuss in the literature: that is, cases where there appears to be a reasonably good fit between the therapist's theoretical model and the clients' needs and capacities, cases that appear to invite rich theoretical formulations and hypotheses. In practice, the story is often different. Here, the need is to constantly mould therapeutic models to suit the particular circumstances of cases in ways that depart significantly from the purity of these theoretical frames. Empirical research findings confirm the practice-based trend towards integrative ways of working (Fonagy, Target, Cottrell, Phillips, & Kurtz, 2002), but integrative theory continues to lag well behind practice.

As a family therapist, I continue to meet clients who do not usually see talking as a route to sorting out their problems and who need much careful engagement in order to construct a potential therapeutic context. While we would not view them as the "wrong" clients, in the sense of being unsuitable for psychotherapy, the challenge of engagement and of opening up a therapeutic dialogue remains formidable, and it is in this area that I see the greatest potential for creative dialogue across the various therapy divides: that point at which we are all, to varying degrees, working with the "wrong" clients; those for whom the "right" therapy may not yet have been formulated; those who bring complex, multi-layered problems requiring responses that combine or integrate different strands of psychotherapy; but also those who see us as the "wrong" therapists, or at least offering the "wrong" therapy, a problem that is perhaps most acutely experienced in publicly funded mental health settings where client choice is constrained by factors such as limited resources and long waiting lists.

A clinical perspective

Mr and Mrs A reluctantly attend family therapy sessions with their twelve-year old son, Adam, an only child. The parents are firmly of the view that their son needs individual help for a range of difficulties, including tics, poor self-esteem, physical aggression, and a deeply negative relationship with his father. My family therapist colleague and I feel that Adam might also benefit from individual work running parallel to the family/parental intervention but, to date, he has resolutely refused to separate from his mother when arrangements have been made. Multi-disciplinary discussion of the case has concluded that, for now, family therapy is the optimum treatment, and it is felt that much productive work is possible within this frame. In particular, we hope that family meetings interspersed with parental meetings might help Adam separate from the acute entanglement in his parents' troubled relationship, which makes consideration of his own needs so difficult both in the family and in the therapeutic context. It is a classic family therapy case with questions and battles around who is the "identified patient" at the heart of the work. It is also typical of many cases worked by family therapists in child and adolescent mental health settings, and I am using it as an example of the routine challenges of our work in engaging families and creating a therapeutic context. For now, at least, we feel we are working with the "right" client, the family, even if Mr and Mrs A do not share this view. How we try to open up space for thinking about the difficulties—including our own hypotheses—with the family in this rather uneasy therapeutic alliance is what interests me here.

In the initial meetings, our impression is of a family stuck together in highly ambivalent relationships. Mr and Mrs A both express acute dissatisfaction with the marriage and air their thoughts about divorce, but seem incapable of making a decision. Marital therapy at another clinic fizzled out. Both parents have past histories of mental health difficulties including hospitalization, and these histories have the status of secrets in the family. They are deeply concerned that their son's current problems may represent the onset of similar mental health problems. A powerful sense of stuckness prevails, and I often feel relieved when my colleague joins me from the other side of the screen for a reflecting conversation in front of the family. I experience these as moments when my own thinking is freed and I begin to play with thoughts and words in a way that feels very difficult when I am with the family. Sometimes, our reflecting conversation simply entails putting into words the stuckness and rigidity of thinking and talking that we experience, and exploring its possible ingredients. We might reflect on our impression that everybody in the family seems deeply attached to their own perspective and is waiting for somebody else to do the changing. We might draw out and think about fleeting moments in the session when something different seemed possible. Over the course of the initial sessions, it seems that my colleague is more likely to take risks in his reflections, which his relative distance from the family appears to facilitate. Sometimes, when this happens, it seems important to share my concern that the conversation might be going beyond what feels comfortable for the family, but I am also likely to welcome this fresh perspective and reflect on what is making it so difficult for this to happen in my own conversation with the family.

In effect, much of our exchange is as likely to be about the process of conversation as it is about content issues. Often it seems that, in our meta-conversation in front of the family, my colleague and I are looking for a variety of ways of saying the same things so that they might be heard and taken in. In the early sessions it is striking that different aspects of the reflecting conversation resonate for different family members, and here we find the spontaneous free-flowing quality of the reflecting process enormously helpful in furthering each member's engagement. Put simply, what seems most important is that we are introducing and constantly reinforcing the value of thinking-and-talking about the family's thinking-and-talking. It is an example of routine systemic practice, which, to my mind, resonates with ideas around mentalization and reflective functioning as a focus for intervention within psychoanalytic discourse. I will return to this later.

At one level, it could be argued that what we are doing is modelling a different kind of conversation with a different way of dealing with differences of perspective: a conversation that places great emphasis on putting feelings into words, on playing with words and ideas, and allowing for contradiction, mixed feelings, and compromise in and through the talking process. But we are also laying the foundations for insight-orientated talking to happen. For example, we are beginning to reflect more directly and openly on the circumstances—including intergenerational issues—that allow Adam to "sit" between his parents and become used in that context. As we push at the boundaries of thinking, feeling, and talking that can be tolerated in the family, anxiety escalates, with further challenges to the family-orientated frame of the work that have to be addressed and worked with.

In my view, there is interesting common ground between our use of the transference–countertransference dynamic, including the processing between ourselves in the reflecting team moments that I have briefly outlined, and family therapy practice that locates itself unequivocally within a psychoanalytic frame. (See Flaskas [1996] for a discussion of transference, countertransference, and projective identification from a systemic perspective. For further psychoanalytic discussion, see Casement [1985, 1990], Kohon [1986], Ogden [1979], Sandler [1987], and Sandler, Dare, Holder, and Dreher [1992].) Obviously, the explicit use of a reflecting conversation observed by the family is particular to the systemic style of practice, but, to my mind, that is primarily a matter of technique and of finding strategies that are effective in promoting less constrained thinking and talking. In this context, I would argue that the systemic clinician has a range of therapeutic tools available that are potentially of value to all clinicians working with families, irrespective of their therapeutic orientation. Difference in technique does not in itself imply difference in therapeutic goals, and should not cloud consideration of qualitative differences between therapeutic orientations.

For Brodie and Wright (2002), who write about family therapy from a psychoanalytic perspective, one such difference from systemic family therapy that they propose is the belief that their work is "taking place at a different subjective level of affective experience and consequently requires something different from the therapist in terms of emotional processing" (p. 219). They cite their personal training analysis (presumably the training analysis required for child or adult psychoanalytic training, given that a separate professional training in psychoanalytic family therapy does not exist in the UK) as the "best way to develop an internal dialogue apropos the unconscious" (p. 211) and, therefore, as integral to their development as psychoanalytic family therapists. They also acknowledge that strand of systemic discourse that emphasizes reflexive practice and the therapist's use of self, and they accept that there are different ways of developing a general capacity for reflection and dialogue. Here, we touch on complex issues concerning what the therapist brings to the work, and their training needs at a personal level, which are outside the scope of this paper. My concern is to think about the very considerable variations that families also bring to the work in terms of their need and their capacity for engagement, for reflexivity, for insight-orientated talking, and for connection at different levels of affective experience. My interest in making connections with psychoanalysis is in what it has to say on these issues, which go to the heart of the challenge in all our work.

Reflective functioning

Within contemporary psychoanalytic discourse, a key strand of debate now addresses the considerable technical challenge of working analytically with people not readily amenable to a traditional psychoanalytic interpretive approach: people who have variously been described as "not ready for interpretations", "unpsychologically minded", or "concrete". These are the "wrong" clients of a previous era who might well have been viewed as unsuitable for psychoanalytically orientated intervention. Some might have a diagnosis of narcissistic or borderline personality disorder. In general, their difficulties are deep-seated and challenging and they are often in considerable personal distress. These are people who also frequently present in child and adolescent mental health clinics with problems firmly located in their children, and they are likely to be well represented in the caseloads of most family therapists working in such settings. The theory of reflective functioning (e.g., Fonagy & Target, 1996, 1998, 2003) has emerged in the psychoanalytic field as an important contribution to the debate about appropriate therapeutic response and technique in working with people presenting with difficulties on this spectrum.

The concept of reflective function refers to our capacity to conceptualize mental processes in self and others; that is, the ability to interpret one's own and others' actions in terms of mental states including thoughts, feelings, beliefs, desires, intentions, and so on. The model of mentalization, or reflective functioning, is an attempt to formulate and understand difficulty in this area, drawing on a developmental psychological perspective.

In early childhood, prior to the age of three, it is suggested that the infant exists primarily in a psychic equivalence mode; that is, ideas or perceptions are experienced not as representations, but as accurate replicas of reality. This oscillates with the pretend mode that is characteristic of the child's play, in which ideas are experienced as representational but are not thought to have a direct relationship to the outside world as such. In the optimal developmental situation, these two modes are eventually integrated, and mental states begin to be experienced as representations. Inner and outer reality can then be seen as linked, and the capacity for mentalization or reflective function is laid down.

Central to this theory is the view that the acquisition of reflective capacity is rooted in the intersubjective process that unfolds between an infant and her parents. In this context, the child internalizes the experience of being thought about by the emotionally containing parent with whom she interacts. In situations of good-enough parenting, this eventually leads to the consolidation of the child's own capacity for reflective functioning. Fonagy and Target (1998) point to evidence suggesting that trauma and maltreatment impair the child's reflective capacity, and an important focus for therapeutic intervention with such patients, either as children or as adults, is the offer of space where thinking about ideas and feelings can be experienced as safe, perhaps for the first time. Here, the relationship between therapist and patient is pivotal, but it entails a way of working that is less focused on explicit interpretation of unconscious content, at least in the early stages of the work, given the limited capacity of the patient for this level of reflective endeavour. Rather, the therapist engages with the patient's world of psychic equivalence; that is, their difficulty in differentiating between internal and external reality. The focus is on helping the patient to gradually learn that mental experience involves representations that can be thought about, talked about, played with, loosened up, and changed. It entails a way of working that has, therefore, much in common with the systemic practitioner's focus on increasing reflexivity in the individual or family's thinking and talking processes, notably through the use of reflexive and circular questioning and reflecting teams. The emphasis, similarly, is on loosening up fixed patterns of perception and belief and increasing the space for people to take up an observer perspective in relation to themselves, their families, and their world generally.

In certain important respects, the psychoanalytic perspective on reflective functioning is broadly consistent with the development of object relations thinking in psychoanalysis (e.g., Klein, 1957; Winnicott, 1965). (See Holmes [2005] for a helpful overview of the links between the model of mentalization or reflective functioning and other strands of theorizing in psychoanalysis.) Both reflect the shift towards moral concerns in contemporary psychoanalysis, in the sense that both try to conceptualize the developmental trajectory of our human capacity to recognize mental states in others and ourselves and to engage, for example, with states of hurt and suffering in the other. Both perspectives underline the privileging of inter-subjectivity and communication in current therapeutic practice and the focus on helping those for whom communication is profoundly limited and distorted by psychological difficulties. Within the psychoanalytic frame, the transference relationship becomes the arena in which these difficulties are played out, understood, and addressed.

The theory of reflective function also represents an important contribution in its own right; not least, because it opens up a very specific and important technical discussion about how best to work with those whose reflective capacity is seriously impaired. It brings psychoanalytic discourse closer to shared technical concerns with other therapies, including systemic therapy, which has long focused on ways of working therapeutically with people who are not moti-vated primarily by an interest in intrapsychic insight. In this respect, reflective functioning could be thought of as something of a bridging concept between the two therapies. Its pivotal status also rests on the fact that it offers a developmental psychological perspective on why some people have seriously impaired reflective functioning capacity, which, in systemic discourse, we might describe in terms of their capacity for reflexivity.

Reflective functioning and reflexivity

Similarity between the concept of reflective functioning and the systemic idea of reflexivity is striking. Karl Tomm (1987a,b) describes the latter as a process in which one is both performing and, at the same time, audience to one's performance. It is this interest in the reflexive process that we might loosely characterize as thinking-and-talking about thinking-and-talking that connects the two models. Tomm conceptualizes reflexivity, as it unfolds in family therapy, as the making of connections between different levels of meaning in the family system. He also emphasizes that "change occurs as a result of alterations in the organisation and structure of the family's pre-existing system of meanings ... the basic mechanism of change is not insight but reflexivity"(1987b, p. 172). Fonagy and Target (1998) similarly emphasize that reflec-tive function should not be conflated with introspection or self-reflection. It is rooted in procedural type knowledge and is understood as an automatic process invoked in interpreting human action, unlike introspection. Within this model, the overarching psychotherapeutic focus is defined in terms of the recovery of this reflective capacity.

Here, we touch on developments relating to therapeutic action and technique that highlight the different mechanisms involved in fostering change. These challenge any exclusive preoccupation with therapeutic action understood in terms of insight, and mean that greater attention is focused on the therapeutic needs of those for whom an exclusive spotlight on insight is unhelpful, alienating, and premature. To the extent that psychoanalysis engages with these debates, it also moves closer to shared challenges with other therapeutic orientations. Most commonly, this is elaborated in a dialogue with cognitive approaches (e.g., Bateman, 2000; Gabbard & Weston, 2003). Yet, on closer scrutiny, the links with a systemic orientation are clear, as I have indicated, in considering shared ground between reflective functioning and reflexivity. Nor is this simply a question of similarity at more abstract levels of theory. For example, in their detailed account of psychoanalytic intervention with a patient with pronounced ruminative thinking, Gabbard and Weston (2003) outline a style of engagement with this aspect of the patient's problem that is strikingly similar to the systemic practice of circular and reflexive questioning. Elsewhere, I have argued that systemic technique has, in fact, much to offer the psychodynamic practitioner (Donovan, 2005).

In one of the more recent elaborations of their model, Fonagy and Target (2003) acknowledge the common ground with allied disciplines in the therapeutic field, but they also admit that, within psychoanalysis, the question has now arisen as to whether what they are describing can still be called "psychoanalysis". This is a useful reminder of the dynamic social construction of borders between therapeutic orientations. It is also a reminder of the problem in relating to psychoanalysis as a reified entity, rather than something evolving and fluid in a changing therapeutic landscape where borrowing and border crossing—acknowledged and unacknowledged—happen all the time. Here, the key issue is not, to my mind, one of large-scale integration of therapies; it is about understanding the already existing points of integration and of difference, about understanding what kinds of intervention are best suited to particular client groups, and about dialogue between orientations at the frontiers of our current therapeutic knowledge and practice so that we might extend the range and effectiveness of our services generally.

Reflecting processes and reflective functioning

I am interested in the different perspectives that systemic and psychoanalytic approaches bring to commonly held concerns and challenges and, in this chapter, I am looking towards psychoanalysis from the perspective of systemic psychotherapy for what it might contribute to our thinking and practice. In so doing, my priority is to establish common ground as a basis for dialogue and for thinking about difference, which is where we are most likely to learn from each other. The themes of reflexivity and reflective function have much in common and highlight points of contact between the two approaches, but there are also important distinctions. The psychoanalytic model presented by Fonagy and Target has an intrapsychic slant, as one might expect, and the technical interventions they propose are predominantly geared towards working in the intimacy of the one-to-one transference relationship. The systemic concept of reflexivity has a much more vigorously relational slant, and lends itself to technical applications that are well suited to the immediacy of relational dynamics in families and other groups, as well as in work with individuals. Fonagy and Target signal their own interest in diversity of therapeutic technique when they write,

> A fundamental task for psychoanalytic theorists is to recognize the weakness of the link between practice and theory, that changes of technique have no power to confirm or disconfirm cherished ideas and that practice may be radically changed with or without changes in theory. We could then see talented clinicians modifying technique while remaining faithful to the core assumptions of psychoanalysis. [2003, p. 312]

To my mind, this clear distinction between theory and technique has therapeutic relevance well beyond psychoanalysis and is highly pertinent to systemic discourse. I will use the systemic perspective on reflecting teams and processes as an example of what I have in mind and, more generally, as a reference point for thinking about the links with reflective functioning.

In the early literature on the reflecting team there is much emphasis on the fact that it should not be understood primarily as a method or technique but, rather, at the level of therapeutic values. Hoffman writes,

> A question people will ask of course is: Is this a new method? Is it a new school of family therapy? At this point my answer would be "No". It enters the picture at a more general level of abstraction, at a level of therapeutic values and therapeutic stance. [1990, p. 11]

While the ethical significance of the reflecting team approach is beyond question, acknowledging this does not imply that we should downplay the value of a technical perspective as if these discourses were mutually exclusive (Donovan, 2003b). There is, I believe, a great loss in not viewing the reflecting team process unambiguously from the perspective of technique, and a danger that its full therapeutic potential might be left unexplored. I also believe that the absence of a well-developed discourse of technique increases the tendency towards uncritical application. Links that might productively be made with other developments in the systemic domain—for example, that between reflecting teams and the therapeutic relationship—remain tenuous. My experience is that reflecting teams can afford an invaluable opportunity for the articulation of complex multi-layered transference dynamics in family therapy. However, I am also aware that the process is one that some families find difficult to connect with, and we need to go on learning about this. Here, I am mindful of Fonagy and Target's psychoanalytic perspective on working with people who have severely impaired reflective functioning capacity, which emphasizes a likely history of trauma, and the centrality of the therapeutic relationship as a safe intersubjective space where thinking about ideas and feelings becomes possible, perhaps for the first time. In working with families with severe difficulties on this spectrum, particular attention needs to be paid to consolidating a safe therapeutic space, and therapeutic method and technique need to be adapted accordingly, including the frequency of sessions, which might need to be greater than for other client groups.

In the case of the A family, described earlier, the need for a safe space where connection at deeper levels of affective experience could become possible was facilitated, in my view, by the consistency and continuity of a reflecting process involving two people whom the family could get to know and connect with as individuals, albeit within a reflecting processes framework. While I would argue that, in such cases, systemic technique in the shape of a reflecting team approach has much to offer the psychodynamic–psychoanalytic practitioner, I also feel that the psychoanalytic perspective on transference–countertransference issues gives the systemic practitioner much food for thought. With the A family it was notable that, early in the work, they returned from a Christmas break in a collapsed state, which, with help, they could tentatively begin to link with the gap in sessions. It was an early reminder of the intensity of the transference that had developed, the intensity of dependency needs evoked, and the need to address and manage these issues very carefully and sensitively in the course of the work. Again, I find Fonagy and Target's reflections on working with cases involving severely impaired reflective functioning capacity helpful in terms of their attention to the intensity of transference phenomena in such work, the process of selective, carefully timed interpretation and management of these processes, and the inadvisability of becoming too insight-orientated too quickly. The latter is similar to Tom Andersen's advice that reflecting team contributions should be "different enough but not too different" from the family's own position (1987, p. 417). My view is that the reflecting team approach is well suited to the technical process of working with people with significant reflective functioning difficulties, but it is a specific and challenging application that needs to be carefully constructed with the needs of this client group firmly in mind, including their great need for—and difficulty in—connecting at deeper levels of affective experience.

I offer the above thoughts drawing on my own clinical experience. I also think that it is only in the context of ongoing dialogue with psychoanalysis that we will get an adequate feel for the creative potential of this interchange, particularly at the level of technique, which I have privileged in this discussion.

Summary

I have explored common ground between the themes of reflective function, reflexivity, and reflecting processes and, in so doing, I have focused on the challenge of working with people with severely impaired reflective capacity. This is therapeutic territory where the technical challenge transcends neat distinctions between systemic, psychoanalytic, and also cognitive approaches, although the latter has not been a specific focus here. It is therapeutic territory where the orientations have much to learn from each other and where constructive communication across ideologically-charged divides can be greatly facilitated by disentangling the levels of theory and of therapeutic technique. In addressing the needs of this client group, it seems to me that the potential for common ground with psychoanalysis is much stronger than in other areas of our systemic practice and where dialogue between the two orientations is, therefore, likely to hold much creative potential.

References

Andersen, T. (1987). The reflecting team: dialogue and meta-dialogue in clinical work. *Family Process, 26:* 415–428.

Andersen, T. (Ed.) (1990). *The Reflecting Team: Dialogues and Dialogues about the Dialogues.* Broadstairs: Borgmann.

Bateman, A. (2000). Integration in psychotherapy : An evolving reality in personality disorder. *British Journal of Psychotherapy, 17:* 147–156.

Brodie, F. & Wright, J. (2002). Minding the gap not bridging the gap: family therapy from a psychoanalytic perspective. *Journal of Family Therapy, 24:* 205–221.

Brown, J. (1997). Circular questioning: an introductory guide. *Australian and New Zealand Journal of Family Therapy, 18:* 109–114.

Casement, P. (1985). On *Learning from the Patient.* London: Tavistock.

Casement, P. (1990). *Further Learning from the Patient.* London: Karnac.

Donovan, M. (2003a). Mind the gap: the need for a generic bridge between psychoanalytic and systemic approaches. *Journal of Family Therapy, 25:* 115–135.

Donovan, M. (2003b). Family therapy beyond postmodernism: some considerations on the ethical orientation of contemporary practice. *Journal of Family Therapy, 25:* 285–306.

Donovan, M. (2005). Bridging the gap: similarity and difference between psychoanalytic and systemic therapeutic orientations. *British Journal of Psychotherapy*, 22: 227–242.

Flaskas, C. (1996). Understanding the therapeutic relationship: using psychoanalytic ideas in the systemic context. In: C. Flaskas, B. Mason, & A. Perlesz (Eds.), *The Therapeutic Relationship in Systemic Therapy* (pp. 111–150). London: Karnac.

Fonagy, P., & Target, M. (1996). Playing with reality: 1. Theory of mind and the normal development of psychic reality. *International Journal of Psychoanalysis*, 77: 217–233.

Fonagy, P., & Target, M. (1998). An interpersonal view of the infant. In: A. Hurry (Ed.), *Psychoanalysis and Developmental Therapy* (pp. 3–31). London: Karnac.

Fonagy, P., & Target, M. (2003). *Psychoanalytic Theories: Perspectives from Developmental Psychology*. London: Whurr.

Fonagy, P., Moran, G., Edgcumbe, R., Kennedy, H., & Target, M. (1993). The roles of mental representations and mental processes in therapeutic action. *Psychoanalytic Study of the Child*, 48: 9–48.

Fonagy, P., Steele, H., Moran, G., Steele, M., & Higgitt, A. (1991). The capacity for understanding mental states: the reflective self in parent and child and its significance for security of attachment. *Infant Mental Health Journal*, 13: 200–217.

Fonagy, P., Target, M., Cottrell, D., Phillips, D., & Kurtz, Z. (2002). *What Works for Whom? A Critical Review of Treatments for Children and Adolescents*. London: Guilford.

Gabbard, G., & Weston, D. (2003). Rethinking therapeutic action. *International Journal of Psychoanalysis*, 84: 823–841.

Hoffman, L. (1990). Foreword. In: T. Andersen. (Ed.), *The Reflecting Team: Dialogues and Dialogues about the Dialogues* (pp. 7–11). Broadstairs: Borgmann.

Holmes, J. (2005). Notes on mentalizing—old hat or new wine? *British Journal of Psychotherapy*, 22: 179–197.

Klein, M. (1957). *Envy and Gratitude*. London: Hogarth.

Kohon, G. (Ed.) (1986). *The British School of Psychoanalysis: The Independent Tradition*. London: Free Association.

Mattinson, J., & Sinclair, I. (1979). *Mate and Stalemate: Working with Marital Problems in a Social Services Department*. Oxford: Blackwell.

Minuchin, S. (1974). *Families and Family Therapy*. London: Tavistock.

Minuchin, S., Montalvo, B., Guerney, B. G., Rosman, B. L., & Schumer, F. (1967). *Families of the Slums: An Exploration of their Structure and Treatment*. New York: Basic Books.

Ogden, T. H. (1979). On projective identification. *International Journal of Psychoanalysis, 60*: 357–373.

Sandler, J. (Ed.) (1987). *Projection, Identification, Projective Identification*. London: Karnac.

Sandler, J., Dare, C., Holder, A., & Dreher, A. (1992). *The Patient and the Analyst*. London: Karnac.

Tomm, K. (1987a). Interventive interviewing: Part I. Strategizing as a fourth guideline for the therapist. *Family Process, 26*: 3–13.

Tomm, K. (1987b). Interventive interviewing: Part II. Reflexive questioning as a means to enable self- healing. *Family Process, 26*: 167–183.

Winnicott. D. W. (1965). *The Maturational Processes and the Facilitating Environment*. London: Hogarth.

CHAPTER TEN

In the thick of culture: systemic and psychoanalytic ideas

Inga-Britt Krause

I n the introduction to a book about cross-cultural psychotherapy, I made the comment that any cross-culturally practising
psychotherapist, in some way, must feel compelled to adopt a
systemic perspective (Krause, 1998). This was a statement that
traced and documented my own personal journey from social
anthropology to family therapy, but I also wanted to call to mind
the historical connection between the two disciplines via Bateson
(Krause, 2006), "culture" as a systemic idea (Krause, 2002), and the
contribution of social constructionism to contemporary systemic
psychotherapy.

In the same book I worked my way through different areas in
which cultural patterns, symbols, and meanings impinge,
constrain, and are implicated in the behaviour and experience of
persons. These included kinship, emotions, ritual, taboos, and
secrets. My argument was that much cultural material is outside the
realm of individual awareness in the form of different types of
knowledge and structures, some of which seem unquestionable and
natural to individuals. (I used Bourdieu's terms *doxic* and *habitus* to
refer to knowledge, which is imprinted on the body and the mind
as the result of the operation of structures that are unconsciously

regulated and that incorporate culturally structured patterns, routines, improvisations, and meanings. I quoted Bourdieu as saying, "It is because subjects do not strictly speaking know what they are doing that what they do has more meaning than they know" [Bourdieu, 1977, p. 79].) I referred to material that is "implicit", "outside awareness", and to those aspects that are not articulated verbally, but I did not use the term "unconscious". This was partly because of the technical meaning of this term in psychoanalysis, but also because I felt a need to be cautious. The evidence of cultural diversity in areas outside consciousness is abundant, but questions about how this works, how we may understand it, and what kind of model or theory we may choose to use are complex. Ultimately, we all have to answer the same ethical questions about our own relationship to that with which we are engaged and to the models for which we make claims.

The paradox (if I may use such a strong description) of my 1998 book was that, while setting out to make important claims for systemic psychotherapy, I ended up moving into an area of our work (that part of life which is outside consciousness), with which systemic psychotherapists had engaged hardly at all as far as cross-cultural work is concerned. Eventually, by suggesting that self-reflection and a kind of cultural and social transference (Krause, 2002) are necessary tools in cross-cultural work, I had moved from advocating systemic ideas to also advocating psychoanalytic ideas as a guide for cross-cultural practice. Through this journey, I have come to believe that, from an individual person's point of view, "culture" is in the same league as "experience" and "reality" (Britton, 1995; Flaskas, 2002) and therefore requires similar engagement and recognition from psychotherapists, whatever their training and background.

Culture in systemic psychotherapy

Despite the inspirational influence of Bateson's anthropological work in the development of family therapy (Bateson, 1958, 1972), the phenomenon of "culture" did not receive much attention in the beginning of the life of the discipline. The Palo Alto Communications Project was set up to research all aspects of communication, but the collaboration between Bateson and his colleague Watzlawick came to an end over a split between them about whether forms of communication could be discussed in isolation from cultural communication (Harries-Jones, 1995). Bateson thought that they could not, but Watzlawick's and Haley's influence signalled a move in family therapy towards behavioural interpretations of human relationships.

Bateson had himself struggled with the tension between local details and general descriptions in his writing about schismogenesis in the Iatmul *naven* ritual. We can trace this struggle through the book *Naven* (1958), and in particular in the development between the two Epilogues of 1936 (Bateson, 1958) and 1958. In the 1936 Epilogue, Bateson was preoccupied with whether or not the labels he was using to categorize behaviour were his or whether they also belonged to the Iatmul people themselves. In the 1958 epilogue, which Bateson wrote after having discovered the relevance of cybernetics and logical typing to his work, he was quite clear that the categories he was using, such as "ethos" and "cultural structure", were descriptions of processes of knowing adopted by scientists. Although there was still an emphasis on ethnographic observation, there was also a notion that what is observed is not solely a result of what is going on between the parties in front of our very eyes. This was conceptualized using ideas such as "meta-position", and "positive" and "negative feedback".

Between the two epilogues, Bateson had moved from investigating a particular ritual, with all its related details of meaning and symbolization, to an attempt to find a generic typology of human relationships and to formulate a general theory about human interaction and communication. It was this "recursive vision" (the phrase used as the title of Harries-Jones seminal book about Bateson and his work [Harries-Jones, 1995]), with all its different layers, from which Bateson thought that Watzlawick and Haley had departed. Accordingly, those of Bateson's papers that achieved a high and even iconic status in family therapy became those papers that focused on behaviour (for example, papers on the double bind, the cybernetics of self, and a theory of schizophrenia [Bateson, 1972]), whereas others, which discussed "meaning" or "culture" more directly (for example, papers such as "Style, grace and information in primitive art", and "Experiments in thinking" [Bateson, 1972]), have hardly been referred to.

Since meaning is ubiquitous, family therapists could hardly practise without working with meaning. However, the question of whose meaning did not seem to arise very much in the early decades of the discipline. The effect of this was that meaning could ride on the back of behaviour, which could be observed and therefore remain relatively unproblematic. So, for example, the early Milan team, who had a reputation of working with meaning, defined ritual primarily in terms of "action accompanied by verbal formulations" (Selvini Palazzoli, Boscolo, Cecchin, & Prata, 1977, p. 452). It was not until a decade later or so when feminist family therapists began to question ideology, that the notion of multiple meanings—of whose categories? whose labels or whose meanings?—began to emerge explicitly as an issue in clinical practice. Since then, it has been extended and developed in many different ways: language generated systems (Anderson & Goolishian, 1988), narrative approaches (Epston & White, 1992; White & Epston, 1990), multiple voices (Hoffman, 1993; Papadopoulos & Byng-Hall, 1997), cultural lenses (Hoffman, 1990), and open dialogues (Seikkula, 1993; Seikkula & Olson, 2003).

However, despite this emphasis on constructionism in the discipline, or perhaps because of it, it has been difficult to consider meaning-making itself as a system. As Flaskas has pointed out in relation to the work of Michael White, the privileging of "new" narratives has led to a de-emphasis on the continuity of experience (Flaskas, 2002, p. 64). It also runs the risk of privileging the therapist's own ideas and notions about relationships at the expense of the views and orientations of clients, which may be more implicit and hidden and therefore not accessible through relatively brief conversations (Krause, 2002, pp. 13–16). This suggests a confidence in the discipline that meaning is not all that difficult to access, that meaning emerges from our dialogues with clients as a result of our skills in using particular techniques, and that we will be able to notice, understand, and attune to them when they do. This entails respect for the role of persons in the construction and co-construction of intersubjectivity, relationships, and communication (often referred to as agency), but it is at the same time inattentive to the limits and constraints against which these processes take place (Hacking, 1999; Flaskas, 2002; Krause, 2002; Lannamann, 1998; Malik & Krause, 2005).

In summary, systemic psychotherapy has a bundle of theories and models, which have been influenced by the early choice of a behavioural direction and are characterized by a theoretical emphasis on the general and the abstract (the meta-), rather than on the process of abstraction. They are also characterized by synchrony rather than diachrony, and by a reluctance to theorize those aspects of life and experience that lie outside awareness or consciousness. These models are also rarely explicit about what is assumed to be universal. Our modes of practice and our understanding of diversity and differences imply that something must be universal, but we do not say what that might be. As a result, we cannot be explicit about what might be the constraints on social construction. Thus, we remain oblivious to what it is that makes possible what we do know about ourselves and our clients in the first place (social anthropologists and ethnographers often find themselves in the same methodological quandary).

Culture in psychoanalysis

But what if some of what we all share lies beyond our awareness? This is highly probable, since each of us sees the world from our particular points of view and what we have in common is therefore only one variation on a theme. This is, of course, also the view put forward in psychoanalysis, where what is of interest in terms of explanation happens in the unconscious. (I am much less qualified to speak about psychoanalytic than about systemic theory. Here, I mainly rely on my own reading of the theories of Klein [1945, 1946], Bion [1962], and Britton [1995].) In many ways, a psychoanalytic approach is the opposite of a systemic one, with an emphasis on diachrony in the form of child development, on unconscious feelings and motivations, and an explicit claim that this is a universal model. In this model, the early experiences of the baby and the processes through which these are addressed become a kind of blueprint for mature persons.

In the world of the newborn infant there are no persons, but only powerful sensations, which the baby experiences as coming from the outside. When the baby is hungry, for example, this is experienced by her as an attack from the outside, as if something outside *is* the bad experience. The baby learns to deal with her anxiety through her carer(s) attending to her, in the course of which the baby's projections are given back to her in a modified way. This helps the baby "contain", or take back into herself (introject), a strong, good, and containing carer/mother. Now the baby is ready to accept a world view in which new things can be contemplated and tested, which allows frustration to be tolerated and discomfort to be recognized, not as an attack, but as the feeling of absence of something that the baby might want.

For Klein, Bion, and Britton, the baby developing an ability to work through to this state (the depressive position) depends on the introduction of the third person, or a triangle, in her life. This person or these other persons challenge(s) the blissful dyadic symbiosis with the primary carer, and this enables the baby to be an observer to other dyadic states (Britton, 1995), to herself (Bion, 1962), and is also implicated in the development of thought and language (Hobson, 2002). If the blissful idealized state of one-ness is unmediated, on the other hand, this is conducive to generating states of mind in which the baby again feels attacked and reacts without being able to think and reflect about this (the paranoid–schizoid position). Because these states and functions are the primitive building blocks of persons in relationships with others, they are also considered to be states of mind into which mature persons may fall again and again.

But what of the specific, the particular, the culturally constructed, and the local in this theory? The theory attends to the position of the infant and the development of fundamental human capacities. The functions of the mother or primary carer are highlighted in so far as they enhance or hinder the development of these capacities. However, in practice these functions are carried out within a cultural context of meaning and convention, which provides the rationale for the interaction and communication for both baby and carer. What the baby experiences from her carer is embedded in cultural conventions and meanings. From this point of view, a variety of ways of offering "containment" and addressing anxiety will be possible in order to reach "normal" development and good enough relationships between carers and infants. An outline of the most rudimentary caring functions therefore does not, by itself, give any clue to how the relationship between cultural variation and universal requirements can be assessed. Instead, it runs the risk that cultural variation is overlooked and that normative expectations are conflated with particular points of view.

How, then, can cultural variation be addressed from a psychoanalytic perspective? This is a tricky question. In the famous discussion about the Oedipus complex between psychoanalysis and anthropology, the debate came to a stalemate several times (see Cohen, 2002, and Krause, 1998, for summaries of this debate). Anthropologists argued that since familial relationships and arrangements do not everywhere adhere to the model of the nuclear family found in North European societies, the Oedipus complex cannot be said to be universal. This was based on observations of kinship rules and behaviour, on myths, and on talking to local informants. However, the psychoanalytic side argued that since some patterns of behaviour and some customs echoed European ones, the meanings that do not fit must be evidence that, far from absent, the Oedipus complex was, in fact, particularly strongly *repressed* in the societies in question. While this may be a somewhat outmoded view in psychoanalysis today, there remain questions as to how rudimentary functions and processes can be accessed through levels of language and cultural symbols, and about the cultural content of the unconscious.

Common ground

In his first ethnography, Bateson approached the Iatmul material (the Iatmul live in the region of the Sepik river in the eastern part of New Guinea) with the idea that the Iatmul ethos in some way distilled the logic of a cultural outlook. To examine this, he used the *naven* ritual as a lens through which to examine Iatmul culture, much in the way systemic psychotherapists have been taught to focus on particular sequences and patterns in therapy sessions and relate these to the system of family relationships. (In the *naven* ritual, a young man who has achieved something that denotes adulthood is pursued by his maternal uncle, dressed up as an old woman. When the maternal uncle finds his nephew, he rubs his buttocks up and down his nephew's thigh in a sexualized gesture, which causes much hilarity among the onlookers. [Bateson, 1958].)

Bateson had already found a tradition of transvestism in large-scale Iatmul ceremonies, and had noticed how proud women were of the men's ornaments, which they wore in these ceremonies. However, it was not until he himself saw the transvestite uncle dressed up in women's rags in the *naven* ritual, and experienced the emotion of this ritual, that he realized that the uncle was a figure of fun, acting like a bedraggled buffoon. The contrast between this figure and the pride women showed in the male ornaments they were wearing in this ritual gave vital clues about the orientation and central themes in Iatmul culture.

This then became the rationale for Bateson's subsequent analysis of Itamul culture and his view of the *naven* ritual as schismogenesis (Bateson, 1958). Later, when Bateson became influenced by cybernetics, he did not refer to emotions very much. But, in the one time when he did, in his argument with Haley over power (Bateson, 1978; Dell, 1989), his position that emotions are culturally constructed (and that therefore particular emotions cannot be elevated to an explanatory principle) was much misunderstood (Krause, 1993). So, when culture went off the theoretical agenda in early family therapy, so did emotions. Since then, this aspect of communication and interaction has, with some recent exceptions (Andersen, 2007; Fredman, 2004; Pocock, 1997), been conspicuous by its absence from theoretical debates in the discipline.

In contrast emotions are at the centre of the theoretical paradigm in psychoanalysis. These are rudimentary feelings, motivations, and experiences that provide the driving force of the infant's emotional and cognitive development. Bion's main concern was how thought is applied to emotional experience at a primitive and unconscious level, and how this cannot be conceived of in isolation from a relationship (Bion, 1962). It is how the carer responds to the infant's anxiety which gives rise to the emotional tone of that relationship. Bion identifies love (L) and hate (H), as well as their negatives, as the rudimentary emotions of the paradigm, and these become transformed into elementary and abstract modes of thought through the stages of the grid (*ibid.*). Despite the rudimentary nature of these emotions, it seems that the analyst is able to access these in practice in therapeutic sessions, much like a key signature in the beginning of a piece of music (Symington & Symington, 1996). Bion suggested that the therapist should approach this "without memory and desire", not by inference, but through intuition, by becoming one with the intuition resulting from the experiencing of different emotions (Bion, 1962). Might we see this as similar to Bateson's idea that ethos will convey something of the logic or meaning of a culture or a pattern of interaction? We could perhaps speculate that this is what happened to Bateson when he was confronted with the fun and buffoonery of the maternal uncle in the *naven* ritual.

Is this what we, systemic psychotherapists, call "knowing" or "not-knowing"? Much has been made of this dichotomy in our discipline (Frosh, 1995; Larner, 1995, 2000; Pocock, 1997). If we approach our clients with a philosophical stance of not-knowing (Anderson, 1999), or a stance of uncertainty or doubt (Mason, 1993), what does it mean to know or to be certain or to be authoritative? Anderson and Goolishian (1988, 1992) did not define this stance with reference to emotions or feelings. Their emphasis was on how the therapist positions herself and how she participates, or not, in the creation of new knowledge. "Not-knowing therapists", Anderson wrote, "value being public, open and honest about their thoughts" (Anderson, 1999, p. 6). But what about their feelings? This seems to exclude those aspects and processes that lie outside awareness or are unconscious. If "not-knowing" is a process that in some way contributes to the emergence of new meanings, which in turn bring other uncertainties, then new meanings must have been outside awareness before.

So how are we to understand the therapist being able to facilitate this process? Larner draws a parallel with the process of containment (Larner, 2000). Very often it is the emotional tone of a client's response, or a shift in emotional outlook of a session against the background of a regular pattern or a "being with", which gives the therapist an indication of whether or not some sort of attunement or engagement has been made. In banishing emotions along with culture in favour of an emphasis on cognitive processes, texts, narratives, and language, we systemic psychotherapists may have been a little disingenuous to ourselves.

Bion's idea of approaching the therapeutic session without memory and desire suggests that the therapist can actively develop this ability by paying close attention to her own emotional activity (Bion, 1962). "Knowing" (K) refers to the analyst's ability of "getting to know something" rather than "having some piece of knowledge" (*ibid.*, p. 65), but the analyst must also become so conscious of her own emotional experience that she is able to abstract "from it a statement that will represent this experience adequately" (*ibid.*, p. 50). In this way, knowing implicates thinking, and, for Bion, thinking is a way of processing emotional experiences and sensations. Ability to think, therefore, has a very special place in both our emotional life and in child development. For Bion and others (e.g., Britton, 1995) early triadic relationships, such as, for example, the Oedipus triangle, provides the context for this, because in such relationships the infant or the baby has an opportunity to step out of a dyadic relationship and become an observer both to this relationship and to herself. In this model, the analyst's own early experiences, as well as her current emotional awareness of these and of herself, become both a reservoir and a screen for her work with patients.

How can we move from this to some notion of how to access meaning in cross-cultural work? By coincidence, Bateson, in a little cited publication (Bateson, 1972), and Freud, in a new translation (Freud, 2006 [1937], p. 78), both give us an intriguing clue. In his essay "Style, grace and information in primitive art", Bateson defined meaning as a synonym of pattern in such a way that an aggregate

> can be divided in any way by a "slash mark" such that an observer perceiving only what is on one side of the slash mark, can *guess*, with better than random success, what is on the other side of the slash mark. [Bateson, 1972, pp. 103–104, original italics]

And, in a new translation of "Constructions in analysis", by Bance, where Freud writes about the analyst's constructions of the meaning of the patient's talk, the German word *erraten*, which is normally translated as "interpreting", is translated as "guessing" (Freud, 2006 [1937], p. 78). Using the word "guess", although perhaps not very respectable (Wood, 2006, p. 5), highlights not a dichotomy, but some sort of tentative or even vulnerable continuity between all human persons and cultures.

With human beings we are dealing with some sort of patterning. It may be difficult to determine the nature of this pattern, but we know that it cannot be a reductionist one, because we know that whatever pattern we are talking about in psychological development or in social systems, it must leave room for individual variation which implicates language, history, tradition, and continuity without being determined by these.

Discursive and pre-discursive

I am not qualified to pursue the extensive and complicated debate in psychoanalysis regarding the content of relationships in pre-discursive modalities and the constitution of the subject. Instead, my assumptions about the subject are as follows: that the attractions and aversions experienced by human infants towards those who care for them and to whom they are attached, as generally proposed by psychoanalytic theory, and what we may nowadays call a "relational self" as a precondition for social life, as generally proposed in systemic psychotherapy, are aspects of a human condition. Other assumptions pertain to basic physiological and psychological human needs and existence such as birth, death, sex and reproduction, generations, maturation, the body, suffering, loss, hunger, thirst, etc. In this, the subject might be said to be situated between what is implicit or unconscious in the context and in him or her, and his or her own agency.

Beyond this, I assume no specific content of these relationships or of the unconscious. How needs are met and functions articulated and attended to is a matter of patterns, which are discursively constructed over time in specific historical, cultural, and contextual localities and not necessarily all within the awareness of individuals. It is this we see in the therapy room. We do not see rudimentary functions, nor do we see generic systems or relationships. We see persons, who are engaged in social and cultural patterns, constructed, developed, contested, and improvised in order to address these needs and functions. In terms of practice, I think there are two processes. First, a process that requires that we engage with what is the human condition, not one asserted by us in our own theories or in our own cultural knowledge, but one that can stand up to cross-cultural scrutiny. As I have suggested, we already have both psychoanalytic and systemic ideas about this, referring to the relational nature of the infant's first experiences with her carers and the social relationships of these carers, and the significance of this for child development and learning. Second, rather than the stances of "knowing or/and not-knowing", there are some things we can know about ourselves; as for the rest, we are guessing.

Case material

In her study of Islam in modern Pakistan, Ewing retells a story which she was told by one of her women informants (Ewing, 1997, pp. 97–110). This is a story about modernity and traditional beliefs, which equally well applies to the workings of different strands of ideologies and discourses that exist in any society.

This story concerns a middle-class, well-off family in which the children are college-educated and who consider themselves as practitioners of "true" Islam. The story was first told to Ewing by the mother in the family.

> A curse (*tauna*) was performed in the form of a goat's head being thrown on to the doorstep. The mother told her son to pick up the goat's head and throw it away, but was warned by a friendly neighbour not to let her son touch it because, if he did, this would transfer the misfortune and badness from the envious person who had thrown the goat's head to him and he would sicken and die. The mother obeyed the neighbour, but insisted to Ewing that she did not believe this and that she thought it was wrong. Ewing then heard another version of this story from one of the daughters, who told her that her brother did take the goat's head and threw it behind the house without any untoward consequences. In telling it, she poured scorn on her neighbour's superstition. To her surprise, Ewing later found this young woman preparing for a protective ritual. When asked, the young woman explained that she had had a bad dream about her father coming to harm and that she was performing this ritual in order to protect him.

It thus became clear that these views were specific to context and situation. Ewing suggests that the mother's locating herself within a different interpretation, and the inconsistency between her story and that of her daughter, covered up her reluctance to acknowledge the pain she must have felt that somebody in the community had wanted to harm her. In the same way, the younger woman's outlook was complex. She wanted to impress her progressive views on the ethnographer, but, when it came to warding off a bad dream, there were some techniques and activities in everyday life which could help her make the world a safer and more familiar place (Ewing, 1997, p. 110). The ethnographer is not in a position to take up this juxtaposition between what is said and what lies behind, but this is the therapist's task, and in this she will surely anchor herself in the human desire to "belong", "to be with" (Molino, 2004) and to ward off suffering and loss, which she recognizes from herself.

A similar theme of a human predicament emerged in my own work with a Pakistani family.

Rohina, who was twenty-three, and the eldest of six siblings, was referred with her daughter Aisha when Aisha was six. Rohina had obeyed her parents' wish to marry a relative from Pakistan in an arranged marriage when she was seventeen. She left school without GCSEs, and immediately became pregnant. On finding this out, Rohina arranged for a termination, but, on her way to the clinic, her mother persuaded her not to go through with it. Soon after Aisha's birth, Rohina's husband attacked her in a violent outburst and she separated from him and moved to live in her own flat. Rohina's parents were disappointed with the separation and the ensuing divorce. Her father stopped speaking to her, but her mother continued to help out by babysitting Aisha. Rohina found it a struggle to attend to Aisha. She could not muster any authority except through hitting and punishing Aisha, and when Aisha was two and a half she was placed on the Child Protection Register.

After some work with social services Rohina managed to stop this style of discipline, but when she and Aisha were referred to my team, Rohina was banging her own head against the wall and scratching herself as a way of containing Aisha and stopping her from doing dangerous things such as running out of the door or turning on the gas stove. I was struck by how compliant Rohina was. She participated in many parenting classes, took Aisha to all her appointments, tried to enforce bedtimes, and provided breakfast. She told me that she wanted to show the world that she could be a good mother, but little useful knowledge and experience was available to her when she found herself in an argument with Aisha. It felt to her, I think, that Aisha always got the upper hand and could get the sympathy and support from professionals, who would then mistrust and blame Rohina in the same way as her parents did. I was present at many of these arguments, and Rohina struck me as being quite desperate and relieved when I intervened.

I was also struck by the angry vehemence with which Rohina denounced arranged marriages and several other traditions that her parents and her sisters observed. This mixture of Rohina being compliant and herself "a good girl", of the whole system spiralling out of control, and of both mother and daughter needing and being grateful for some containment, gave me a feeling of contradiction, stuckness, and acting out. I myself felt protective towards both Rohina and Aisha, and angry with the social workers. Rohina's attempts to be a good daughter and a good mother and a good person seemed always to fail. In respecting her parents by having an arranged marriage, an outlook highly valued by her parents, Rohina had had the best intentions, but she had disappointed and distressed them, as well as herself. Her vehement opposition to Pakistani values now functioned, I thought, as a barrier between herself and the everyday outlooks, desires, and fears which characterized her parents and the traditions and everyday practices with which she herself had grown up.

With this impression in mind, I asked to meet with Rohina and her mother. I thought that we might be able to go back to something which could stand for "being with", or "being attached to", something more fundamental from which, rather than reducing Rohina's experience to events in the past, we might be able to open them up for the future. I had three sessions with Rohina, Mrs Begum (Rohina's mother), and an interpreter. We noted that we were four women who were all mothers and daughters, and also that the person who had the most children, and therefore was perhaps the most experienced, was Rohina's mother. With this starting point, we were able to talk about how to manage when children are naughty and when a mother is not feeling good. We were also able to talk about Rohina being distraught at not being welcome in her parents' house, and how this interfered with her feeling that she could be a good mother and a good person. After some discussion of the pros and cons of marrying a Pakistani man, Mrs Begum was able to say that she was sorry for making Rohina marry so young and that she accepted that now Rohina would choose her own husband if she wanted to marry again. This marked a turning point in the therapy and opened up more reflexivity and the prospect of fewer splits for Rohina and Aisha.

Closing remarks: culture as a process

I have argued that, paradoxically, perhaps cross-cultural work high-lights the need for a place for both universality and difference in our therapeutic models and thinking. Psychoanalysis has made contributions to the universal domain, whereas systemic psycho-therapy theory has been built around the idea of difference. Yet, universality and difference as ideas implicate each other. In both bodies of knowledge, access to meaning has not only remained the central concern, but has also been problematic as far as cross-cultural work is concerned. I have argued that the therapist may combine the two models by clarifying what, on the one hand, might be assumed to belong to the pre-discursive and, on the other, how the social-cultural context as expressed through discursive relation-ships might be accessed.

One aspect of the pre-discursive, or what I have called the human condition, is the psychoanalytic assumption regarding the anxiety of the infant, the adequacy of the carer's response, and the re-emergence of primitive states of mind throughout human life. This fits quite well with the social processes, which we know take place in the definition of identity and ethnicity (Banks, 1996; Bau-man, 1999; Jenkins, 1997), with the fundamentalist projections of "good" and "bad" in the formation and maintenance of rasicm (Dalal, 2002; Fanon, 1952; Khanna, 2003), and with the idea that culture is prejudicial (Krause, 2002). Cultural conventions and meanings enter the infant's experiences from the first interaction with carers, providing a process for the negotiation of conflict, anxi-ety, communication, and dilemmas. This process might sometimes be reflective and sometimes not, but always it is a kind of work that weaves between discursive and pre-discursive domains.

I do not think that we can avoid a double approach. We need to recognize emotions as an aspect of the human condition in our theoretical model. We cannot banish them, and we also need to acknowledge that they are in part culturally constructed. As Bateson observed, if we fail to arrive at "a preliminary sketch [of an ethos or emotional outlook] our attribution of emotional value to behaviour can only be guided by general and probably fallacious assumptions about human nature" (Bateson, 1958, p. 268). Cross-cultural psychotherapy, it seems to me, must continuously move between these two levels.

References

Andersen, T. (2007). Crossroads. Tom Andersen in conversation with Per Jensen. In: H. Anderson & P. Jensen (Eds.), *Innovations in the Reflecting Process* (pp. 158–174). London: Karnac.

Anderson, H. (1999). Reimagining family therapy: reflections on Minuchin's invisible family. *Journal of Marital and Family Therapy, 25*: 1–8.

Anderson, H., & Goolishian, H. A. (1988). Human systems as linguistic systems: preliminary and evolving ideas about the implications for clinical theory. *Family Process, 27*(4): 371–393.

Anderson, H., & Goolishian, H. A. (1992). The client is the expert: a not-knowing approach to therapy. In: S. McNamee & K. Gergen (Eds.), *Therapy as Social Construction* (pp. 25–39). London: Sage.

Banks, M. (1996). *Ethnicity: Anthropological Constructions.* New York: Routledge.

Bateson, G. (1958). *Naven.* London: Wildwood House.

Bateson, G. (1972). *Steps to an Ecology of Mind. Collected Essays in Anthropology, Psychiatry, Evolution and Epistemology.* London: Jason Aronson.

Bateson, G. (1978). Comments to John Weakland. In: M. M. Berger (Ed.), *Beyond the Double Bind* (pp. 81–82). New York: Brunner-Mazel.

Bauman, G. (1999). *The Multicultural Riddle. Rethinking National, Ethnic and Religious Identities.* New York: Routledge.

Bion, W. (1962). *Learning from Experience.* London: Karnac.

Bourdieu, P. (1977). *Outline of a Theory of Practice.* Cambridge: Cambridge University Press.

Britton, R. (1995). The missing link in the Oedipus complex. In: R. Britton, M. Feldman, & E. O'Shaughnessy (Eds.), *The Oedipus Complex Today. Clinical Implications* (pp. 83–102). London: Karnac.

Cohen, P. (2002). Psychoanalysis and racism: reading the other scene. In: D. Y. Goldberg & J. Solomos (Eds.), *A Companion to Racial and Ethnic Studies* (pp. 170–201). Oxford: Blackwell.

Dalal, F. (2002). *Race, Colour and the Processes of Racialization. New Perspectives from Group Analysis, Psychoanalysis and Sociology.* Hove: Brunner-Routledge.

Dell, P. F. (1989). Violence and the systemic view: the problem of power. *Family Process, 28*: 1–14.

Epston, D., & White, M. (1992). *Experience, Contradiction, Narrative & Imagination: Selected Papers.* Adelaide: Dulwich Centre Publications.

Ewing, K. P. (1997). *Arguing Sainthood: Modernity, Psychoanalysis and Islam*. London: Duke University Press.

Fanon, F. (1952). *Black Skin, White Masks*. London: Pluto Press, 1986.

Flaskas, C. (2002). *Family Therapy Beyond Modernism. Practice Challenges Theory*. Hove: Brunner-Routledge.

Fredman, G. (2004). *Transforming Emotions: Conversations in Counselling and Psychotherapy*. London: Whurr.

Freud, S. (2006) [1937]. *The Penguin Reader*. A. Phillips (Ed.) London: Penguin.

Frosh, S. (1995). Postmodernism versus psychotherapy. *Journal of Family Therapy, 17*: 175–190.

Hacking, I. (1999). *The Social Construction of What?* Cambridge, MA: Harvard University Press.

Harries-Jones, P. (1995). *A Recursive Vision. Ecological Understanding and Gregory Bateson*. Toronto: University of Toronto Press.

Hobson, P. (2002). *The Cradle of Thought*. London: Macmillan.

Hoffman, L. (1990). Constructing realities: an art of lenses. *Family Process, 29*: 1–12.

Hoffman, L. (1993). *Exchanging Voices: A Collaborative Approach to Family Therapy*. London: Karnac.

Jenkins, R. (1997). *Rethinking Ethnicity: Arguments and Explorations*. London: Routledge.

Khanna, R. (2003). *Dark Continents. Psychoanalysis and Colonialism*. London: Duke University Press.

Klein, M. (1945). The Oedipus complex in the light of early anxieties. *International Journal of Psychoanalysis, 26*: 11–33.

Klein, M. (1946). Notes on some schizoid mechanisms. *International Jorunal of Psychoanalysis, 27*: 99–110.

Krause, I.-B. (1993). Anthropology and family therapy: a case for emotions. *Journal of Family Therapy, 15*: 35–56.

Krause, I.-B. (1998). *Therapy Across Culture*. London: Sage.

Krause, I.-B. (2002). *Culture and System in Family Therapy*. London: Karnac.

Krause, I.-B. (2006). Hidden points of view in cross-cultural psychotherapy and ethnography. *Transcultural Psychiatry, 43*(2): 181–204.

Lannamann, J. W. (1998). Social constructionism and materiality: the limits of indeterminancy in therapeutic settings. *Family Process, 37*: 393–419.

Larner, G. (1995). The real as illusion: deconstructing power in family therapy. *Journal of Family Therapy, 17*: 191–218.

Larner, G. (2000). Towards a common ground in psychoanalysis and family therapy: on knowing not to know. *Journal of Family Therapy*, 22: 61–82.

Malik, R., & Krause, I.-B. (2005). Before and beyond words: embodiment and intercultural therapeutic relationships in family therapy. In: C. Flaskas, B. Mason, & A. Perlesz (Eds.), *The Space Between. Experience, Context and Process in the Therapeutic Relationship* (pp. 95–110). London: Karnac.

Mason, B. (1993). Towards positions of safe uncertainty. *Human Systems: The Journal of Systemic Consultation and Management* (Special Issue), 4(3–4): 189–200.

Molino, A. (2004). Rethinking relations between psychoanalysis and anthropology. In: A. Molino (Ed.), *Culture, Subject, Psyche. Dialogues in Psychoanalysis and Anthropology* (pp. 20–42). London: Whurr.

Papadopoulos, R., & Byng-Hall, J. (1997). *Multiple Voices. Narrative in Systemic Family Psychotherapy*. London: Karnac.

Pocock, D. (1997). Feeling understood in family therapy. *Journal of Family Therapy*, 19: 283–302.

Seikkula, J. (1993). The aim of the work is to create dialogue: Bakhtin and Vygotsky in family session. *Human Systems: The Journal of Systemic Consultation and Management*, 4: 33–48.

Seikkula, J., & Olson, M. (2003). Open dialogue approach to acute psychosis. *Family Process*, 42: 403–418.

Selvini Palazzoli, M., Boscolo, L., Cecchin, G., & Prata, G. (1978). Family rituals. A powerful tool in family therapy. *Family Process*, 16: 445–454.

Symington, J., & Symington, N. (1996). *The Clinical Thinking of Wilfred Bion*. London: Brunner-Routledge.

White, M., & Epston, D. (1990). *Narrative Means to Therapeutic Ends*. New York: Norton.

Wood, M. (2006). There is no cure. Review of A. Phillips (Ed.), *The New Freud Reader*. *London Review of Books*, July 6th: 3–7.

CHAPTER ELEVEN

What does the other want?

Stephen Frosh

> "O let them be left, wildness and wet;
> Long live the weeds and the wilderness yet"
>
> (Gerard Manley Hopkins, 1970, "Inversnaid")

After a rocky start, which resulted in accusations (particularly from feminists) of normative politics and blindness to social inequality, systems theory has developed an honourable and now long tradition of engaging with oppression—gender, sexual, race, and class—and advocating democratic and emancipatory practices within therapy (e.g., Burck & Daniel, 1995; Mason & Sawyerr, 2002; McGoldrick, 1998). The shift from first order to second order cybernetics was crucial here, as it forced systemic therapists to consider their practices in a reflexive mode, a move that has resonance with the "relational " move in psychoanalysis that has also struck a chord amongst feminists (Benjamin, 1998). Given the very large number of women working psychotherapeutically with children and families, it was perhaps predictable as well as necessary that systems therapy would have to deal with feminist concerns. Yet, subsequent extensions of the political critique to engage with "race " and culture have provoked a very extensive and impressive attempt to come to terms with what is experienced as an even more challenging block in the therapeutic way of thinking. That is, female systemic therapists spoke from *within* their immediate experience when confronting sexism, and with the intellectual and political backing of a very powerful movement. In addressing issues of racialized oppression and conflict, family systems theorists and therapists—overwhelmingly white and western—have had to think through what it might mean to be confronted with "otherness", including how they are incorporated into it and also how they might face the limits of understanding and of the appropriateness of their methods. In this context, the efforts of several senior and influential members of the systemic community to address cultural and "race " concerns have been exemplary (Mason & Sawyerr, 2002; McGoldrick, Giordano, & Pearce, 1996), and some powerful attempts have been made to institute actively anti-racist procedures in family work (for example, by the "Just Therapy" group [Waldegrave, Tamasese, Tuhaka, & Campbell, 2003]).

This work has been very significant in shifting the perceptions of psychotherapists concerning "race" and culture issues, but there are ways in which it can also be seen as reflecting not just the strength, but also the weakness, of systemic thinking. On the positive side, encounters with "otherness" are supported by a fundamental premise of systemic theory: that the relational has precedence over everything else and that it is only through understanding relationships systemically that one can fully grasp psychosocial phenomena. Once one focuses on the relational in this intense way, it is pretty much a given that one will come face to face with what it means to be in relationship with others of all kinds, and have to theorize the impact that this has. The "metatheoretical" stance of systemic theory frees it from too many assumptions about individuals and instead directs it to concerns over types of relationships and their effects, including relationships in which one person does not easily understand another. This gives systemic approaches great leverage, especially when the injunctions towards reflexivity are properly observed, since, in every single encounter, one can ask the question of what impact the observer or therapist is having on the system as a starting point for exploring the new "system plus outsider" conjunction.

However, the ability to use systemic thinking to help compre-hend any possible system produces its own limit feature. The "link-ing" approach makes it possible to construe all encounters between human subjects as relationships, and hence as available to negotia-tion and amelioration; yet one possibility is that this underestimates the degree of "alienness" that otherness entails. This alienness might not be just a *problem* to be treated and overcome; instead, as some contemporary philosophy and psychoanalysis suggests, it might be a central and precious feature of the "other" that otherness cannot be colonized as "same", can never, that is, be regulated or fully understood. Systemic theory has many advantages over the individualism of much western psychology, including traditional psychoanalysis, and its flirtation with postmodernism (whatever its other drawbacks) has ensured it shows awareness of the "multiple positions" from which all social and relational phenomena can be perceived or articulated; but it maintains the tradition of western philosophy that everything that exists can be known, and that in such knowledge lies the key to power. Relational, systemic thinking makes sense of the other in much the same way as all rationalist approaches do: it works with the belief that even if alternative modes of experience are not reconcilable, they are at least overlap-ping: they are, that is, commensurable with one another, translatable into the terms of the relational, even if that is a difficult thing to do. My suggestion here is that this might not be the most productive way to think of the other; that otherness might be something we are compelled to stand in awe of, not to make comprehensible, and that this might constitute its challenge and also its humanizing core.

Recognizing others

The stance that otherness is something to be bridged is by no means unique to systemic thinking, and, of course, it has many positive consequences. In contemporary psychoanalysis, it is reflected in a relational position which takes the self–other link as constitutive of human subjectivity; from this position, relationality does not need to be explained, but is rather the starting point out of which all analysis flows. Jessica Benjamin's take on "intersubjectivity", which is rooted in feminist scholarship and critical theory and hence

orientated towards emancipatory practice, is an especially significant variant of this general approach. For Benjamin, the intersubjective stance is a specific move within the general domain of
relational theorizing, one that holds on to a position in which the
other is related *to* but is not appropriated: that is, it is a stance that
acknowledges the appeal of omnipotence (in knowing the other
we come to colonize her/him) but works against it. The manner in
which omnipotence is contested is through a process that Benjamin
calls "recognition", which denotes a stance towards the other that
acknowledges her or him as a source of subjectivity, giving rise
(in an echo of the Buberian "I–thou") to what Benjamin (1998) calls
a "subject–subject" psychology. This means that recognition is built
out of an understanding of the other's continuing otherness, maintaining the subjecthood of both participants in the exchange, who
are thus both autonomous and yet also exist in relation to one
another: "in the intersubjective conception of recognition, two
active subjects may exchange, may alternate in expressing and
receiving, cocreating a mutuality that allows for and presumes
separateness" (*ibid.*, p. 29).

(Parenthetically, the term "cocreating" is a familiar one from systemic work and indicates the shared assumption with relational
psychoanalysis that subjects actively engage with one another in
"world building".)

What is being traced here is a particular form of relationship
between selves and others, a certain handling of the trope similar-
ity/difference, in which neither is collapsed into the other. Indeed,
Benjamin's approach specifically seeks a balance between theories
that emphasize difference and those that promote a vision of subjectivity as involving disappearance in or of the other, either through
self-effacement (as in many theories of mothering), or through
instrumental use of the other (the main thrust of rationality). Recognition staves off the absorption of self into the other, just as it
prevents the other being colonized by the self; rather, the possibility is raised of allowing difference, yet also appreciating similarity.
Benjamin herself makes explicit the distinction between omnipotence and recognition:

> The tension between recognizing the other and wanting the self
> to be absolute (omnipotence) is, to my mind, an internal conflict

inherent in the psyche; it exists independent of any given inter-action—even in the most favourable conditions. It is not interper-sonally generated but is, rather, a psychic structure that conditions the interpersonal. The problem of whether or not we are able to recognize the other person as outside, not the sum of, our projec-tions or the mere object of need, and still feel recognized by her or him, is defining for intersubjectivity. [Benjamin, 2000, p. 294]

Recognition of this kind is not a merely cognitive event, nor is it a passive reflection or mirroring of what is already somehow "in" the other. It is, rather, something actively reaching out that makes what it finds, yet also lets the other be; it is, in this sense, a process of *sanctification*, in which what is found in the other is also cherished specifically for its capacity to be different, and its otherness.

Building on the rather contrary work of both Winnicott (to whom Benjamin [2000] states herself to be deeply indebted) and of Lacan (to whom she is mainly opposed), the argument can be restated as a privileging of the role of respect for the other *as other*, with whom one has connections, but whose inner space cannot be colonized. This is a surprisingly difficult aspiration to realize, even in theory. In many psychoanalytic accounts, for example, the high-est point of an intimate relationship is a process of identification, or even incorporation, rather than recognition of the otherness of the other; and, more generally, there is a small space between the liberal urge to understand the other and the wish to remove the other's otherness, as can be seen in recent debates about the limits of "multiculturalism". Clearly, just seeing the other as different is not the solution: that can be a defence against recognizing relatedness where it exists, of noting and experiencing the similarity of human experience. There is plenty of circumstantial evidence, indeed, that this kind of "othering" can be a source of social hatred, especially when "different" is cast as "alien": for example, in ethnic and racist hate (Frosh, 2002). Rather, the idea of recognition embraces the acknowledgement of existence of the other as other in the context of relatedness: there is a real difference, yet this difference is not necessarily marked by preference, it is "just" difference. There is an other who or which cannot be made "same", but that does not mean that there is a lack of connection, only that this connection is for the sake of bridging, not for invasion or incorporation. The Benjaminite idea, read this way, suggests that becoming "real" is premised on the situation in which one's otherness is noted and acknowledged, and valued for what it is.

In her analysis of the implications of Benjamin's theory for mothering, Baraitser (2008) describes how Benjamin's account draws on Winnicott's (1969) ideas about a developmental phase that comes after object relating and involves "object use", which is made possible through seeing that the (paradigmatically, maternal) object survives unconscious destruction. Attacks on this object—in fantasy, *destruction* of it—support the infant's perception of the existence of an external other so long as the mother survives and is non-retaliatory in her response. That is, what the infant is supposed to discover is that the mother is not subject to the infant's "internal" experience of having destroyed her, and hence is an object with more than merely imaginary existence. Baraitser (2008, p. 94) comments,

> In Benjamin's view there is an ongoing and endless cycle of the establishment of mutual recognition followed by its negation, constituting a never ending tension between complementarity and mutuality, between relating to the other as object or like subject.

("Complementarity", here, is not being used in the systemic sense, to mean ways of reducing positive feedback, but rather to denote the reassuring but potentially sterile polarities that constitute the subject–object state of mind, with masculinity *vs.* femininity being the most obvious example.) Further,

> In Benjamin's work, we are not fundamentally constituted through loss, but through processes of separation that are tempered by the pleasures of mutual recognition and the possibilities of shared understanding made possible through surviving destruction. And if we follow this through, difference can then be experienced as something that can be identified with, not just repudiated, negated or controlled. The infant can enjoy the fact that the mother has a life of her own to get on with, as it means that she is like me, with desires of her own. [Baraitser, 2006]

The idea of "enjoyment" here is an important one, as it conveys the sense of erotic charge existing when the subject confronts the other in its *difference* from the self. Indeed, the threat of the other, which produces the impulse towards omnipotence in the subject, always has erotic components, something reflected in much of the discourse of racism as well as in the attractions of the "exotic" (Frosh, 2006). Baraitser's use of the term "enjoy" here, though, has a less sexual connotation and points to the domination of the relational stance (including Winnicott's sometimes annoyingly sexually-anodyne theorizing) by concepts such as "holding" and "containing"; it seems to mean something more akin to "feeling secure and satisfied" than to feeling excited. At its extremes, it sometimes seems as if the humanistic component of this work trumps its analytic rigour; even the notion of "destruction" lacks the passion of, for example, the Kleinian concept of envy, with its connotations of greed and murderous violence.

The bridging-across-differences element in Benjamin's work reflects both the strengths and, perhaps, the dangers of this stance, and can be seen too in her more recent and highly productive concern with "thirdness" (2004). This is a concept that has a considerable history in psychoanalysis and, in the guise of Oedipal thinking, has been the main element in its approach to social theory, from Freud (1930a) onwards (see Frosh, 1999). While acknowledging the utility of Oedipal scenarios for understanding aspects of development, however, Benjamin (in line with other relational theorists, such as Guntrip, 1973) has long been critical of the Oedipal framework as the overriding element in analytic theory, seeing it as fixing a bipolarity (father *vs.* mother; reality *vs.* narcissism) that is not only misogynist in its assumptions, but also misses the true "overdeterminism" of psychic life. Benjamin's approach to this is to question the final authority of the Oedipus complex, which she sees as too easily accepting traditional bipolarizing notions such as that the father is the primary symbol of reality and maturity, while the mother's pull is always to fantasy and narcissism. As she notes in her major work on domination, *The Bonds of Love* (1988), versions of the Oedipus complex which draw on this "Oedipus *vs.* Narcissus" mentality in which the father "liberates" the child from the regressive pull of dependency and incest, produce misogynistic and lifeless accounts of the possible arrangements of masculinity and femininity, based firmly around idealization and denigration:

> Paradoxically, the image of the liberating father undermines the acceptance of difference that the Oedipus complex is meant to

embody. For the idea of the father as protection against "limitless narcissism" at once authorises his idealisation and the mother's denigration . . . Difference turns out to be governed by the code of domination. [*ibid.*, p. 135]

What has to be achieved is a capacity to sustain identification with "sameness in difference", a capacity to recognize the other yet also appreciate the other's subjectivity and "authorship". Benjamin implies that this is to be achieved neither by a regression to the pre-Oedipal mother, rather characteristic of object relations theory and involving a denial of the sexualized nature of gender differentiation, nor by the traditional Freudian or Lacanian adherence to the structuring power of the Oedipal situation, with its focus on lack and denial:

In linking identificatory love to the rapprochement [i.e. pre-Oedipal] father, I was emphasizing that the father figure is used not merely to beat back the mother, to defensively idealize someone other than mother, but also to extend love to a second . . . I also emphasized that the boy does not need to forgo identification with mother so early, unless difficulties in separation lead to an early defensive repudiation. [Benjamin, 1998, pp. 61–62]

On the basis of this "over-inclusive" pattern of identifications, in which the child incorporates gendered aspects of all her or his loved objects into the self, it is possible to see the entry into the Oedipal order as one in which greater differentiation is made, but not necessarily (depending on the quality of actual object relationships) at the expense of the valuing of difference. Here, Benjamin distinguishes between the traditional kind of Oedipal complementarity, in which the other is repudiated so that the self can be sustained, and a more mature, post-Oedipal complementarity which brings back together the various "elements of identification, so that they become less threatening, less diametrically opposite, no longer cancelling out one's identity" (*ibid.*, pp. 69–70). It is only through the achievement of this kind of integrative complementarity that the idealization–denigration split so characteristic of Oedipal thinking can be overcome, hence making it possible for gender to become an arena of encounter between necessarily fragmentary subjects, relating to one another as agents rather than as threats. Multiple identifications forge the basis for gender identities which themselves are multiple and fluid, less defensive, and hence less caricatured and stereotyped. *Connectedness* is emphasized here, recognizing difference but not discounting the other because of it.

In developing the idea of the "third" away from Oedipal structures, Benjamin formalizes her interest in connectedness and relationality through postulating a "space" in which contact occurs. This space is a dynamic space, "a principle, relationship or function which is constantly collapsing and needing to be repaired" (Baraitser, 2006). It has two elements (Benjamin, 2004): the "third in the one", which is the capacity (paradigmatically of the mother or the analyst) for a subject to hold in mind what subject and other can create together, a kind of reparative capacity to believe that it is possible to comprehend the other even when the other is destructive and alien; and the "one in the third", a pattern of being that links subject and other and produces something new, a space (for example the projected space of the analytic encounter) for meeting, reflection, and newness, owned by neither party but an aspect of them both. For Benjamin, this links further with the idea of the therapist being actively present in the therapeutic encounter, ready, for example, to acknowledge errors, and hence very much engaged in the process of negotiating the relational dynamics of the session. Thus, Benjamin (2004) rejects the Kleinian tendency to speak from the countertransference but not to become relationally involved with it, to insist "that the patient is ultimately helped only by understanding rather than by being understood" (*ibid.*, p. 35). For Benjamin, it is necessary for the analyst who is "caught in enactment" (*ibid.*) to acknowledge it in relation to the patient, a stance or position that Benjamin refers to as the "moral third". It is this that differentiates the relational from the Kleinian perspective and also provides a further link with the characteristically active and open stance of systemic therapists: Benjamin (*ibid.*, p. 33) comments, "The analyst says, in effect, 'I'll go first'. In orienting to the moral third of responsibility, the analyst is also demonstrating the route out of helplessness".

"I'll go first", or "After you"?

Benjamin's emphasis on responsibility has direct implications for working with others, and, indeed, has been used by her as a way into reconciliation work in Israel–Palestine (Altman, Benjamin, Jacobs, & Wachtel, 2006). Political involvement in this specific instance is coded as the need for engagement with Palestinian suffering from the perspective of acknowledging responsibility as a Jew, and Benjamin links this with the analyst's realization that, while she or he might be the "activator of old traumas, old pain" rather than their instigator,

> you acknowledge that you have, you know, bumped into the person's bruise, and you acknowledge that there is hurt and pain and that you may have responsibility for that, and in doing this, you alleviate a whole level of tension that makes it possible, then, to talk about, to explore. [*ibid.*, p. 170].

In both the political and the therapeutic context, recognition and responsibility go hand in hand, with each entailing the other. Taking responsibility for the other arises from recognition of their existence as a genuine centre of subjectivity, not just possessing rights but also having the capacity to be hurt. The analyst "bruises" the patient merely by being there, though her or his infelicities might make this bruising greater (hence, in the tradition of object relations theorists, Benjamin advocates acknowledging mistakes rather than simply interpreting their effects). "Bumping into the person's bruise" is bound to occur; it is a necessary part of therapy because, if one is to look truthfully at what exists, then pain is bound to be felt. But this does not mean it can all be put back onto the other; the subject/analyst has responsibility, even if the damage is unavoidable.

Despite the analytic "I'll go first", Benjamin is cautious about always making the other's needs primary, always taking responsibility in this way, because she wants to warn against a kind of self-abasement in which the subject gives up her or his agency and, indeed, her or his rights. That is, taking responsibility is not the same thing as always giving way; and indeed the analytic situation (characterized by "analytic abstinence") is precisely one in which not giving way (paradigmatically, at the molar level by becoming involved in the patient's life, or at the molecular level by allowing even small shifts in the time boundaries of the session) is seen as crucial both for the containment of a patient's anxiety and for the exploration of deep trauma. The analyst does not say, "Tell me what you want and I will meet your need". A kind of robustness is required, again to match Winnicott's idea that the existence of the other is realized through her or his capacity to survive the subject's destructive attacks. The analyst has to hold firm not only to maintain her or his sanity, but in order to become "real" for the patient; this must be tempered with acknowledgement of errors and readiness to participate in the intersubjective exchange, but not at the price of obliterating one's own subjectivity.

There is an important comparison here with Levinas's approach to "ethics as first philosophy", which is one of the most influential areas of work in which the "face-to-face" encounter has become central to comprehension of human subjectivity. The intensity of his argument for the prior recognition of the other as the foundation of ethics is immense and extraordinarily demanding, taking, if one can think of it this way, the notion of *hospitality* to an extreme. However, in many therapeutic encounters we are dealing with extreme situations, extreme states of mind and extreme politics. In that context, there is something to be said for starkly presenting the impossible ideal, that towards which we have continually to gesture.

> In my analysis . . . the relation to the Face is the relation to the absolutely weak . . . and there is, consequently, in the Face of the Other always the death of the Other and thus, in some way, an incitement to murder, the temptation to go to the extreme, to completely neglect the other—and at the same time (and this is the paradoxical thing) the Face is also the "Thou Shalt not Kill". A Thou-Shalt-not-Kill that can also be explicated much further: it is the fact that I cannot let the other die alone, it is like a calling out to me . . . at the outset I hardly care what the other is with respect to me, that is his own business; for me, he is above all the one I am responsible for. [Levinas, 1991, pp. 104–105]

This Levinasian primacy of the other has given rise to a great deal of philosophical debate, and it is not clear that all its implications stand up to scrutiny. However, there is something powerful here: nothing contingent is assumed in relation to how the other will treat the self, there is no expectation of there being any pay-off from "love of one's neighbour", no Buberian or Benjaminite reciprocity. Being responsible for the other does not mean that something positive will come back to the subject; it exists simply as an ethical imperative, as that which makes one human.

Indeed, Levinas makes it clear that this relationship of responsibility—this ethical relation—is, in his view, *primary*, rather than following on from something pre-existent. It is not the case that the human subject exists and then engages in ethical relations; rather, ethics is the defining feature of subjectivity itself.

> I understand responsibility as responsibility for the Other, thus as responsibility for what is not my deed, or for what does not even matter to me; or which precisely does matter to me, is met by me as face. [Levinas, 1985, p. 95]

Levinas insists that responsibility for the other comes before the subject can even know what the other is; it is, consequently, an absolute given, and the recognition which is part of it is as non-contingent as can be. Indeed, the term "recognition" is inappropriate within the Levinasian domain, because of its implication that somehow, through the act of recognition, the other becomes known. Realizing that one "does not know and has never seen" the other, yet that the other exists, is not the same as recognition in the conventional sense. Rather, it is an absolute refusal of the impulse to believe that the other can ever be brought within the realm of the self. Even more so, Levinas states, "at the outset I hardly care what the other is with respect to me"; knowledge of what the other might be, what use or reciprocity might derive from it, is irrelevant; the other is not any *specific* "person", but that which is outside what can be claimed by the self. Knowing the other would be part of the colonizing act of reducing it to the same; in the Levinasian scheme, the otherness of the other is always maintained.

Levinas's ontology here is distinct from Benjamin's in a number of ways that have a bearing on the opening issue of this paper, the limitations of an account that assumes the bridgeability of difference. Benjamin, in fact, is not making an ontological claim. In focusing on the "third", she is extending her analysis of complementarity in intersubjective relations into an attempt to think about how recognition and reconciliation go together. The point about the third is that it offers a space in which intersubjective recognition can take place; in demonstrating a capacity to think beyond the dyad, the subject creates a third space in which the other can also move. What family systems theorists conventionally call "going symmetrical", in which the stakes between warring parties get escalated (positive feedback) rather than reduced, can be understood as a failure to take up the prospect of a third, a space for meeting: not for compromise, but for encounter. If the analyst abjures the responsibility to move "first" into this third, then the analyst's fear of losing the safety of complementarity is blocking the possibility of an encounter of this kind. This is best thought of as a mode of "practical ethics" in which the route to taking responsibility is to move both participants in the intersubjective exchange into a new domain, making thought and mutual recognition possible.

For Levinas, there is no intersubjective meeting; there is, rather, the construction of the subject *as an ethical subject* through responsibility for the other, whatever that might be constituted by, whatever strangeness it might imply. In Levinas, this is an assertion of the irrevocable otherness of the other as something that stands over and above us and is best coded as the infinite. In relation to other subjects, this means seeing the infinite in the face of the other, in all its inapproachability; acknowledgement of this primary mode of being, this "You go first", links us with the infinite and, irrespective of desire, understanding, or contact, makes us human.

Perhaps Lingis (1994) expresses a variant of this idea most compellingly in his appositely entitled book, *The Community of Those Who Have Nothing in Common*. Writing about the experience of being in the presence of someone who is dying, he shows how some kinds of communion rest not on the belief that it is possible to exchange "meaning" through the transmission of messages in which each is the recipient of the other's sense, but rather on an acknowledgement that we are all rooted in something elemental. This kind of encounter constitutes the subject not through a mode of reaching agreement, but of drawing on the other's existence in all its alien form, so that one has marked out the vista of a world that is not the same as one's own.

> We do not relate to the light, the earth, the air, and the warmth only with our individual sensibility and sensuality. We communicate to one another the light our eyes know, the ground that sustains our postures, and the air and the warmth with which we speak. We face one another as condensations of earth, light, air, and warmth, and orient one another in the elemental in a primary communication. We appeal to the others to help us be at home in the alien elements

into which we stray: in the drifting and nameless light and warmth of infancy, in the nocturnal depths of the erotic, and in the domain of dying where rational discourse has no longer anything to say. [*ibid.*, p. 122]

The appeal of the other here is less harsh than as represented in Levinas, but it is just as unbridgeable. We are linked in the elemental, not through some mediated communication, but as a response to an appeal. The "third" is transformed into the light of each other's face, its recognition of the mutual being and enlivening power of subjects who are nevertheless not just distinct, but alien from one another. We have here, in its austerity, a different model from one that assumes the potential linkage of subjects through shared perspectives, drawing together of narratives or meta-level transformation of points of view. We have here, that is, an invocation of otherness as what we need to maintain, the "weeds and the wilderness" always about to be destroyed

What does the other want?

Stretching out the ideas developed in this chapter so that they meet the systemic focus on the relational as primary, the suggestion is that the impulse to link, to see everyone as potentially in a comprehensible relationship to everyone else, might seem obviously "therapeutic" and humanitarian. The risks, though, lie in missing the specificity of an other that is irreducible to the same, and gathers its force from this very irreducibility, this enigmatic, slippery sense of the existence of something else which the subject cannot understand, yet has to take into account. Where systemic thinking focuses on connection, and relational psychoanalysis also seeks out a space in which such connections can be made, the "ethical turn" in philosophy focuses on the task of how to live face to face with an other with whom one has no possible connection, in a community of those "who have nothing in common". This task is urgent, both socially and interpersonally; it also demands recognition of the incommensurability of different forms of human experience.

Perhaps the way to think about this is to consider the other as always posing a *question* to the subject; hence, the troubling sense of oppression and disturbance when faced with the other is a way of articulating a question of one's own in response to the one being offered: "what does the other want?" (This is itself a variant of Freud's famous question about the woman, experienced as the site of otherness for him.) The other, in this formation, presents each subject—wherever they are located culturally, sexually, ethnically or socially—with what can be construed as a classic psychoanalytic and systemic challenge: to remain open to the other's question, their way of being, with all the threat and excitement that it may offer to the self, and without closing it down in a defensive attempt to *manage* difference. We do all have something in common: the pun in "The community of those who have *nothing* in common" is that the thing we have in common is *nothing*: the disappearance into death, the need to face various kinds of abyss, "the alien elements into which we stray" (Lingis, 1994, p. 122). Because we have this nothing in common, we reach out to one another in the elemental, seeking signs of recognition and care, of "community". But we also have *nothing in common*; we look out at each other uncertain of what we are seeing, able only to gain access to the other through various mediations, all of them events (linguistic, symbolic, physical) involving potential and actual misrecognition. Building a community out of this (a deeply paradoxical task) requires not just a "respect" for difference in the multicultural sense, out of which we can learn about the other sufficiently to make her or him seem "same"; it requires a continuing, rigorous self-scrutiny to avoid assuming that we have knowledge of the other, that any one of us can feel as the other feels, know what they might know.

Systemic and relational psychoanalytic theories and therapies seem to have been on similar paths, trying to work respectfully with difference in order to bridge it without colonization, and alighting on various related conceptualizations of thirdness in order to enable them to do so. The gains in doing this have been very significant: for systemic therapists, an increasingly sophisticated appreciation of gendered and cultural contexts for their work; for (some) psychoanalysts, a growing appreciation of the way the analyst contributes actively to the construction of an encounter with an other who is not reducible to a context-independent internal world. Both approaches consequently have adopted a more democratic and open stance, and perhaps a more humble one, too. The argument here is not that these gains should be ditched in favour of a kind of awe-struck appreciation of the impossibility of ever knowing anyone fully. Instead, in a spirit of never-ending criticism, the obverse of the relational attitude is being emphasized: the other should always be a surprise, a question, an uncertainty, and a challenge; something renewed each time we come across the "nothing" that unites and divides us; something that survives our attempts to destroy it through too thorough, seeming understanding; something resilient and thing-like in itself. Maintaining this attitude is a considerable task, as it goes against what one might think of as a defensive need to feel safe in the presence of the other, to ward off an experience of what, echoing Freud (1919h) evokes the "uncanny" as known and strange at one and the same time. The tendency is to grasp after knowing, but, as both systemic and psychoanalytic psychotherapists have long argued, resisting this tendency is an important component of any non-instructive therapeutic approach. Standing back from too desperately trying to comprehend the other is part of this necessary, resistive enterprise.

References

Altman, N., Benjamin, J., Jacobs, T., & Wachtel, P. (2006). Is politics the last taboo in psychoanalysis? In: L. Layton, N. Hollander, & S. Gutwill (Eds.), *Psychoanalysis, Class and Politics* (pp. 166–194). London: Routledge.

Baraitser, L. (2006). Introduction to seminar with Jessica Benjamin. Centre for Psychosocial Studies, Birkbeck College.

Baraitser, L. (2008). Mum's the word: intersubjectivity, alterity and the maternal subject. *Studies in Gender and Sexuality, 9*: 86–110.

Benjamin, J. (1988). *The Bonds of Love.* London: Virago.

Benjamin, J. (1998). *Shadow of the Other: Intersubjectivity and Gender in Psychoanalysis.* New York: Routledge.

Benjamin, J. (2000). Response to commentaries by Mitchell and by Butler. *Studies in Gender and Sexuality, 1*: 291–308.

Benjamin, J. (2004). Beyond doer and done to: an intersubjective view of thirdness. *Psychoanalytic Quarterly, 73*: 5–46.

Burck, C., & Daniel, G. (1995). *Gender and Family Therapy.* London: Routledge.

Freud, S. (1919h). The uncanny. *S.E., 17*: 217–256. London: Hogarth.

Freud, S. (1930a). *Civilization and its Discontents. S.E.,* 21: 57–145. London: Hogarth.

Frosh, S. (1999). *The Politics of Psychoanalysis.* London: Palgrave.

Frosh, S. (2002). The Other. *American Imago, 59*: 389–407.

Frosh, S. (2006). *For and Against Psychoanalysis.* London: Routledge.

Guntrip, H. (1973). *Psychoanalytic Theory, Therapy and the Self.* New York: Basic Books.

Hopkins, G. M. (1970). *The Poems of Gerard Manley Hopkins.* W. H. Gardner & N. H. Mackenzie (Eds.). Oxford: Oxford University Press.

Levinas, E. (1985). *Ethics and Infinity.* Pittsburgh, PA: Duquesne University Press.

Levinas, E. (1991). *Entre Nous: On Thinking of the Other.* London: Athlone, 1998.

Lingis, A. (1994). *The Community of Those Who Have Nothing in Common.* Indianapolis, IN: Indiana University Press.

Mason, B., & Sawyerr, A. (Eds.) (2002). *Exploring the Unsaid: Creativity, Risks and Dilemmas in Working Cross-Culturally.* London: Karnac.

McGoldrick, M. (Ed.) (1998). *Revisioning Family Therapy: Race, Culture and Gender in Clinical Practice.* New York: Guilford.

McGoldrick, M., Giordano, J., & Pearce, J. (Eds.) (1996). *Ethnicity and Family Therapy.* New York: Guilford.

Waldegrave, C., Tamasese, K., Tuhaka, F., & Campbell, W. (2003). *Just Therapy: A Journey.* Adelaide: Dulwich Centre.

Winnicott, D. W. (1969). The use of an Object. *International Journal of Psychoanalysis, 50*: 711–716.

Intersecting Levinas and Bion: the ethical container in psychoanalysis and family therapy

Glenn Larner

I n a previous publication, I defined a common ground between psychoanalysis and family therapy as constructing a narrative or dialogical space to explore personal and relational meaning in the therapeutic relationship (Larner, 2000). Whereas the focus for family therapy is the systemic pattern of relationships, including the therapist–family interface, in psychoanalysis it is the emotional intensity of the transference relationship over the long term (Bertrando, 2002). I suggested that analyst and family therapist both integrate not-knowing and knowing in a both/and or deconstructive stance of *knowing not to know*. Following Bion, this creates a narrative container, or reflective space, for thinking to emerge in the therapeutic conversation (Flaskas, 2002).

In this chapter, I intersect Bion's thinking with the ethical philosophy of Emmanuel Levinas in the idea of the "ethical container". For Bion, containment is a relational process: a being with the patient in thoughtful reverie where emotional and symbolic meaning is held, interpretations are ventured, and thinking develops. For Levinas, the foundation of thinking is the ethical relation to the other. The "ethical" is the incomprehensible, the disruption of knowing by not-knowing in face-to-face encounter with the other

(Larner, 2004). This intersection proposes that therapy is, first and foremost, an ethical relation where the therapist's stance of knowing not to know constructs an ethical container for thinking and for relational meaning to grow.

The experience or practice of therapy is always larger than theory can contain, and recognizing this is already to enter the ethical relation. As Carmel Flaskas (2002) has commented,

> Therapy is a human activity—indeed at times, alarmingly personal—and the stuff of therapy is the lived experience that clients bring, regardless of the framework of therapy we find ourselves working in. [p. 8].

For this reason, the chapter begins with a detailed description of a piece of family therapy practice. Then I describe the ethical philosophy of Levinas and its intersection with Bion's thinking. More systemic reflection on practice follows to illustrate the ethical container. "Containment" is defined as an ethical relation to the other that takes in the person's affective experience, beginning a process of thinking and reflection in the therapeutic conversation.

Ghost of the rabbit ears[1]

James, aged fourteen years, was referred by his mother for a range of problems including anxiety, angry outbursts at school and home, truanting, refusing schoolwork, lack of motivation, depression, and sleeping difficulties that had him sharing her bed over several months. Four years previously, his father abandoned the family to live with another woman, making no subsequent contact. In the first family interview, attended by James, his mother, and grandmother, the sudden loss of this relationship was presented as a major issue. As the mother put it, "His Dad not being around; it's always James and I." The grandmother chipped in, "He feels insecure." James agreed he felt insecure, saying he had recently made another unsuccessful attempt to contact his father. A related discussion explored the question of who steps into father's shoes to provide discipline. James complained of being bossed around by women of the house, including his older sister. "I feel like I'm not allowed to do anything. And then you say how much you hate Dad for what he had done."

During the interview, I was mindful of my own similar experience at ten years of age when my father disappeared to live with another woman and I never saw him again. I could feel the depth of James' sadness stirring my own emotions. I thought about the massive impact of the pain of abandonment on my life, its effect on my mother, and the years of psychoanalytic therapy I needed to deal with it. The experience touched me deeply as I thought, "This could be me many years ago."

The next family session tracked family interaction and conflict around James' sleeping problem and not attending school. James denied feeling scared about sleeping in his own room, but admitted it was isolated and "creepy", complaining that his bed was uncomfortable. We discussed buying James a new bed if he slept in his own room for two weeks. James' anger towards his father was raised, which he separated into two parts: "Because he left me" and "Because of what he did to my mother". I ventured a possible link between James' anxiety, sleeping problem, school resistance, and his anger about being abandoned by his father. For the mother and grandmother, James had become a "bully" in his own family "throwing his weight around" as the only male in the household.

In the third family interview with James, his mother, and his older sister, they reported that he slept upstairs in his grandmother's bed for one week while she was away on holiday. In the subsequent week, the mother purposely locked her bedroom door, so James bedded on the floor in his sister's room, going to sleep watching TV. Our conversation touched on the verbal abuse the family had suffered from the father: as the sister explained, "When Dad was angry it wasn't because of anything we had done, he let his anger out on the family." At this point James said he couldn't sleep in his own room because it had a creaky floor: "It feels like someone walking in the room." I asked whether having a TV in his room might make a difference and he answered, "It would drown out the creaky noises." However, the aerial extension would not reach his room, so I suggested, "What about getting some rabbit ears?" I was thinking of a portable antenna sometimes called, in slang, "dog's ears". In response to my *faux pas* the whole family broke into prolonged laughter; James, in particular, cackled and repeated my phrase several times. After this merry interlude his sister said a TV in James' room might make a difference, and she offered hers, though the mother was sceptical. James repeated, "It's a freaky room", and talked about the possibility of ghosts in the house and the scary movies he had been watching, such as *The Ring*.

Still in reverie about the resonance with my own emotional experience, I ventured the interpretation that the "creaky noises" James heard brought to mind the footprints of his absent father. James appeared to wince under the brutality of my suggestion and, turning towards me, said with biting sarcasm, "Oh you're good, very good." During the family interviews I had been aware of his frequent put-downs and demeaning attitude towards me. The "joke" and laughter about the rabbit ears was really at my expense, showing me to be the "clown" I really was. Perhaps I made the error unconsciously, as an ethical gesture in the hope that exposing my own emotional vulnerability to James might be reciprocated. Reflecting on this later, I saw my interpretation as thinking-through the emotional experience of fear, sadness, and anger James evoked in me that led to my reverie about my father.

A moment after James's sarcastic comment, he conceded, "I've never really thought about it that way before." Perhaps, initially, he was angry with me for exposing his vulnerability, his sarcasm concealing that what I said had hit the mark; it was James's cry of pain and anger about his father directed at me as a good–bad therapist. Then he acknowledged thinking differently about himself, that I could be "good" or helpful in clarifying his experience; he accepted my meaning and began to *think* it. This was a crucial moment in the therapeutic relationship.

After James acknowledged my interpretation, I sensed an invitation to continue, and offered, "The footprints of a father who could give you a sense of security and look after and protect you." Ghosts not only *haunt* with the terror of death, loss, or absence but are visitations from a familiar figure, for James the absent presence of his father as protector in the house. The mother contributed, "I felt that as a child—you know, safe." Mindful that James' teasing posture towards me meshed with my anger about my father-abandonment, I repeated, "Could someone walking around, making creepy and creaky noises in your room like a ghost, be your angry feelings about Dad not being there for you?" James rebuffed me, saying, "I'm still thinking about that", but appeared to take it in. The sister said that she was sometimes scared of ghosts and the family recounted a memorable, though scary, Ghost-tour four years ago, coincidentally around the time the father left. The session ended with the mother saying that James was better behaved after our sessions, and he agreed, saying, "I don't feel as angry."

For various reasons I did not see James and his family again; an ironic repetition of both our histories. On follow-up, six months later, the mother reported James had "settled down" and was sleeping in his own room, with plans to have TV connected in the near future. He had "come a long way", he was more mature, and talking about his feelings had been beneficial. On further follow-up nine months later, James was "getting there" and attending school consistently.

Levinas and the ethical relation

> To approach the Other in conversation is to welcome his expression, in which at each instant he overflows the idea a thought would carry away from it. It is therefore to receive from the Other beyond the capacity of the I, which means exactly to have the idea of infinity. [Levinas, 1969, p. 51]

Emmanuel Levinas is a post-structuralist French philosopher and pre-eminent thinker of our age, influencing diverse fields of study including philosophy, theology, feminism, and psychology (Critchley & Bernasconi, 2002; Davis, 1996; Diprose, 2002; Hutchens, 2004). He was a contemporary and colleague of Derrida, inspiring him to define deconstruction in terms of hospitality, justice, and the ethical. As Derrida (1999) says in his eulogy *Adieu*, Levinas awakened us to ethics and responsibility. The ethical philosophy of Levinas is an emergent voice in postmodern psychology and therapy (Gantt & Williams, 2002; Larner, 2004; Sampson, 2003).

For Levinas, the ethical is distinct from traditional "ethics" as morality; rather, it concerns the *face-to-face* encounter with another person as a foundation for thinking, subjectivity, and being. This "ethics-first" philosophy is radical. In contrast to hermeneutics, which begins with the interpreting subject, it starts with the *other*, who breaches our understanding: "The face is present in its refusal to be contained. In this sense it cannot be comprehended, that is, encompassed" (Levinas, 1969, p. 194).

Levinas's account of the self and thinking is systemic or relational. The self is awareness of the other-in-me. Thought is not contemplation of a unity, totality or the same, but of difference, separation and the other: "Thought and freedom come to us from separation and from the consideration of the other . . ." (*ibid.*, p. 105).

The ethical relation to other is what forms our person: "I" is always *you–I*. The other is a condition of subjectivity or having a self at all; one cannot know oneself except through the other. The other comes first and this ethical relation makes knowledge and thinking possible (Larner, 2004).

What, then, could the above statement by Levinas about infinity possibly mean for therapy? At first glance it appears to throw into doubt any notion of what therapy *is*. Certainly, it becomes less what I do *to* others and more what my experience of the other does to me. Taken beyond my understanding, I am moved to *respond* to the other. I move away from objective knowing and categories that put my experience of the other into words, what Levinas called the *"Said"*, into the relational encounter of not-knowing, that he calls *"Saying"*. As a therapist, I become aware that the other is so much more than I can possibly think: the very idea of transcendence or infinity.

What changes in the encounter is how I see *myself*; in part, therapy is a gift I receive from the other. This calls to mind the *irreverent* stance of Cecchin, Lane, and Ray (1994), where the systemic therapist takes responsibility for changing his or her beliefs and prejudices rather than those of others: "But it is at the moment when the therapist begins to reflect upon the effect of his own attitude and presumptions that he acquires a position that is both ethical and therapeutic" (*ibid.*, pp. 8–9). In relation to other, I become aware of my responsibility in the face of the unknown, which, as Derrida (1999) explains, "is the element of friendship or hospitality for the transcendence of the stranger, the infinite distance of the other" (p. 8). In therapy, welcoming the other—or hospitality— comes about by exposing the inadequacy of what one knows, which is tantamount to coming face to face with the suffering of another human being.

Translating this ethical philosophy to therapy as a person is always beyond my grasp or understanding, I resist totalizing or violent knowledge: ideas that assimilate the other's experience and story in terms of preconceived categories, ideas, theories, or approaches to therapy, whether these are theories from psychoanalysis, cognitive therapy, or family therapy. The ethical therapist, open to an experience of *other*, is moved by the uniqueness of each therapy encounter. In receiving the other, I become aware she is separate from me; as *other* he overflows the "I", who thinks only in terms of knowledge and understanding. This does not throw meaning to the wind; rather, it becomes grounded and thickened in relational experience. In a face-to-face encounter with another human being, my understanding is enriched beyond possible understanding. There is relation in difference, connection in separation, space in the between.

What is interesting is the framing of this ethical process within the context of family therapy practice. The painful feelings that James evoked in me can be described as a systemic mingling of our subjectivities, a resonance between our experiences that allowed me to frame the thought that feelings of abandonment fuelled his angry and defiant behaviour. However, to James, my interpretation seemed to feel like an attack on his person, bringing home the pain of his father's abandonment, leading to his sarcastic response about me being "good".

Yet it was in the context of my *faux pas* about rabbit ears, a moment later, that he seemed able to take in my meaning. Perhaps the joke exposed my vulnerability, humanness, and lack of knowingness in the face-to-face relational encounter with his person. More than merely comprehending or interpreting James' predicament, I was *disturbed* by it, taking it in as emotional experience at the level of the body. Whatever else happened, this ethical gesture of welcoming and being host or hospitable helped James to participate in a dialogue of shared meaning and to begin to think differently.

For Levinas, thinking is not a private activity of cognition, or self-knowledge, but acted out in a relational field. To have a self is to be thought by the other, to become aware of the other thinking in me and to put myself in their place. Peter Fonagy and colleagues describe this relational process as developing a mentalizing or reflective capacity. In human attachment, the infant develops a sense of self by internalizing the experience of feeling known to the other. They describe a similar process occurring in the therapeutic relationship, where the therapist's thinking fosters the patient's mentalizing: "The crux of the value of psychotherapy is the experience of another human being's having the patient's mind in mind" (Fonagy & Bateman, 2006, p. 415).

I am suggesting this relational process of thinking is ethical in Levinas's sense. In proximity to another, it is to let oneself be *affected* or disturbed by the other, to *take in* their experience and think it, which, as we shall see, is what Bion calls containment. As Alphonso Lingis says, introducing his translation of Levinas's (2004) *Otherwise Than Being*, "Being exposed to the other is being exposed to being wounded and outraged" (p. xxiv). This requires the therapist to be in a state of receptivity towards the other's pain and fragility, feeling it *as if* it were one's own. Yet, the other is infinitely more than I can ever attune to or understand. While beyond my understanding, only through the other can I understand at all. Under-standing takes place *in relation to* other, where I am extended to think beyond myself; it is literally to *stand under*, to approach the infinitely other with curiosity, wonder, and awe.

Bion's thinking container

Bion's metaphor of containment elaborated Klein's notion of projective identification from an intrapsychic mechanism into a relational process of interpersonal communication between infant–patient and mother–therapist (Vaslamatzis, 1999). In a state of reverie, the mother takes in the infant's emotional experience, providing reassurance and preventing anxiety from overwhelming the infant's developing self. Likewise, the analyst, in partly unconscious reverie, begins to experience, think, understand, and put into words the projected pre-verbal emotional distress of the patient (the contained). Containment can be described as an intersubjective process in the countertransference relationship. As Vaslamatzis describes it, the container–contained relationship is reciprocal, where the therapist's reverie is resonant of the patient's emotional struggle: "He was now the person who contains and who suffers (annoyance, wondering); he was the container of her projections" (p. 436).

As I have suggested previously (Larner, 2000), postmodern psychoanalysts influenced by Bion, like family therapists (cf. Flaskas, 2002), frame such analytic ideas in terms of an intersubjective or relational model, which "considers relations with others, rather than drives, the fundamental element of mental life" (Marzi, Hautmann, & Maestro, 2006, p. 1302). Following Bion, reverie, thinking, and reflection to contain emotional experience are seen as central ingredients of psychoanalysis. Can a similar process occur in systemic therapy? Possibly, in a different way.

The work with James and his family described a thinking container where the therapist helped to shift the emotional culture or *ethos* of the participants (Pocock, 2005). As a systemic therapist, I received their emotional experience, constructing a thinking space for reflection and conversation in the therapeutic relationship (Flaskas, 2005). Here, the systemic therapist integrates a key ingredient of containment: what Fisher (2006), reading Bion, calls the emotional experience of "feeling curious". In psychoanalysis, the container is provided by the analyst "wanting to know and understand, not from an emotional distance, but by experiencing those emotions and yet retaining a K-state of mind" (*ibid.*, p. 1231). The analyst's curiosity is contagious, inviting the patient to do likewise so "they might too begin to wonder" (*ibid.*, p. 1235).This stance of negative capability, described by Bion, is not-knowing, the capacity to remain in doubt and not find answers too quickly.

This is the link between Bion's notion of containment and the ethical relation in family therapy: the desire to know in a totalizing way is relinquished (Larner, 2004). In Levinasian terms, the Said gives way to the Saying; the intellect gives way to the heart, and knowing to not-knowing. Thus, in the clinical example, what I *said*—my therapeutic knowing or interpretation about James' father's abandonment—had meaning for him only in the context of not knowing or *Saying*, where my experience of his emotional pain was transformed into a *faux pas* about rabbit ears.

The ethical is a disruption of ordinary experience by the transcendent, where the other as not-me overwhelms or ruptures our thinking. Containment, in psychoanalysis and systemic therapy, is the therapist thinking through this emotional experience or disturbance (what Flaskas [2005] calls *impasse*) and communicating its meaning reflexively or dialogically in the therapeutic conversation.

The ethical as knowing not to know

The ethical relation is the container for receiving and thinking the emotional experience of the other. It concerns how to know in a way that resists knowing *all* as totalizing knowledge, being open to what is other, or beyond, knowing. As I have described it, *knowing not to know* is an ethical stance in psychoanalysis and family therapy that concerns less what we know, and more *how* we know in the therapeutic relationship (Larner, 2000). Knowledge and expertise is still there, but there *for* the other. As Levinas notes, without knowledge, science, and technology there would be no ethics, because the world would starve (Larner, 2004). Our responsibility as therapists is to *know* enough to be helpful in therapy, as I could be with James, but knowing as not-knowing while participating in the Saying of relational encounter.

This is where the ethical relation, like the therapeutic relationship, is asymmetrical: like the mother with her baby, as a therapist I am there *for* the other. I think and reflect as a therapist on what knowledge is available to help influence stories of suffering and adversity. As for Levinas, not knowing is really *ethical knowing*, where the other is put first. Here, *knowing not to know* takes up the ethical responsibility to know in order to alleviate suffering; at the same time, it acknowledges one can never know, understand, or comprehend the suffering of another person, but only be moved to respond. As Large (2005) explains Levinas, "To think the experience of the Other, which is nothing less than to think suffering, is to refuse to allow this thought to fall into the image of thought" (p. xiii).

The ethical is an attempt to think the other as in Bion's understanding of psychoanalysis. The attempt to represent the other by image, interpretation, or theory can get in the way of providing a container for their emotional pain (Symington, 1986). Containment is a reflective or narrative space where the therapist/analyst thinks the client's suffering and gives it back as shared meaning in the dialogue of therapy. Where the therapist is *disturbed* by the experience and resists imposing preconceived meaning, the encounter is ethical. It is *how* we know and act towards the other, an ethical stance that gives knowing a human or relational face. This *knowing not to know* is the common ground between psychoanalysis and systemic family therapy (Larner, 2000). As Ogden (2004) explains, reading and understanding Bion, like doing psychoanalysis, involves "a progressive cycle of knowing and not knowing" (p. 290).

The ethical container

The suggestion here is that the container in Bion's thought has an ethical shape. The analyst's not-knowing is an ethical positioning of being open to relational encounter with the other. To understand *other*, one must give up understanding as a merely intellectual or rational exercise: give up memory and desire, and take in the experience of the other in the room. This is to experience the other as a person, not as an extension of the therapist's meaning, interpretation, or image of them. The therapist's first step is ethical: to suspend theory and expectations, to stop the internal chatter of mind in order to listen, feel, and be there *for* the other. Is this so far from Freud's original advice to the beginning analyst to "simply listen" rather than be bothered about keeping anything in mind (Epstein, 1995)? Yes and no!

As a self-reflective therapist, I put myself in the place of the other, containing and thinking their emotional experience; this is the ethical relation. However, the thinking container is less in the mind of the therapist (as knowledge or interpretation of meaning) or the patient, and more in the *relation* between them, in the narrative of therapy that unfolds as dialogue between relational selves. As Bion (1962) says, thoughts wait for thinkers to think (and say) them. This yet-to-be-said, unspoken experience James stirred in me, leading to my reverie and thinking about the footprints of our fathers.

The therapist allows herself to be *affected* by the emotional experience of the other, constructing a thinking container in the relational mind or dialogic space between. This containment begins with the ethical gesture of receiving and thinking the other's pain. As Noreen O'Connor (1998) says, "one can be a psychotherapist only through the interhuman emergence of one's own suffering" (p. 233). Thus, my experience with James was a confluence of my old wound and his fresh one. Although I was able to think what belonged where without reacting to his sarcasm, his experience, reflected through mine, opened up something useful for both of us.

In systemic therapy and psychoanalysis, the therapist moved by relational experience of the other constructs a conversational space for thinking and reflection. Carmel Flaskas (2005) charts this containing process as experience of impasse, and Peter Rober (1999) calls it dialogue between inner and outer conversation. Building on these excellent notions, I reference it as an ethical container that unfolds between therapist and client in the discourse of therapy (Larner, 2000, 2004).

Thinking arises in the intersubjective curvature of space, as Levinas calls the interhuman. In experiencing you, I am moved to reverie and thought. Your suffering holds up a mirror to my own experience, through which I begin to understand and hold you "in mind". You, in return, hold me in mind by taking in what I have to say. Yet, the mind or thinking container is defined in discourse made possible by the ethical relation. Thus, when James says, "I'm still thinking about that" in response to my posing a link between the ghost of his father and his anger, he becomes host to my thought. Perhaps, realizing that I am holding him in mind, he is able to return the ethical gesture and take what I have to say seriously, not merely as a "joke".

Reflecting on systemic practice

I invite the reader for further reflection on systemic practice in relation to the ethical container. First, it needs to be said that family therapy is not the same as psychoanalysis. There is no comparison between the emotional and relational intensity of three to six sessions of systemic therapy and a thousand or more psychoanalytic sessions over several years. The two therapies have distinct traditions, with their commonalities and differences well addressed in the family therapy literature (Pocock, 2006). While the perspective of systemic therapy is undoubtedly *external* relationships (Bertrando, 2002), both approaches work with internal representations of self and others to different degrees.

Both modalities share a common ground of postmodern thinking and constructing a reflective dialogic space for thinking *self* and *other* in the therapeutic relationship (Larner, 2000). In such relational therapies, emotional understanding develops in the intersubjective or dialogic space *between* persons. This is what Pocock (2005) nicely calls a "system of the heart", where the therapist, moved by the therapeutic encounter, "makes him or herself available to be affected and to think in the newly forming ethos of the therapeutic relationship" (p. 133).

Derrida (2000), inspired by Levinas, defines "ethos" somewhat differently, as hospitality and the ethical: "It is always about answering for a dwelling place, for one's identity, one's space, one's limits, for the ethos as abode, habitation, house, heath, family, home" (p. 149). In these terms, both systemic therapy and psychoanalysis welcome the other into an ethos, habitat, or reflective space where thinking of self in relation to others is possible. As Frosh and Baraitser (2003) state, the key question for contemporary psycho-analysis is: "What are the conditions under which it is possible to think?" (p. 772).

In the clinical vignette with James, the inner thinking or dialogue of the therapist became part of the outer conversation between therapist and family (Rober, 1999), grounding relational meaning in shared emotional experience. As a systemic therapist, I was able to take in the hostile and derisive projections of James' abandoned, fearful, and humiliated self, spooked by the footprints of his absent father, which, resonating with the "ghost" of my own father, enabled me to think and contribute meaning in the therapy narrative. His fear of going to school and sleeping in his bed suggested anxiety about further abandonment, his omnipotence and derision towards me, a defence against his helplessness. In face-to-face encounter with James and his family, this heightened my emotional disturbance sufficiently to enter a relational thinking space on the theme of father abandonment, all in the virtual nether-land of the "what if" of imagination, a ghostly reception made possible by a "joke" about rabbit ears. This is part of what I call the ethical container.

In terms of Levinas, I put myself in the place of the other, receiv-ing James's angry jibes without retaliation (even though I felt their barbs in my person), allowing trust and thinking to develop in the nether space between us. This ethical gesture provided a Bion-like container for receiving and thinking the emotional experience of James via my own struggle with father ghosts. So we both might eventually say, as Hamlet did to the Ghost of his father, "Rest, rest perturbed Spirit". As Derrida (1995) notes in deference to Levinas, deconstruction is a "thinking of the gift", a "gratitude without thanks", and a "justice" that is "beyond exchange", where one "learns only by receiving" from the other.

As in Hamlet, the murdered absence of a father contributed to my own emotional dreaming and a kind of madness about rabbit ears. Following Derrida (1995), for both James and I this unspoken experience would have, I speculate, put our narrative histories and minds "out of joint", trapping us in a haunting mourning for the father ghost who never returns; yet our yearning and expectation of imminent return leaves us anxious and alert to the silent creak of footsteps in the house. Perhaps, like Hamlet, for James the footprints belong to the ghost of the father he has killed, and kills every day, in oedipal rage as revenge for the injustice of what has been done to him and his mother. It is his own anger come to haunt him, an apparition of the missing father in him; is he the monstrous Uncle who now shares his mother's bed?

Thinking about thinking

Systemic supervision—thinking about thinking—introduces another level of the ethical container. In bringing this therapy narrative to a systemic consultant, I wanted her to take in and think about my experience, much as I did with James and his family. This constructs a new understanding and ethos for the therapeutic work; call it "fine-tuning" if you like or "adjusting rabbit ears" to improve therapeutic reception. Among other things, the consultant saw my use of humour as a "soothing balm" that allowed the unspeakable to be spoken. The family sessions touched on the dilemma for James about stepping into his father's shoes while still grieving for him; they raised the spectre of the ghost that could not be spoken about by gradually introducing the theme of the *no-father*.

For Bion, the prototype of thinking is the infant's "thought of the breast, imposed by the reality of the no-breast, which is necessary for thinking in the object's absence" (Sandler, 2006, pp. 190–191). Or as Eisold (2005) puts it, "We continually seek containers for our painful experiences of absence, and the thoughts they give rise to in us are continually experienced as persecutory or insufficiently gratifying" (p. 361). In this way, thoughts exist before there is a thinker to think them; the thinking self begins with emotional experience first contained and thought by the other.

Now, for Levinas, maternal receptivity is the ethical relation *per exemplar*. As the psychoanalyst Chetrit-Vatine (2004) notes, maternity, pregnancy, and the womb is a metaphor for the capacity to make a place for the other "a space of a relationship to an other in me" (p. 845). Thus, the French for womb is *matrice*, but in Hebrew it is *Rechem*, from which derives the word *Rachamim*, or compassion. Like the mother who acts as a receptacle, or container, to receive and modify through reverie the emotional experience of her infant, the analyst turns towards the face of the other in a gesture of unconditional hospitality, empathy, and ethos. In therapy, it is the other who brings forth my thinking as an abode for unspoken experience to be thought and narrated.

This ethos, or ethical relation, formed part of the therapeutic container in systemic therapy for James and his family. The consultant suggested that TV acted as a transitional-like object for James' anxiety, allowing it to be safely received and named, providing a container for the family narrative to emerge. My gaffe helped to provide a space for reflection about what could not previously be thought. Linking father absence and the footprints to the rabbit ears allowed imagination to enter the narrative. It put my therapeutic interpretation *on* TV, where the painful could be talked about in acceptable form as in a *show*. Thinking now, it became a kind of family ghost-tour, a playing with unreality where fantasy provided a portal into the real world.

The consultant commented that this medium provided a way of thinking *no-father* without really doing it. My interpretation was a no-interpretation; my knowing a laughable not-knowing that could be taken on board by James in his own time. The humour and laughing with/at the therapist was an important part of the container, allowing the experience of fear, anxiety, and belittlement to be approached as father abandonment. Rabbit ears, like the therapist, are not "all there" or there at all (think of the mad rabbit *alter ego* in the cult film, *Johnny Darko*); they are ghost's ears, like footprints or "flags" of our fathers.

Conclusion

In terms of Bion and Levinas, therapy is an experience of the mysterious and impossible; it is reaching out to other in the imagination. I imagine your suffering even though I cannot experience it, because it is not mine but yours. You are who you are and I am who I am, though who we are depends on our relation to each other. I reach out to you and you reach back to me, and then we reach out to each other, like me to James and, finally, James to me. The difference for me as a therapist is that I do this *for* you; that is my job, or positioning in relation to you, the ethical context for coming together in dialogue.

Together we come to experience, think, and say the unbearable, that which cannot be said except in this context of therapy, where one person tells another what they cannot tell anyone else. What you tell me, I receive as a gift in wonder that you privileged me to hear your story. I give back to you my attempt to feel and think about your pain. I put myself in your place and think the possibilities for change *as if* you were me, as if I were in therapy and you were listening to my story. This thinking as containment is the ethical relation. I think for you, yet you think through me. There is an exchange of thinking in the abode of our relationship. This is the intersection between Bion and Levinas and between psychoanalysis and systemic therapy.

Note

1.   I thank my co-therapist Emerick Kovacs for his wisdom, sparkling sense of humour, and opportunity for reflective dialogue.

References

Bertrando, P. (2002). The presence of the third party: systemic therapy and transference analysis. *Journal of Family Therapy*, 24: 351–368.

Bion, W. R. (1962). The psychoanalytic study of thinking. *International Journal of Psychoanalysis*, 43: 306–310.

Cecchin, G., Lane, G., & Ray, W. A. (1994). *The Cybernetics of Prejudices in the Practice of Psychotherapy*. London: Karnac.

Chetrit-Vatine, V. (2004). Primal seduction, matricial space and asymmetry in the psychoanalytic encounter. *International Journal of Psychoanalysis*, 85: 841–856.

Critchley, S., & Bernasconi, R. (Eds.) (2002). *The Cambridge Companion to Levinas*. Cambridge: Cambridge University Press.

Davis, C. (1996). *Levinas: An Introduction*. Cambridge: Polity Press.

Derrida, J. (1995). The time is out of joint. In: A. Haverkamp (Ed.), *Deconstruction is/in America: A New Sense of the Political* (pp. 14–38). New York: New York University Press.

Derrida, J. (1999). *Adieu: To Emmanuel Levinas*. Stanford, CA: Stanford University Press.

Derrida, J. (2000). *Of Hospitality*. Stanford, CA: Stanford University Press.

Diprose, R. (2002). *Corporeal Generosity*. Albany, NY: State University of New York Press.

Eisold, K. (2005). Using Bion. *Psychoanalytic Psychology, 22*: 357–369.

Epstein, M. (1995). *Thought Without a Thinker*. New York: Basic Books.

Fisher, J. V. (2006). The emotional experience of K. *International Journal of Psychoanalysis, 87*: 1221–1237.

Flaskas, C. (2002). *Family Therapy Beyond Postmodernism: Practice Challenges Theory*. Hove: Brunner-Routledge.

Flaskas, C. (2005). Sticky situations, therapy mess: on impasse and the therapist's position. In: C. Flaskas, B. Mason, & A. Perlesz, (Eds.), *The Space Between: Experience, Context, and Process in the Therapeutic Relationship* (pp. 111–125). London: Karnac.

Fonagy, P., & Bateman, A. (2006). Mechanisms of change in mentalization-based treatment of BPD. *Journal of Clinical Psychology, 62*: 411–430.

Frosh, S., & Baraitser, L. (2003). Thinking, recognition and otherness. *Psychoanalytic Review, 90*: 771–789.

Gantt, E., & Williams, R. N. (Eds.) (2002). *Psychology for the Other: Levinas, Ethics and the Practice of Psychology*. Pittsburgh, PA: Duquesne University Press.

Hutchens, B. C. (2004). *Levinas: A Guide for the Perplexed*. New York: Continuum.

Large, W. (2005). *Emmanuel Levinas and Maurice Blanchot: Ethics and the Ambiguity of Writing*. Manchester: Clinamen Press.

Larner, G. (2000). Towards a common ground in psychoanalysis and family therapy: on knowing not to know. *Journal of Family Therapy, 22*: 61–82.

Larner, G. (2004). Levinas: therapy as discourse ethics. In: T. Strong & D. Pare (Eds.), *Furthering Talk: Advances in the Discursive Therapies* (pp. 15–32). New York: Kluwer Academic.

Levinas, E. (1969). *Totality and Infinity*. Pittsburgh, PA: Duquesne University Press.

Levinas, E. (2004). *Otherwise Than Being: Or Beyond Essence*. Pittsburgh, PA: Duquesne University Press.

Marzi, A., Hautmann, G., & Maestro, S. (2006). Critical reflections on intersubjectivity in psychoanalysis. *International Journal of Psychoanalysis, 87*: 1297–1314.

O'Connor, N. (1998). The personal is political: discursive practice of the face-to-face. In: R. Bernasconi & D. Wood (Eds.), *The Provocation of Levinas: Rethinking the Other* (pp. 57–69). London: Routledge.

Ogden, T. H. (2004). On holding and containing, being and dreaming. *International Journal of Psychoanalysis, 85*: 1349–1364.

Pocock, D. (2005). Systems of the heart: evoking the feeling self in family therapy. In: C. Flaskas, B. Mason, & A. Perlesz, (Eds.), *The Space Between: Experience, Context, and Process in the Therapeutic Relationship* (pp.127–139). London: Karnac.

Pocock, D. (2006). Six things worth understanding about psychoanalytic psychotherapy. *Journal of Family Therapy, 28*: 352–369.

Rober, P. (1999). The therapist's inner conversation in family therapy practice: some ideas about the self of the therapist, therapeutic impasse and the process of reflection. *Family Process, 38*: 209–228.

Sampson, E. E. (2003). Unconditional kindness to strangers: human sociality and the foundation for an ethical psychology. *Theory and Psychology, 13*: 147–175.

Sandler, P. C. (2006). The origin of Bion's work. *International Journal of Psychoanalysis, 87*: 179–201.

Symington, N. (1986). *The Analytic Experience: Lectures from the Tavistock*. London: Free Association.

Vaslamatzis, G. (1999). On the therapist's reverie and containing function. *Psychoanalytic Quarterly, LXV111*: 431–440.

INDEX